AS I RECALL . . .

AS I RECALL...

William A. Clark

This book was printed in the United States of America.

To order additional copies of this book, contact:
Xlibris Corporation
1-888-795-4274
www.Xlibris.com
Orders@Xlibris.com
16472

CONTENTS

Introduction 11

Letter 1 : Was It Better or Worse? 13

Letter 2 : Dogs in School 16

Letter 3 : Parents and Teachers vs. Kids 19

Letter 4 : Feelings About Time 22

Letter 5 : Good Things, Nasty Things 25

Letter 6 : Going To War 28

Letter 7 : The House At 405 31

Letter 8 : Choosing Hobbies 34

Letter 9 : Great Ears 37

Letter 10 : Uncle Walter 40

Letter 11 : Feelings About Money 44

Letter 12 : Food—Some of It Edible 48

Letter 13 : Two Splendid Files 51

Letter 14 : A Bit of Wartime Fun 54

Letter 15 : Sniffing 57

Letter 16 : You're Not What You Eat 60

Letter 17 : Brain Waves 64

Letter 18 : That Wretched Corsage 67

Letter 19: What Happens To Imaginations? 70

Letter 20 : Getting Scared For Fun and For Real 73

Letter 21: Quirks and Flaws 77

Letter 22 : Marriage and Luck 80

Letter 23 : The Toilet Paper Trail 83

Letter 24 : Laughing Loudly 86

Letter 25 : Mother's More Personable Dogs 89

Letter 26 : Mistreated People and a Mis-made Pie 93

Letter 27 : What's the Very Best Time of Life? 98

Letter 28 : My Grandfather Pop 101

Letter 29 : Careers and Office Pranks 104
Letter 30 : Attitudes Toward Learning 108
Letter 31 : Big Changes esp. in Females 111
Letter 32 : Water and I 114
Letter 33 : Those Foxy Folks 117
Letter 34 : Our Cottage's Door Panels 120
Letter 35 : To-Do Lists, Not Got-Done Lists 123
Letter 36 : The Soaps of My Boyhood 126
Letter 37 : Medicine Cabinets and Sick Beds 129
Letter 38 : How Female Logic Was Destroyed 132
Letter 39 : Those Once-only Encounters 135
Letter 40 : Rules, Rules, Rules 138
Letter 41 : Our Non-Dog Pets 141
Letter 42 : That Busy Old Kitchen 144
Letter 43 : Life in Stages 147
Letter 44 : House Maids 150
Letter 45 : First Impressions 153
Letter 46 : Hanging Onto Intangibles 156
Letter 47 : The "Why" of Love 159
Letter 48 : The Sidewalk at 405 162
Letter 49 : What Games Do for Folks 165
Letter 50 : Fiddling with Strange Headlines 168
Letter 51 : Fascination with Crimes 171
Letter 52 : The Color Gray 174
Letter 53 : Old Customs, Old Toys, Old Folks 177
Letter 54 : On Being a "Different" Sort of Father 180
Letter 55 : Emotions 183
Letter 56 : What To Do About Your Mind 186
Letter 57 : Cars, Now and Then 189
Letter 58 : My Chemistry Set 192
Letter 59 : Tree Frogs and Sharks 195
Letter 60 : Studying Hands 198
Letter 61 : When Folks Take Chances 201
Letter 62 : The Cobbler and the Hardware Man 204
Letter 63 : The Dime Store and One-Cent Sales 207
Letter 64 : A Blackfoot from Up North 210

Letter 65 : Having Fun With Language............... 213
Letter 66 : What Your Great-Grandmother Was Like.......... 216
Letter 67 : How Folks Copy Nature 219
Letter 68 : The Flat Cat 222
Letter 69 : Skate Keys and Rumble Seats 225
Letter 70 : The Tin Lizzie Worth Fifteen Cartwheels 228
Letter 71 : What It's Like To Grow Old 231
Letter 72 : Our Ailing English Language 234
Letter 73 : My Happiest Day 237
Letter 74 : The Number One Invention 240
Letter 75 : Memorable Meals in Faraway Places................. 243
Letter 76 : Idioms That Have Kicked the Bucket 246
Letter 77 : Collar Buttons and Debut Parties 249
Letter 78 : Greenbelt Musings 252
Letter 79 : Writing As a Pastime 255
Letter 80 : Sorting Stuff 258
Letter 81 : Parent-Child Conversations 261
Letter 82 : Dirt............ 264
Letter 83 : A Fine Friendship Cut Short 267
Letter 84 : Taking Trips Long Ago............ 270
Letter 85 : Homemade Stuff 273
Letter 86 : Shrinking 276
Letter 87 : Chairs: Easy and Not So Easy 279
Letter 88 : Huge Mistakes..................... 282
Letter 89 : Sleeping 285
Letter 90 : Conversations With Plants 288
Letter 91 : Hopes For Grandchildren 291
Letter 92 : I've Got Dibs 294
Letter 93 : My Knickers Years 297
Letter 94 : How the Young View the Old 300
Letter 95 : Zany Laws and Lawmakers 303
Letter 96 : Those Capital Sins of Youth 306
Letter 97 : Catching Up With Long-Gone Sounds 309
Letter 98 : Paid-for Discipline............ 312
Letter 99 : The Importance of Timing 315
Letter 100 : To Plant a Tree 318

DEDICATION

To Josie,
Who excels at three of the world's top careers:
Wife,
Mother, and
Grandmother

INTRODUCTION

Several friends of mine have started to write their memoirs, but are not apt to finish. That's too bad, because they very much want their legacies to include more than money and snapshots. Maybe their approach is wrong. They try to write year-by-year accounts of their lives. The trouble is, memories don't arrive in chronological order, but pop up instead in a most disorderly way. At least that's how my memory bank works. I can't simply request the memories of, say, 1938 and get them. The process is passive, not active. I have to let my brain decide which memories it wants to serve up and when.

And that's how I've put together my memoirs. Whenever my brain gave me a worthwhile thought, I wrote a letter about it—no more than two typed pages in the original. I numbered the letters consecutively as I wrote them and added one by one to a slow-growing stack. Although the stack was to be just for our sixteen grandchildren, various folks have urged me to share with others these recollections of mirth and fright, joy and sadness, from the 1920s on.

Those "worthwhile" thoughts I wrote about cover quite a range: animals, people, happenings, places, secrets, and emotions. The lack of order within the stack should keep the reader alert, not bored. Letter 20, for example, is about getting scared; Letter 22 is about long marriages; and Letter 23 is about misbehaving in high school.

There were but four rules I followed in writing these letters. Keep the tone folksy but not overly slangy. Don't be preachy. Don't claim that times were a lot better or a lot worse long ago than they are now. Don't write descriptions of living descendants, lest one of them be irked or grow envious.

Because these were letters to grandchildren, I should identify a few relatives for non-family readers of this book. My maternal grandparents were Mom and Pop; my favorite uncle was Walter. My mother was known as Mother to her children and Gommie to her grandchildren. My wife is Josie. Our six children are Ken, Josie, Jr., Steve, Chris, David, and Mark.

The letters-to-grandchildren approach seems to have been a good choice. As the stack grew, I realized that my manuscript was always finished because there could be no real ending of the sort found in other memoirs. I was also pleased to find that what had begun as a gift to grandchildren was also a gift to myself. To write properly about a memory and hold it to two typed pages, I was able to (and *had* to) truly relive events just to bring forth the right details. As I wrote about the soaps of my youth, for instance, I had to recall not only the rings of dirt on the tub, but also what I had done to create such wonderfully *dark* rings.

LETTER 1

Was It Better or Worse?

This is out of character for me. My favorite tenses are the present and the future, yet here I am pondering the past. It's probably an age-related mental disorder. Lately, I have heard quite a few of my contemporaries, when they were not talking about food and failing body parts, recall their pasts. Evidently they enjoy doing that. Instead of brooding over the fact that there is way more sand in the bottoms of their hourglasses than there is up top, they dream of those halcyon days so long ago when life was hard but good. And they remember achievements known only to themselves.

I think that they truly hope to be remembered, for a while at least, for what they accomplished and for having had profound thoughts about how life should be lived. Whether they will reach that goal is doubtful, but the pursuit of it pleases them and pushes aside those worries that oldsters harbor.

With a past as uneventful as mine, I am not apt to be long remembered. Throughout my life, I have been more a witness than a doer. I know now that those who make lasting impressions are people who do things I never thought of doing: compose catchy sonatas, discover cures for dreaded diseases, head up Mafia families. I simply watched, sometimes smiling, sometimes frowning, as the world changed.

About all I can offer by way of remembrance is a stack of letters, this being the first. I'll write one whenever I think of something worth passing along to you, and I'll try not to be preachy about it. I don't intend to mail each letter as I finish it. There are fifteen of you, some too young to read, maybe some waiting to be born.

Besides, I don't fancy addressing fifteen envelopes every time I have a proper random thought and write about it.

Old folks, when they tell of the past, tend to exaggerate, to make the past seem much harsher or much rosier than it really was. For example, some old codger may tell you he had to slog through five or ten miles of snow to get to or from school. Not I. My school was only a mile and a half away. True, I often *did* slog through snow to get there, but I was seldom, if ever, alone. I was with friends who lived along the way, and those friends had mothers who knew how to cook up hot cocoa and cap it with molten marshmallow. I was also warmly dressed. I had leather boots, wool mittens, a fur-lined helmet with ear flaps, a heavy sweater, and a sheepskin jacket. When I spent too much time making snowballs, my fingers and toes got achy but never frostbitten. As I recall, those walks home, whatever the weather, were lots more fun than sitting and squirming at my schoolroom desk.

Was it more fun than riding a school bus? Who knows? Where I grew up the only school busses were for kids who went to expensive private schools. There were streetcars, but to ride one cost a nickel each way—a week's allowance—and only a sissy would ride one rather than walk a mile or two.

Most likely you'll hear old folks crow about how great things were. Things *were* a lot cheaper. For a nickel you could buy a loaf of bread, a coke, a sack of so-called penny candies or a phone call from a booth. For a dime you could watch a double-feature movie plus at least two short comedy films. If you were old enough to drive, you could buy a gallon of gas for a dime. To buy a *new* car was expensive—$495 for a black Chevy coupe—but the used cars that high-school and college kids drove were much cheaper. My first car, which I drove for three years, cost $35, and there was no sales tax.

Prices really *were* like that. Still, when someone tells you about it, ask about wages and salaries and allowances. The typical allowance for the grade-schoolers I knew was 5-10 cents, and once a kid got old enough to do summertime work, he earned about 10 cents an hour. Ask, too, about that bargain-priced car. It wasn't like today's cars. It had no radio, no air conditioner, no automatic shift.

So you see, those times long gone were neither bleak nor golden. They were something in between, and the challenge for you is to capture the best of the *then* and *now*.

LETTER 2

Dogs in School

About that grade school to which I slogged or walked . . .

It was made of bricks the color of week-old scabs and must have had eight classrooms, because that's how many grades there were. If it held up for many years with all those kids going through there, it was must have been built to last, but what I remember better than the strength of the building is the way it was kept up. Although the floors creaked in spots, they were always polished, and at the end of each day, every blackboard was washed, every desk cleared, every classroom swept.

We entered only by the front door each morning and walked—never ran—silently to our classroom; but before sitting down we hung up our jackets, if any, on one of thirty-five hooks in the cloak room. That's where we also put our baseballs and bats and gloves and jump ropes, and occasionally our soaking wet shoes. Now and then we ourselves were put in one of those cloak rooms for misbehaving.

It was a no-nonsense parochial school run by Dominican nuns who smelled of starch and Ivory soap and talcum powder. They wore heavy white robes with black headdresses. Rumor had it that beneath those black headdresses were shaved heads, but no one was absolutely positive about that. What we *did* know was that the nun in each classroom had czar-like authority. She would make us learn, she would tolerate neither disrespect nor disruption, and she would punish us promptly enough so we knew why our ears were being twisted or our knuckles rapped with a ruler. Most of the time—almost all the time—it was a boy who got punished.

Girls, it seemed, never got into trouble. Whether that was because they had tender ears and knuckles or simply because they were just plain well-behaved I don't recall.

I think that, despite the punishments, those nuns really liked us. Certainly each of them was dedicated to the notion that she would see to it we didn't stumble on one step of our march to adulthood. We were all destined to go through college, probably to have families, and certainly to succeed in life. None of us would go to jail or become a moral pygmy. But first things first. In grade school, that meant learning how to spell, how to write legibly, how to crunch numbers, how to listen, how to read. We also learned the principles of our religion, the rules of grammar, and the fundamentals of geography and history.

Uncharacteristically, some of these very strict nuns let us bring our dogs into classrooms, provided they sat or lay quietly. As I look back on those days, I wonder what would have happened if some kid had brought a female in heat to school. Of course, none of the boys I knew owned a girl dog. It was a time when almost every boy had as his constant companion a dog, preferably a large one. Boy and dog slept together, played together, roamed together. There were no leash laws.

Then, as now, the best parts of the school day were recess, lunch, and the 3:30 school's-out bell. We spent our recesses, whatever the weather, in a spacious playground, which was rather like a big yard, unpaved, and with none of the playground equipment found around today's schools. We were a noisy bunch, being mostly unsupervised outdoors, and we segregated ourselves as though it were the natural thing to do. Boys went one way, girls another. No boy picked up jacks with girls or jumped rope or played hopscotch. No girl shot marbles with the boys or played mumbletypeg, softball, or touch football.

Lunch hour was partly an extra recess. We brought our lunches in metal boxes: two sandwiches, a piece of fruit, milk or cocoa in a thermos strapped to the underside of the top of the lunch box, and cookies for dessert.

When did boys stop shooting marbles and playing mumbletypeg? And why? I don't know. I'm just glad those games were popular when I was of an age to enjoy them.

LETTER 3

Parents and Teachers vs. Kids

More about that grade school of mine . . . .

I've already told you about some of the differences between my school and yours. We had a lot less equipment and a lot more discipline than you do, so perhaps you are better off all around. We lacked just about everything you take for granted: a gym, a cafeteria, athletic equipment, a school nurse, musical instruments, visual aids for teachers, computers, labs, counselors, even a hoop for shooting baskets. For that, we rigged a bushel basket with the bottom cut out.

There was also a difference in the relationships between parents, teachers, and kids. Parents and teachers were in cahoots. They neither had nor needed a PTA. They met one-on-one whenever either a parent or a teacher thought it was necessary, and we kids were victims of their conspiracy. Parents gave teachers the right to do whatever it took to make a kid behave and learn. If that meant keeping one of us an hour or two after school, so be it. If it meant a bit of (mild) physical punishment, that was okay, too. And if tutoring was required, the parents either did it or hired it done.

Provided a child behaved well and kept up his or her grades, parents and teachers pretty much left him or her alone except in classrooms or when there were household chores to do. Play time belonged to us kids. There were no Little Leagues, and parents didn't horn in on kids' games. When we played, we often had disputes, some so spirited that we socked one another; but we had to settle our own differences, for there were no adult officials to impose their rulings. In the process, we learned a lot about truthfulness and sportsmanship and temper control and getting along with one another.

We were also slower to master athletic skills than we would have been, given a bit of coaching. That didn't matter, though. It still doesn't. We played games for *fun,* not because we had ambitions to become pros.

Our school clothing was different from yours. The boys wore knickers and shirts, and I used to have an awful time keeping my shirttails tucked in. They'd come out as soon as I threw a ball or corked some kid's arm, and I never could remember to tuck them back in. My mother, who hated to see me run around with shirttails flapping, knew how to cure me of my sloppy habit. She sewed strips of lace to the edges of my shirttails knowing I'd never let anyone see me flash lace. A very perceptive woman, my mother. No son of hers would let himself be sissified like that. I was a regular boy, and regular boys did not wear necklaces or bracelets or grow long hair or flash lace.

The girls wore skirts and blouses that had big bibs in back. I never did figure out what those bibs were good for except pulling on if you happened to have a girl at a desk right in front of yours. Even then it was more fun just to dip her hair in your inkwell. I never did see a girl use her bib. I don't see how she could have. When stuff spills down your front you can't catch it in a back bib.

Then as now, we boys carried knives. We didn't slash or stab with ours, though. We used them to sharpen our pencils, to whittle, and to play mumbletypeg. I wonder, with all the spelling exercises I endured, why I never learned to spell mumbletypeg.

Each October, my mother used to buy me a pair of leather boots. They cost $4, so I had to take real good care of them. I rubbed neatsfoot oil into them, same as I did with my baseball glove. Their brand name was either Buster Brown or Red Goose, and they had a most important feature: a narrow pocket on the outside of the right boot. It was in that pocket that I carried my knife during the fall and winter months.

If I were to criticize my grade school for anything, it would be the way we were taught too much by rote. We memorized and memorized: multiplication tables, poems, spelling words, historical dates, state capitals. We learned handwriting by the Palmer Method, which involved repeated exercises in making spirals and saw-tooth patterns. All this memorization and repetition got to be a drag at times. No wonder we were so squirmy at our little desks. I wish our teachers had spent more time getting us to *think* and to *imagine.*

Still, all in all, those grade school years were a good time of life. My marks were pretty good except the ones for conduct. I had good friends, a few of whom I still see or hear from now and then. I played hard, ate gluttonously, slept soundly, and only once worried about my personal safety. That was when Ted M., who was four years my senior, threatened to beat the tar out of me. He never did. I didn't go near him unless my dog, Jerry, was with me, and Ted knew better than to touch me when Jerry was close by.

LETTER 4

Feelings About Time

Gurus, I have been told, know the secret of life and will share it with anyone who goes to where they squat and asks them politely. Since they apparently do their squatting on Tibetan mountains where the ground must be very cold, I wonder whether they really have discovered the secret of life.

I have neither met a guru nor known anyone who has, and I can't help but wonder whether there really is a single, all-purpose secret of life. My notion is that there are a bunch of smaller secrets that we find, one at a time, as we go through life.

A good example of a small secret has to do with *attitudes*. Think about the people you know. What do the happy, contented ones have in common? Chances are, each of them has a proper set of attitudes and can switch from one attitude to another as the need arises to be glad or sad, competitive or content. The attitudes I have in mind are those a person really *feels*; they may or may not be the same as the attitudes he or she displays in public.

As best I can tell, we build our broad attitudes—of contentment, sadness and the like—bit by bit. We form narrower attitudes: toward money, toward time, toward sense of humor, toward types of people, toward authority.

So what is your attitude about, say, time? You'll notice, if you haven't already noticed, that people have weird ideas about time. They make up such slogans as "Time is precious" and "Time is money." Some of them keep checking their watches; others do zany things to save time.

Some years ago, I was driven by a young Brit named Mark

down a stretch of the Autobahn. We hadn't far to go—only about 20 miles—and we had at least an hour until our appointment, yet Mark drove as though pursued by demons. He was intelligent, well-educated, and, I think, a responsible person; yet here he was barreling along, risking life and limb and fender while I sat white-knuckled beside him.

"What's the hurry?" I asked. "We've got lots of time, and the guy we're calling on won't care if we're a few minutes late anyway." Mark mumbled something about there being no harm in getting there early.

Perhaps to take my mind off the thought of a fatal crash I whipped out my pocket calculator to convert kilometers to miles, and in a few minutes I said, "If we average 50 miles an hour we'll be there in 24 minutes. If we average 80 we'll be there in 15 minutes. Of course to *average* 80 we'll have to go 90 some of the time to make up what we lose by slowing down to avoid collisions. But let's assume we *do* average 80, and we *do* arrive in one piece. What will we do with the nine minutes we save? That's hardly enough time to get our blood pressure and pulse rate back to normal."

I once had a wonderful daughter-in-law, Gail, the mother of four of you grandchildren. She was a cardiologist who believed that stress was the No. 2 cause of heart attacks, heredity being No. 1. She ran a lab in a hospital. In that lab, patients were put through tests to see whether time pressures made them stressful. They were, for example, confronted with TV movies taken from a car that got honked at, cut off, stopped too long at red lights, and bumped. The effect on some patients was dramatic. Pulses, blood pressures, and heart rates rose.

When I was in high school, there was a lot of talk about an eccentric scientist named Einstein who was said to have discovered a fourth dimension: time. Until then, we had been content to think that dimensions were supposed to be measured with rulers, not clocks. If we wanted to know how much space a box took up, we measured its width, length, and height. While doing that, we saw no need to check a clock or calendar. I still don't.

Einstein caused quite a stir, though. Some thought he was a genius who could write papers that only three other people in the world could understand (I don't recall anyone's naming those three people). Others thought he was batty, and still others thought he should find time to buy a comb and a change of clothes.

He had a different effect on me. He got me thinking how we measure our lives in terms of time but could just as easily measure the lengths, widths, and heights of the spaces we occupy. We start with small ones: wombs, cribs, baby buggies, playpens. We move on to somewhat larger spaces: yards, houses, whole neighborhoods, schools. As adults, we have access to virtually unlimited space: the whole world, the sky, maybe even outer space. As we age, our space shrinks progressively: nursing home, hospital bed, casket.

And what is my attitude about time? I'll tell you, but don't feel obliged to agree. I think time should be *used*, not just *passed*. I try not to waste time checking my wristwatch (which I stopped wearing the day I retired). I figure that for most of us, the happiest hours are those we spend without checking the time. Instead, we get lost in the fun of the moment, whether because we are partying or courting or creating something. I try not to waste the time of others because I hate having other people waste mine. I resent being put on hold or told to wait in the office of a doctor who wants me to know his time is more important than mine.

In retirement, I don't budget my time. Instead, I make sure there is a big enough backlog of things to do that I never wonder whether all my hours will be filled. Still—and this is important— I let myself feel pride of workmanship by using however much time it takes to do things right.

LETTER 5

Good Things, Nasty Things

Some thoughts about *THINGS,* all sorts of inanimate *THINGS,* expensive and cheap, some lovable and some not.

To collect things seems to be a normal human trait. What sets us apart from pack rats is that we tend to be choosier. They collect whatever they can carry. I also think we have more fun than rats do as we build our collections, but never having conversed with a rat, I can't be sure.

There are, in our midst, two types of human collectors: the *Actives* and the *Passives.* The *Actives* are the more deliberate, the more dedicated. They are careful in choosing what to collect, and settle on something rare or expensive or both. Antiques or paintings, for example, or stamps, coins, hard-to-find rocks, or butterflies. For the *Active* collector, the fun is mostly in the search. That and in bragging about the collection.

Passive collectors are a different breed. I know, because I am one. So is your grandmother. We collect things less for the fun and more to satisfy a miserly urge. Being driven by that urge—or pulled by it—is, in fact, the reason we're called passive. We can't help ourselves. We can't scrap things that just might one day become useful.

Your grandmother's box collection fills the shelves of two walk-in closets. If ever she needs a box, the right one is there waiting to see whether it can be found. There are boxes of every color whose name you could spell. The largest one would hold a pygmy, the smallest only a ring. A few of her boxes were custom-designed. Like the one that was made to hold a two-pound smoked salmon.

That box has been in her collection for years. I wonder when she'll catch a fish just that size and want to ship it.

I'm just about as irrational as I add to my collection of wood scraps. I can't bear to see a piece of good hardwood burned, so I rescue it, rub it, wonder what I might make of it, and store it.

Jim Lugers, a tennis friend of mine, was not what anyone would call a philosopher, yet he once gave me an enduring thought. It was this. Throughout our lives, we concern ourselves with *things*. Early on it's toys, later it's trikes and bikes and cars and houses, maybe planes. To get a real kick out of a *thing*, you have to meet three requirements. You have to want that thing intensely; you have to want it for a long enough time; and you have to get it at last.

Jim was convincing if not also dogmatic. And why not? He had had the experience, and what he said made sense. When *things* have come to me too quickly, too easily, I haven't really appreciated them. And when I never did get what I had longed for, I wasn't at all happy.

As I later discovered, Jim was only 95% percent correct. Some people can get a huge kick by getting something they hardly knew they wanted. A woman goes to a mall to shop for nothing in particular, maybe just to see what's available. She simply likes to shop. Now and then she finds a real bargain. Is she very pleased? I should think so. Will her joy last for long? Possibly. At a garage sale, a man spots a wonderful old tool for which he has no need. He buys it, restores it, and cherishes it.

My grandfather gave me another thought about *things*. He said I should look closely at them and figure out what they were trying to tell me—which struck me as strange because the only talking things I could think of were radios and phones and record players. My grandfather, seeing I was puzzled, explained that most things wouldn't talk out loud to me. "They'll give you messages by brain waves," he said, "if only you'll let them."

He then gave me some examples. "A puffy white cloud will tell you to imagine what it looks like. Maybe you'll see a five-legged hippo or the face of an ogre or a pile of sparklingly clean white laundry or the whipped cream atop a sundae. Look closely at a piece of antique jewelry, a lady's ring for instance. It may ask you to guess where it has been over the years, and what sorts of ladies wore it."

I've grown quite fond of *things,* at least certain *things,* these past few decades. Thanks to my grandfather, I look closely at lots of *things.* What I had to learn on my own was that *things* quite often pass me messages about people. A carefully made quilt tells me its stitcher had patience and pride of workmanship. A piece of furniture held together with staples tells me its maker had neither. Flowers and tidal waves and walnut burls tell that no man could make them, however hard he tried. Certain pieces of jewelry tell me their owners are show-offs. A pair of well-worn shoes describe an owner who cares less about show than about comfort. Roughly treated *things* tell me their owners are the sort who would beat their dogs.

Before I end this letter on *things,* I should mention those that are unfriendly, the ones that plot against you if you treat them badly. If you shut a few clothes hangers in a dark closet, they'll reproduce; you may even catch them tangled in a huge embrace. If you buy tools just because you have to, and not because you want to, those tools will sense your ill will. They will scare you and scar you. An unwanted hammer may blacken your thumbnail and make you think it was all your fault.

Years ago, my toaster and I were fast friends. It handled home-baked bread and spongy store-bought bread. It let me watch my toast get golden brown, and it kept my hands and its toast warm. But it died, and I had to get a new one, a very unfriendly one that probably sensed my ill will. It undercooked home-baked slices, blackened spongy bread, and threw both onto the counter top and floor.

So my parting message in this letter is: If you have a *thing* you don't like, don't let that *thing* find out how you feel.

LETTER 6

Going To War

This morning, I write about the BIG War, WW2, saving the gory stuff for a later letter.

I volunteered to be trained as a naval officer. Until then, I had never held a real job, only summer ones, but I had a degree in chemistry and was engaged to your grandmother. The Navy sent me to Notre Dame (30 days) and to Northwestern (90 days), and commissioned me an ensign. Four days later, your grandmother and I were married in Montclair, N.J.; a week later we were on our way to the University of California. There, the Navy said, I was to earn a Certificate in Diesel Engineering. Which I did, and was then assigned to a small converted tuna boat (the FIRECREST, out of San Diego), and was taught very briefly how to sweep mines.

The FIRECREST was an interesting experience. It rode the waves like a cork, rolling 58 degrees on my first day aboard, and was great at inducing seasickness in queasy newcomers. On the FIRECREST, only the captain and I were white. There were 14 blacks (courteously called Negroes in those days), and they took great pride in that tiny vessel. They kept the decks holystoned, the brass gleaming, the galley spotless, and the machinery humming. Even so, they found time for a ritual they had for each new man coming aboard. Typically, the new man got seasick and leaned over the side. When he turned around, thinking his sickness has ended, what he saw was a crewman holding up a cold pork chop covered with congealed grease.

The FIRECREST duty was easy: out in the morning, never out of sight of land, back in the afternoon, and home in La Jolla every other night. It lasted only two months. My next orders took me to a ship being built near Los Angeles: the USS YMS-393, a wooden-hulled minesweep. Your grandmother, by now getting close to the time for Ken to be born, went to stay with her parents in Neenah, Wisconsin. My home was a YMCA room, and I spent my days supervising the installation of equipment on my ship. I became a father, and the Navy *did* let me go see Ken when he was ten days old. I would not see him again until he was nearly two years old.

Before long, our crew of 29 men and 4 officers were aboard, and we took the 393 for shakedown cruises. She—that was the right pronoun to use in referring to a ship; I wonder why?—had a top speed of 14.6 miles an hour; the guns and generators and stoves and compasses and minesweep gear all worked.

There were just four problems, none considered serious at the time. After we dropped a pattern of depth charges, the ship sprang a few leaks. The chronometer, our only way of keeping accurate time, stopped whenever we fired our (big?) 3-inch gun. Only one man on board had ever been out of sight of land on a Navy ship. And the captain got seasick, really seasick, each time the ship left the dock.

The Navy didn't wait for us to fix leaks, get a new chronometer or a captain with sea legs before we set off for the war zone. We went first to Hawaii (Pearl Harbor), accompanied by a tanker and several other small ships unable to carry enough diesel oil for the trip. By the time we got to Hawaii, it was clear that the ship's leakage problem and the captain's seasickness problem had worsened. Although I was still an ensign, I was the second in command, and my problem, once we got the leaks plugged, was to take this ship (now alone) on an island-hopping journey to New Guinea via Australia.

Here's what I was up against as we steamed away from Pearl Harbor. The island (Palmyra) that we had to reach was no larger, as I recall, than a city block. We had just enough fuel to reach it, but should we fail to find it, we could reach no other land in any direction. To know where we were at any moment, we had to identify stars, measure their heights with a sextant and note the time very precisely. Our only way to tell time precisely was that chronometer watch which would stop if we fired the 3-inch gun, so I decided we simply wouldn't fire it. If a Jap sub were to spot us, we were goners anyway, because that sub could outrun us, stay out of range of our 3-incher and pick us off with its 5-incher. We had a radio telephone which would transmit 50 miles, no more, and that was our only way to holler for help. We had no radar with which to spot ships or planes or land.

My feelings at the time were quite a mixture. I was worried: 33 lives in my hands, no real navigational experience beyond textbook exercises, and the chance we'd be attacked en route. I was angry at the Navy for sending us out alone with a captain too sick even to stand watch. I was exhausted from spending nights on the bridge, sextant in hand. I was more reverent than usual as I prayed for our safe arrival in Palmyra. And when that tiny island finally appeared, I was wonderfully relieved, self-confidant, grateful, and so tired that I slept for 20 hours.

I had a reason to tell you about this short period in my life. There was a lesson for me in that experience. I learned that in almost everything, war included, there is *some* good. War, in other words, is at least 98% bad and the 2% good is hard to find. That tiny bit of good is the pressure war puts on people to achieve way more than they think they can. Scientists speed up their rates of discovery, factory workers set new production records, and green ensigns grow up faster than they ever could have in civilian life. I learned in short order how to assume awesome responsibility, how to be decisive, and how to stay calm in crises.

So here's a game for you. Look at the worst things around you—even the worst people—and see whether you can find a smidgeon of good. Just don't start with turnips. I've looked hard for good in them. There isn't any.

LETTER 7

The House At 405

Would you like to read about my home and boyhood neighborhood? Here goes, but this may take more than one letter. My home was near the top of a hill in the heavily wooded section of Webster Groves, Missouri, known as Sherwood Forest. That section was not a housing development. Instead, houses were built one at a time, slowly, carefully, and with high-quality materials. The tools of construction were, of course, primitive by today's standards: no bulldozers or power drills or nail guns, for example. Horses pulled scoops to dig foundation holes. Men felled trees with axes and mixed concrete with shovels.

Ours was one of the smaller houses in Sherwood Forest. We five kids never felt cramped in it, though. Upstairs there were four bedrooms, two bathrooms, and a large sleeping porch. Downstairs were a living room, dining room, sunroom, kitchen, breakfast room, maid's room, and half-bath. It was a frame house with white, painted shingles, a slate roof, solid copper gutters and downspouts, solid oak flooring, and a two-car garage, all on a corner lot (100' x 125').

You will find, if you're lucky enough to live in a house for very long, that its shape and size are far less important than the memories it gives you. I lived in that house for about twenty years, and my mother stayed on for another three decades, so for over fifty years, it was either my home or my second home.

After my mother died and the house was set to be sold, I walked into every room, taking pictures of even the most insignificant objects: light fixtures, framed mirrors, the scorched underside of the fireplace mantel, and so on. And oh, how the

memories of my childhood surfaced! Right next to that light fixture
was an unpaintable spot. I made that spot long ago. With my first
chemistry set I managed a minor explosion that sent a thistle tube
and some strong acid into the ceiling. One framed mirror was
something I stared at while bedridden with scarlet fever. The
carvings in the top of the frame were not supposed to look like the
face of an ogre, but they certainly did to me as I lay in that bed.

The scorched mantel touched off a series of memories: boots
drying and numb hands warming in front of those roaring fires,
my having to stack five cords of oak logs before cold weather set in,
roasting marshmallows and hot dogs indoors, the night our roasting
chestnuts exploded, sending hot bits of shell onto the living room
rug.

There were also sad memories in those pictures. The one of
the sleeping porch took me back to a cold February morning in
1928. Three of us kids had spent the night on that porch, windows
open, snowflakes blowing in, down comforters up to our chins or
higher. I was nine years old. That morning our mother woke us
early to tell us our father had gone to heaven; he wouldn't be back
home. Not ever. We formed a huddle, and wept.

If the inside of the house was rich in memories, so was the
outside. The yard itself wasn't all that big—until you had to cut
the grass with a powerless push mower or rake all those leaves from
all those oak trees. We had a lot of sidewalk, ours being a corner
lot, so there was plenty of snow to shovel in the winter, and a heap
of weeds to dig from the cracks in summer. At some point, my
mother thought it would be nice to plant barberry bushes all along
those sidewalks. Having them, she felt, would make kids and dogs
take the long way around rather than cut through the yard. They'd
look nice, too, with scarlet berries and leaves that changed from
green to russet. What she didn't reckon with was the way a barberry
bush traps oak leaves and scratches the hands of anyone who tries
to remove them.

Even the picture of the little back porch (stoop) sparked
memories. During the mid-1930s, we were visited almost daily
by men who were hungry and broke, victims of the Great

Depression. My mother never turned any of them away. She didn't feel safe inviting them inside, and she couldn't give them much money, so she fed them and asked them to eat out on the back porch. Sometimes I sat with them, and although few of them ever spoke of their plights, I felt sorry for them and grateful for what we had. Not until many years later, while I was off fighting the war, did I learn from experience what it is like to go without food and wonder when I would eat again, if ever.

There were plenty of vacant lots in and around Sherwood Forest up until my late high school years, so we had no trouble getting up games. Of course we seldom had a regulation complement of players because there were too few boys the right age in the neighborhood, but we made do. Our dogs didn't wait to be invited to play, and they didn't learn the rules. I never forgave that airedale, Bing, for robbing me of a homer. He grabbed that ball I hit and took off like a greyhound after a rabbit.

Our neighborhood had something even better than games: houses under slow-motion construction. When the builders were on site we begged all sorts of materials. We got scrap boards and nails to build wagons and racers and roofs for our tunnels. We got wire to make little signal lights so we could send Morse code messages from one house to another. We got lead to melt and mold into lead soldiers. I now wonder, in view of the current fuss about lead poisoning, why we didn't go batty at an early age. Lead was a big thing in our lives, and not just for lead soldiers. We used it to weight toys; we shaped it into sinkers for our fishing lines; we made paint out of white lead, japan dryer, linseed oil, and turpentine.

After the workmen went home, we had skeletal structures to climb. Who could shinny up to the top of the roof support? Who could walk, tightrope fashion, a 20-foot length of 2 by 6? Who could climb to the attic and get back down when there were no stairs? Such explorations wouldn't be allowed today. Someone would whisper "liability," and the fun would end. But when I was young, parents simply told their kids to be careful, then let them learn for themselves what climbing was all about.

LETTER 8

Choosing Hobbies

Most of what I know about my father has come from pictures, relatives, and newspaper clippings. He was stocky, had dark hair, wore wire-rimmed glasses with perfectly circular lenses, worked extra hard, and died at age 36. He was raised in Arkansas by staunch Baptist parents who were absolutely certain that Catholic churches were stocked with guns. Parishioners awaited word from the pope to shoot every Protestant in sight.

My father had little formal education. Some say he got to the tenth grade, others that he didn't make it past the sixth. All agree that the family was too poor to let sons dawdle very long in school. He must have made the most of what education he had, though, because with his brother and his father, he built a successful publishing business: a trade magazine, *The American Paint Journal.*

He was a family man. That is to say he really liked having a family and was determined that his children would have more of everything than he had had. This, I think, drove him to spend too much time making money, and too little time just hanging around with us. The result was that I have few memories of him. I remember that he liked Model T Fords, and had one with a sun visor of cobalt glass. I remember he once gave me four boxing gloves for my birthday and scheduled a bout with Jimmy Rodgers, a boy my age who lived a block away. Jimmy bloodied my nose and ended my ring career before it began.

My one really delightful memory was his introducing me to fishing. He didn't mean to teach me a lesson that day. It just happened. He took me to a farm owned by one of his business friends, Mr. Van Hoffman, a farm with a fish hatchery. In perhaps a half-hour, I caught 22 rainbow trout. I remember the number because my father said, "Twenty-two, the same as your birthday, May 22." I was immediately hooked on fishing.

And what was the lesson I learned? It dawned on me years later: A child's first experience with a sport or game or hobby should be a successful one. There will be plenty of time to learn later that there will be bad days, but why not start out with a warm feeling to a new sport or game?

I wanted to give each of my children some happy first experiences. I ran out of ideas of how to do that though. My best was for Ken, who at age 3 or 4 decided my gardening work looked like fun. He'd like to plant some seeds. What kind? Watermelon, of course. (Boys that age like to grow *big, good tasting* crops. Carrots and beans are for the birds—or rabbits). So we planted watermelon seeds, and they sprouted, and the vines grew and had blossoms. But alas, no melons, and time was running out: Ken would soon go to Michigan with his mother. He needed success with his first gardening venture, so as he napped I bought the biggest melon I could find, lifted it into his patch, draped a vine over it, and waited for him to discover it.

Did I deceive him? Yes, just as my father had when he got me to think that whenever I had a half-hour to fish, I could catch 22 trout. I know better now. And Ken knows that blossoms don't turn into huge melons overnight. But my first experience with fishing didn't turn me against the sport—as that bloody nose had turned me against boxing—and Ken didn't get turned against gardening.

When I started this letter, I meant to write about a delightful decision you get to make all on your own. Don't let anyone make it for you. The decision is what hobby or hobbies to have, and it's delightful for several reasons. You have only yourself to please. You don't have to weigh pros and cons. You have lots of possibilities from which to choose. You can take as much time as you like. You can even change your mind if you choose the wrong hobby the first time.

It's probably a good idea to listen to others tell you why they like the hobbies they've chosen, and why they've rejected others, but *your* hobbies should be *your* call. Now, hang onto that thought as I ramble on about *my* likes and dislikes.

I'm biased in favor of hobbies. I wouldn't be without one. Hobbies are a way to be alone with happy thoughts, to escape the sometimes worrisome or humdrum aspects of life. I have known very few likeable people who were without hobbies.

I also have a pro-creative-hobby bias. I tried a few collective hobbies (stamps, baseball cards, coins) but gave up on them. Some other collective hobbies didn't catch my fancy at all. Collecting paintings was too expensive, butterflies too cruel, ancestral names and dates too uninteresting. I don't even like the *spelling* of genealogy; it ought to be spelled geneology. I have friends who are fascinated with their collections of genealogical data. To add a birth date, a death date or a begat name excites these people. That hobby is right for them. Not for me. I'm less interested in when a person started and ended life than in what he did in between. Even what an ancestor did might not interest me unless he or she won the Nobel Prize or rode shotgun for Capone or something else really noteworthy.

The only things I collect are those that come my way more or less automatically. That's not a hobby. For hobbies, I like to *make* things. I call them *creative* hobbies; they might better be called *constructive* hobbies since I use raw materials.

For the last few years, my hobby time has been split between making tangibles and intangibles. The tangibles are items I make of wood: a ship's wheel, furniture, turnings, and carvings. The intangibles are my writings and my computer software models.

Two observations about my hobbies. First, the end-product must please me, no one else. If someone else is pleased, that's fine but not essential. I want to be able to pat my ship's wheel or manuscript and say, "I did my best." Second, for a hobby to be right for me, it must have this effect on me: It must be able to grab me on short notice and completely absorb me, blocking out all other thoughts.

Enough said. Go find yourself a hobby or two. You won't regret it.

LETTER 9

Great Ears

Did you ever notice the way a single thought can take you on a mental ride down winding and branching roads? I often find it fun. Like this afternoon. It's December, with signs and sounds of Christmas everywhere. My initial thought was of gifts: the ones your grandmother will buy because she enjoys shopping a lot more than I do. She also has an uncanny knack for knowing *what* gifts various friends and relatives would like. She even makes great guesses at peoples' *sizes*.

I recalled gifts I have been given: children's toys, grown-up toys, clothes. When I was a lad, I had relatives who gave me clothes. I don't know what they had in mind. Maybe they thought I looked in need of new clothes—which I probably did. I didn't want new clothes. I wanted something to play with, and something good to eat.

I began my mental ride on a road called Intangible Gifts, the kind for which people thank God: health, family, freedom from want. Why is it, I wondered, that those people use such broad terms? Each year after Christmas and my birthday, I had to write thank-you letters, even for gifts of clothing, and they had to be specific. I had to thank Aunt June, not for clothes, but for dark blue wool socks, which would keep my feet toasty on the skating pond. I figure that people who are grateful for good health should at least mention their five senses.

Off to the right I went, down an Avenue called Sound. As gifts go, the gift of hearing is high on my list, and not just because it adds to the pleasure of day-to-day living. It also fetches memories stashed deep in the brain. I hear the bark of a big dog, and I remember my Great Dane, Horace. He used to sleep in bed with me, a single bed beside a wall. More than once, Horace stretched those long legs of his, and, with his back against the wall, shoved me out of bed onto the floor.

Horace was the only dog I ever had who bayed at the moon. He was good at it. He didn't even need a full moon. A half moon was enough to make him wail long and loud. If he bothered the neighbors, they never said so, maybe because big dogs were popular around there. But then one morning the police came to our house. It seems a woman who lived blocks away said she'd been wakened from a sound sleep by the baying of a dog. When the baying didn't stop she got up, got into her car, searched for the source of the eerie noise and found it. And I had thought Horace's voice couldn't carry even a block.

At one of your little league baseball games, I heard the crack of a bat. It's a more metallic sound than what I used to hear when all batters swung Louisville Sluggers made of wood—ash, I believe, or hickory. Still, the sound of a ball coming off today's bat takes me back in time. Son Ken had persuaded me to take him to a Sunday afternoon Cardinal double-header. He could hardly have chosen a better day. Stan Musial hit a homer, then another, and another. After that, the stadium got quiet as a tomb whenever Musial stepped up to the plate. When we heard the cracks of the bat for those fourth and fifth homers, we just knew those balls were long gone, and records had been broken. So many sounds, so many memories.

Seldom these days do I hear a hoot owl. When I do, I think of the family of owls that lived in the vacant Papin lot and spooked little kids for the fun of it. I hear the bang of a firecracker, probably not so loud as the bang from the cherry salute Johnny Longmire lobbed onto the window sill near my bed one night. That was some firecracker! It blew a hole in the screen and woke everyone in the house except me. I was a sound sleeper.

As I thought about the sound of trains, I found myself on yet another street in my mental ride. The street sign read Tragedy. It didn't seem right because I am, in many ways, fond of trains.

As a boy I rode them, slept, and ate on them, stood outside on the rear platform and let them flatten pennies for me. I waved to engineers, befriended conductors, and played with electric trains. Two railroads, the Frisco and the Missouri Pacific, had tracks close enough to our house that we could hear the engines chug. It was a happy sound.

But one day a train did something ugly. It killed someone I liked. His name was Tom, who, as far as I could tell, had never hurt anyone. I don't know how old he was. I do know he was a Negro who seemed ever able to flash a smile and carry on a happy conversation even though his life must have been tough. He whistled, too—lively tunes with rhythm. That was unusual. Most Negroes in those days didn't whistle; they sang. Tom worked on the grease rack at the local Socony-Mobil station.

What I had seen in Tom was a facade, a front. Within him were depression and desperation. He walked down the Frisco tracks and just let the train end his misery. Later I learned that others during the Great Depression did what Tom had done. It was, they felt, the only way to provide for their destitute families. The railroads were compelled by law to pay damages to the families of people run down by trains.

Do I blame trains for what happened to Tom? Of course not; but when I hear a train, my memories are not just happy ones. I remember Tom.

Well, that's how today's mental trip went: Gifts? Intangibles? Sound? Tragedy. I'll probably explore a few more side streets before it's time for bed, but that's enough to give you the idea, and maybe to convince you to try a trip of your own.

LETTER 10

Uncle Walter

This seems a good point in my letter writing to tell you about my Uncle Walter, who had and then lost one of those great gifts I wrote about in my last letter.

On my mother's side of the family there were my grandparents, known to me as Mom and Pop, and three children: my Auntie May, my Uncle Walter, and my Mother. At about the turn of the century, while the children were quite young, the family lived on Chicago's south side. When Uncle Walter was a toddler and just learning to speak, he was chased by a mastiff, fell down, and got a nasty cut. Within days, infection set in, and a bit later Uncle Walter had spinal meningitis. Whether the meningitis actually came from the cut is anyone's guess. The family always thought so. Whatever the cause, Uncle Walter was rendered totally deaf. The auditory nerve had been wiped out. Never again would he hear a bird chirp, an orchestra play, or a person speak.

Mom and Pop were devastated but not beaten. In the years that followed, they were as heroic, I think, as anyone on any branch or twig of my family tree. They set themselves a near-impossible goal. They would see to it that Uncle Walter led a normal life. He would not spend his days with deaf children. He would not use sign language. He would read lips, and he would speak. He would be taught those skills at home, first by his parents, later by his sisters. By age five, he would be skillful enough to attend a regular school. He would not attend a school for the deaf—if there even was one at the time.

His boyhood evidently went well. In school he lip-read what

teachers said except when they spoke while facing the blackboard, and he got help on his homework from his family.

He must have learned, early on, how important it was that he avoid hanging around the house. At his parents' urging, he ventured forth, made friends, played games, and had the usual boyhood adventures. After school one day, he wandered toward Lake Michigan and found the Jackson Park Yacht Club where a kindly boat owner showed him around. The boat owner invited him back for a sail that week-end provided he had a note from home. By the time he finished grade school, he was hooked on sailing and was often asked to be a crewman. In more than one year he was in the 300-mile long Chicago to Mackinac race; he had an internal sensor that enabled him to predict oncoming storms—a valuable trait in such a long race.

High school also went well. Month by month his self confidence grew. He seemed to view his affliction more as a challenge than a handicap. Why shouldn't he try doing whatever his classmates could do, he wondered. He went out for football. Now football in those days was a bit different from today's game. The quarterback always stood in the shotgun position to holler out signals and receive the ball from the center. Uncle Walter knew where he should be. He should play center. He could learn to read the quarterback's lips upside down. Which he did, apparently quite well. His team won the Chicago city championship, and he cherished that little gold football for life.

College didn't go so well. He couldn't always lip-read the bearded professors, and his family couldn't always tutor him on college level courses. He learned a trade: maintenance and operation of linotype machines.

The family moved to St. Louis in time for the World's Fair there in 1904. Mother and Auntie May graduated from college; Auntie May moved to Birmingham to do social work; Mother married and had my brothers, sisters, and me. Uncle Walter continued to live with Mom and Pop, at first in a house a mile away from ours, and later (after my father died) in a house only a block away.

Still living his "normal" life, he learned to drive (a new 1928 Studebaker), held down a job, became a co-owner of a series of sailboats, joined an athletic/social club, and went to the movies (silent with subtitles).

He drove for nearly four decades with nary a ticket or dent. Lots of miles, too. Weekdays he drove to and from work in downtown St. Louis. On summer week-ends in the 1940s and 1950s, he and I drove to and from Michigan. He liked Chryslers at that time. He'd buy one, a coupe with jump-seat space, take great care of it, and part with it when the odometer read 200,000 or so. I remember when he got the 1950 car, and brought it around to show me. "I just made a salesman's day for him," he said. "How so?" I asked. "I let him sell a deaf man a car radio. I bet he'll brag about that to his boss and his wife and anyone else who'll listen." We used that radio on our many Michigan trips. I'd turn it on, usually to a ball game, and repeat the play by play account of the game while Uncle Walter read my lips. When we drove at night he got help from the map light.

In the 1930s, Pop died. Mom lasted a little longer, growing peculiar enough toward the end to hide dollar bills under the wallpaper. With her passing, Uncle Walter lived alone. He went to work, came home, and most nights ate supper at our house. There was something he'd have to take care of. Without a hearing person in the house, he had no way to tell when an alarm clock or a doorbell rang. He got a cocker spaniel, a smart one whom he named Chief. Chief quickly learned that whenever he heard a knock or a bell or other unusual noise, he was to alert Uncle Walter and lead him to the source of the noise. Uncle Walter, for reasons unknown, had not disconnected the phone after Mom's death, so Mother phoned to him to let him know that dinner was about ready. She'd call his number, the phone would ring, Chief would lead Uncle Walter to the phone, and he (Uncle Walter) would lift the receiver, replace it, and walk to our house. Except for the occasional wrong-number caller, the system worked well.

The rest of Uncle Walter's life was fairly normal, fairly full. Auntie May retired from her social work in Birmingham and came back home, where she kept house for him. He went on working and playing and seeking challenges. He'd have me check out movies (without subtitles) and tell him whether there were so many dark scenes that he'd have trouble lip reading. Amazingly, he got interested in music! He played records on our Magnavox and "listened" with his fingers on top of the record player.

A remarkable life.

LETTER 11

Feelings About Money

A guy I know just bought a new car. It's German, expensive, bright red, and, according to Jimmy, high-powered. He's quite proud of it and worries about its well-being. He parks it on a slant, using up two parking spaces, because he dreads seeing that first scratch. Whether he takes it out in the rain I can't say.

If I had ever taken a psychology course, I might be able to hoke up an explanation for his having bought this car. But I didn't, and I can't. He's too old to go cruising around in it in search of gullible young girls. It's too small to use to haul anything. It doesn't even get decent gas mileage.

Mutual friends, some of whom must envy Jimmy, have a very simple explanation. They say Jimmy thinks the only thing to do with money is spend it, preferably on stuff he can brag about or show off. They speculate that he never shook a childhood habit of rushing to stores whenever he had money in his pocket. Could be.

The thing is, Jimmy has found a comfortable attitude toward money. Although it wouldn't suit me, he likes it, and that's what counts. While he was growing up, there were periods of dreadful inflation. If he didn't buy a car one day, its price went up, up, up. And if he didn't have the full price of the car, he simply borrowed. It was the thing to do. His peers all did it. They didn't wait until they had saved the full price. The idea was why wait? Buy now, enjoy now, and don't worry about the future.

During the Depression, when I saw too often what happened to those without money, I became a saver. I saw families with no wage earners, families who lost their homes, families forming makeshift communities, like Hooverville on the Mississippi levee, where the shacks were made of scraps: cloth, wood, metal, cardboard. When you see enough of that sort of poverty and despair, you decide to save and not to put too many eggs in a single basket, and above all to avoid going heavily into debt.

I sometimes wonder why so few people use logic as they decide whether or not to borrow. Let's say you want some furniture that costs $1200 and that you're able to save $100 a month. You could save for a year and buy the furniture outright. Or you could borrow the money, and, over the next year, pay maybe $1400 for the furniture. You pay an extra $200 in interest to a lender who will see to it that you save more than $100 a month and pay it to him or her. I hate the idea of paying someone to force me to save.

Now what will your attitudes toward money be? Will you come by them automatically, the way Jimmy and I did? If I had it to do over again, I'd work at it. I'd *think* about each of a bunch of verbs that go with the noun money. *Save, spend, find, lose, borrow, repay, squander, give, gamble, lend, invest.*

All in all, I rather like money. The quest of it made me ambitious and industrious. Earning it let me raise a family. Making myself save some of it was an exercise in self-discipline. I enjoyed buying tangible things with it—tools and sensible cars, for instance—but buying intangibles was even better. I bought warm feelings when I gave away some of it. I bought a feeling of relief when I mailed the last college tuition check. And I bought a glorious feeling of independence when I picked up enough stocks and bonds to see us through retirement.

One day, when our children were fairly young (mostly grade-schoolers), I had a twinge of conscience. With six kids, a none-too-handsome salary, and a commitment to save something each month, there wasn't much to spend on frills. Was I being too stingy? Was I depriving my children of the many toys and clothes their friends had?

I came up with a plan, a totally irresponsible plan according to my father-in-law. He felt that children could learn the value of a dollar only by *earning* money. My plan was to let them learn by *spending.* I went to the bank and withdrew $600, all in brand new one-dollar bills, and gift- wrapped six packages of $100 each. After supper that night the whole family squatted on the living room floor. With a tape recorder running I had them guess what was in the packages. They squeezed those packages, shook them to listen for telltale rattles, checked them for heft, and sniffed them. Most of the kids were stumped. Only one was absolutely sure that his package was a jumbo-sized Hershey bar.

The squeals when they opened those packages—and later on the tape replay—were really something. In those days $100 was a heap of money, especially to a grade-schooler. Once I had set their minds at ease that this wasn't play money, I gave them the simple rules. "This is money you must *spend*, not save or give away. Just take as long as you like to decide what you want to buy."

The plan turned out well. The kids mulled over all sorts of things they might buy, some of them for months. They learned something about the value of money all right as they read price tags. They also surprised your grandparents by buying things we had not dreamed they had wanted.

One thing that the kids decided to do was to pool some of their money to buy a Sailfish—a small sailboat similar to a Sunfish. The kids knew that their grandfather (my father-in-law—the one who thought my plan was so irresponsible) had been saving his spare change to buy the boat for them. Here he was, a retired vice-president of Kimberly-Clark, slowly depositing into a big jar the loose change that he accumulated each week so he could save up the $425 necessary to buy the boat for them. He had intended this method to be a lesson for the kids in the value of saving up for things they wanted rather than just going out and impulsively buying. Well, each of the kids contributed $25 to the kitty, and the next summer (and for many years afterward), they enjoyed that sailboat. Maybe everyone learned something that year about spending, saving, and sharing.

I tell you about this plan, this experiment, because it showed me one more thing that money is good for. It can buy wonderful memories. Ask your parents and aunts and uncles if that's not so.

LETTER 12

Food—Some of It Edible

Some folks, as they grow old, don't *do* much. With little of interest to talk about, they jabber about ailing body parts, feeble friends, and food-diets, recipes, bargain restaurants, cholesterol.

And wouldn't you know it! I've chosen *FOOD* as the topic of this letter. I'd apologize for this, but it was inevitable. I come from a family of eaters, I like food, and I've had some memorable experiences with food.

Just about every aspect of food has changed during the years that separate your generation and mine. In grocery stores during my childhood, there were no frozen foods, no microwaveable foods, no prefabricated pizzas, no prepackaged meats, no canned soft drinks, no mysterious labels about the contents of our food, no foods marked lite or fat-free. We bought fresh food from experts we knew on a first-name basis. If they said it was good, it was. In most homes in my neighborhood, mothers chose the menus, got the food, cooked it, and served it. The kids were stuck with cleaning up. In our house, Mother had certain rules-of-thumb about this whole process. We had to have variety in our meals. We had to have proper amounts of protein, carbohydrate, fat, and vitamins each day—even if that meant swallowing a spoonful of cod liver oil. We ate supper each night at 6 PM with the whole family in attendance, hands washed, elbows off the table, dogs with anxious looks not far away.

Those 6 PM suppers were a big part of what made us a family. Around that oak table, we laughed and argued and reported on the day's doings. We also fussed on the nights Mother served liver or Brussels sprouts. To qualify for dessert, we had to eat a certain amount of main course stuff, so we went to great lengths to win the prize. I recall wrapping pea-sized pellets of liver in whole strips of bacon. The desserts Mother fixed made it all worthwhile. She loved to bake, and turned out all sorts of yummies: pies, cakes, tarts, cookies, caramel rolls, coffee cakes, cream puffs, chocolate eclairs (with *real* whipped cream), shortcakes, cobblers, and apple dumplings.

Sunday nights in our house were different. On Sundays we kids were in command. We made up the menus, paying attention only to taste, not nutritional value, and we took our meals standing up in the kitchen. Let's say our main course (or only course) was doughnuts. Mother mixed the dough and got the caldron of grease piping hot. We kids rolled and cut the dough, watched the doughnuts turn tan, then popped them into sacks, added powdered sugar, and shook. There was no waiting for doughnuts to cool. We had *hot* suppers, hot enough for an occasional burnt lip. On other Sundays we feasted on popovers, cinnamon toast (made from home-baked bread), cornbread sticks soaked with pure maple syrup, and waffles.

For better or worse, suppers like those are a thing of the past. Fast food is now easy to get. Little league games are played at supper time. Kids can fend for themselves, given a microwave and a few frozen packages. Mothers care little about cooking and less about baking. Seldom does a whole family gather around the dining room table.

Mother had one weakness when it came to cooking. She liked to experiment, and when she did, we kids shuddered. We just knew we'd hate whatever she made, and we knew, too, we'd have to eat it. Remember, in those days a kid wasn't allowed to turn down food just because he or she didn't like it. But seldom did Mother push us to the edge. The closest she came was the day she served brain fritters. The next day my sister, Mary, scissored a slue of foul-sounding recipes from Mother's cookbooks.

Mother's urge to experiment may have come from my grandfather, Pop. He didn't cook. He just looked for odd foods to eat, and, for reasons known only to him, he chose to introduce me to some of his favorites. He saw to it that my first bite of catfish was right. "It has to be a channel cat with a bluish gray belly, not over a foot long, and caught in cold moving water," he told me. Good advice. Raw oysters were hard for me to swallow the first time, but were great later on. By the time he finished teaching me about odd foods, I had tastes for smelly cheeses, snails, frog legs, and suckling pigs cooked head and all.

What Pop didn't prepare me for were a few later eating adventures. Live fish, for example, raw octopus, and fried agave worms. And I wonder what Pop would have thought about a meal Bruce Reeves once had. Bruce was a New Zealander who served aboard our ship for a year or so. Early in the war, he had been trapped in Borneo when the Japs invaded that country. To escape, he needed, sought, and got help from natives (Dyaks) who took him through jungles and down streams, hid him, sheltered him, and fed him. Most of the meals were pretty bad, but one day the Dyaks handed Bruce a coconut bowl of delicious meat stew. He had seconds, complimented them on it, and insisted on knowing what kind of meat it was. He shouldn't have. It was human!

There's another eating adventure I was going to tell you about here, but I've decided to put it in a later letter. Look for the story of Steve and the key lime pie.

LETTER 13

Two Splendid Files

Shortly after I retired and bought my first computer, I remembered what a programmer told me back in the late 1950s or early 1960s. "The computer is mighty nice to people who change their minds as often as they change underwear," he said. "It lets them erase or add or move numbers and words. If they think a report would be better with graphs instead of tables and with a few new paragraphs of explanation, the computer will oblige."

With that thought in mind, I asked my first computer to set up two files, one called NUMBERS, the other IDEAS, and to assume that I would change both files often.

Let me tell you about those files. The NUMBERS file began because I was struck by the way numbers seem to touch us at every turn. At first I put in the more obvious numbers: bank accounts, credit cards, car licenses, birth dates, insurance policies. Later I added some less obvious ones: serial numbers for cars, cameras, and computer, the combination of the bicycle padlock, prescriptions for eye glasses, formulas for house paints, the codes needed to make car keys when the originals are lost.

It has been a handy file for me. I update it maybe three times a year, usually to take care of changes in phone numbers, licenses or insurance policies. Meantime, I know where to look first when someone asks me for a number. And someone often does.

My IDEAS file is a lot less practical and a lot more interesting. As the name suggests, this is where I stash ideas—all sorts of ideas. Some of them are original, some from books I read or pictures I see or conversations I hear. What do these ideas have in common?

Only that at one time or another they struck me as worth jotting down.

Here now is an ample sample of items from my IDEAS file. In collecting figures of speech, I have found John Updike to be a great source: "Her shaved armpit gleamed like a piece of chicken skin . . . ." "The doomsday hiss of a wife who at night smells gas . . . ." "His heart beat like a wasp in a jar . . . ." "He exclaimed 'Darling,' and their heads fell together like bagged oranges . . . ." "Behind him, the bus doors closed: pterodactyl wings . . . ." "As valuable as a 1939 MoPac timetable . . . ." "Sugar hit the floor with a sound like one stroke of a drummer's brush."

John Irving writing about older women: "There was nothing for her to do in the sun but burn . . . ." "She had the vague, unfocused look of someone over forty who might be sixty—or would be tomorrow . . . ." "Her skin (from make-up) was clay."

And here are a few of my own: "Moral fiber makes good fabric but dissolves in alcohol." "A last name that sounds like a Polish sausage on a stick." "Young boys settle happily for empty calories and full stomachs." "Culture is what you find in museums, music halls, libraries, and petri dishes." "A grin like a gash in his face." "Headmaster: a man in charge of a navy bathroom." "As rare as a Baptist belly dancer."

To live up to its name, the IDEAS file has to contain more than figures of speech, and it does. In it are various thoughts which would have long since been forgotten had I not recorded them. Some, I am sure, should have been forgotten. Still, it's fun for me to read them now and then.

In this world of ours, which thinks *change* and *progress* are synonyms, I once thought about what hasn't changed in the last fifty years. Deer still don't cross at deer crossing signs. Tornadoes still like to buzz trailer parks. Adolescents and parents still bug one another. When babies cry, it's still for one of three reasons: hunger, gas, or leakage, and no adult can be right on the first guess. Dogs are still choosy about the trees they'll anoint. Politicians still lie and charge others with perjury. Restaurants still give seconds on coffee but not on tea. Getting a breakfast without grits down

South is still most difficult. Swallows, whales, and crocuses still show up more or less on schedule.

About fifteen percent of my IDEAS file is the "Memories" section. The entries there are cryptic—usually an isolated word or two, just enough to jog my memory. For example, there's the name of a chemical: methyl salicylate. It's the chemical that gives root beer its taste, liniments their sting, and wintergreen life savers their flavor and tingle. When I see the name of that chemical, I recall a summer in Michigan.

We were in a cottage Mother had rented from Mrs. Wrenn. As a normal thirteen-year-old, I knew how to make root beer. In a large ceramic crock, you mix a lot of sugar, a fair bit of water, a smidgeon of root beer extract (containing the methyl salicylate), and a cake of yeast. Using a wooden paddle—metal won't do— you stir until the sugar and yeast are dissolved, then pour the mixture into bottles, cap the bottles, and let the root beer age.

For me, that was the hard part: letting it age. I was long on thirst, short on patience, and the yeast wanted several days to make the right amount of fizz. I hurried things a bit by letting my bottles sunbathe in the side yard.

Once the fizz was just right, the bottles had to be kept cool, and the root beer had to be drunk fairly soon; otherwise it would taste yeasty or get gassy enough to explode the bottles. This called for serious drinking. Each batch was five gallons, and I always had a new batch ageing while the one before it was being drunk. There were bottles of root beer everywhere: in the ice box, in the pantry, under my bed, on the back porch.

It was a fun summer, and I didn't lose my taste for root beer, and as we left for home, Mother told Mrs. Wrenn we'd be back next year. We were, too, even though in May Mrs. Wrenn wrote Mother to say she would have to pay extra for the damage done by bottles of root beer having blown up under my bed.

Why do I tell you all this about my IDEAS file? I'm not sure. I think it's to make the point that fascinating ideas have a way of getting away from us if we don't record them. I hate to lose them, don't you?

LETTER 14

A Bit of Wartime Fun

This will be about two guys on two consecutive days during the war. Commander Fairchild was *Regular Navy*, which is to say that he was overly fond of picky rules and not at all fond of Navy Reservists. Lt. (j.g.) John Montgomery was the captain we got after his chronically seasick predecessor was beached. John had been a lawyer and judge in civilian life. He knew very little about navigation and seamanship and ordnance, but he understood *people*, and that's what made him a splendid choice for captain of our ship, the USS YMS-393. Like all but two enlisted men aboard our ship, he was a *Reservist*, just the sort of junior officer Commander Fairchild would happily bully.

That didn't worry John a bit. He had the Regular-vs-Reserve thing all figured out. The Regulars were in the war for glory. To get that, they needed to be on *fighting* ships, big ships with clout and speed. Reservists had merely signed on for the duration. They had to settle for small ships: landing craft, subchasers, minesweepers, PTs. Most of them—us—were content to forget the glory and mouth the slogan, "Back alive in '45."

What John saw in all this was a chance to run his ship his way with no fear of retaliation. We were a small group having to live together under tough circumstances. We had no need for fat books of rules. If the Regular Navy guys didn't like the way John did things, what could they do? He was, after all, captain of his ship. To reprimand him, they would have to relieve him of his command and court-martial him, probably back in the U.S. Any Regular Navy officer who made such a fuss when he was supposed to be fighting a war would get in trouble himself.

Just a tad more background before I describe the two days John and Commander Fairchild had. The locale was New Guinea during the early days of the war. Our ship had orders for the first few months to escort convoys along the southern coast of New Guinea. Every month, in the dark phase of the moon, we rode at the outer edge of a convoy, pinging away with our Sonar, listening for echoes off enemy subs, and standing ready to drop depth charges. The ships we escorted were a ragtag lot: landing craft, good sized supply ships, little motor launches, even a few sailboats without engines. Ships were in short supply in our part of the world, in the Pacific, because more ships were needed in the Atlantic; so we used whatever would float and carry men and supplies.

We were not very good at this. The nights were black as a coal mine at midnight, and in war zones, ships didn't turn on outside lights. Luckily, the Japs had few subs in the area.

(This will seem out of place but it's not). There was some question about the legality of my keeping my handsome beard. The Navy's Uniform Regulations said it was O.K. if my commanding officer, John, agreed, and he did. But some sort of wartime fleet orders said no beard, no how.

On one of our escort trips the convoy included the USS OTIS, a good-sized supply ship, a *Regular Navy* supply ship with Commander Fairchild aboard. We were to stay 300 yards off the OTIS's starboard beam as the convoy zigzagged throughout the night. We were to vacate that position only to go depth charge a sub. As luck would have it, we were a good 1500 yards out of position by the first light of dawn. By late afternoon we were anchored, and John was on his way to the USS OTIS, having been ordered there by Commander Fairchild, USN (not USNR). To hear John tell about it, Fairchild was furious at our failure to protect the OTIS, got all trembly and purple in the face, and didn't appreciate John's advising him to calm down. John just couldn't back off, though. He told Fairchild that a Jap sub commander would take one look at the OTIS and decide it wasn't worth a torpedo.

The very next day I took a working party to the OTIS to pick up food for our ship, and right away I ran into Commander

Fairchild. Well, darned if he didn't order me into the wardroom, where he told me to shave and report back to him within the hour. So I quoted Uniform Regulations about how I could have a beard if my commanding officer agreed, and right away he did what John had described. He trembled and got purplish, and his speaking voice got ever so loud. He wanted to know the names of my ship and my captain, and when I told him USS YMS-393 and John Montgomery, I thought he'd explode. He grabbed his cap and called a launch alongside to take us back to the 393. Silly as it seemed to me, this three-striper was going to all this trouble to order John to order me to get rid of my beard. There just had to be more important matters for someone of that rank to handle.

We rode back in strained silence. I wasn't aware, as we got near the ship, that one of the crewmen, a lad named Pourcelli, would add to the excitement of the moment. A week or two earlier, Pourcelli had gone ashore and found, in the wake of fleeing Japs, a complete Jap marine uniform. Above the left pocket of that uniform Pourcelli then painted fake campaign ribbons—lots of them, so many that they went up over the shoulder. As we pulled alongside the 393, there he was: Pourcelli in full Jap uniform standing the deck watch. It was he who would give Fairchild a hand coming aboard. Now even on a fairly loosely run ship, the men don't stand watch in enemy uniforms. And who, other than Pourcelli, would do all that and stand there polishing his fingernails on fake campaign ribbons?

I led the way to the wardroom for the second Fairchild-Montgomery bout. John hadn't expected this visitor, but it wouldn't have made any difference. He had his bare feet propped up when we entered. All he wore, in fact, was a pair of khaki shorts, and he didn't rise to greet the visitor, but simply said, "Hi ya Commander."

Whereupon, Fairchild fumed and shouted before he finally got around to ordering John to order me to shave my beard. John just smiled and spoke softly, "I like it. It stays."

I was sure we had now done enough to get John a court-martial, but I was wrong. None of us even got a scolding. Not John or Pourcelli or me. And I kept my beard for another year.

LETTER 15

Sniffing

Until half an hour ago this letter was to have been about flaws. That will have to wait. Instead, I'll now write about sniffing. For thirty minutes, give or take five, I've been sniffing and thinking about sniffing. No, I don't do that often. It was an experiment, and, as I found, a pleasant diversion, though not the sort that bears frequent repetition. Should you find yourself with a bit of free time and decide to run your own sniffing experiment, as I hope you will, you'll want to do it in private. The sight of someone wandering around sniffing strikes folks as odd.

Several summers ago, a friend of mine was hospitalized after having had a bad fall. Once he passed the crisis period and was fit to roam the corridors, he had a new worry: how to dress for his walks. Hospital regulations called for his wearing a flimsy gown with a back door that didn't want to stay shut. He could wear a bathrobe over the gown, his keepers told him, but alas, he owned no bathrobe. Never had. Didn't believe in them.

Well, your grandmother, one of your great aunts, and my friend's wife conspired. Instead of buying a bathrobe, which would be used for a few days at most, they'd simply borrow mine. That was just fine with me, so your grandmother put it through the washer and dryer, and I thought no more about it until mid-afternoon. Out in the driveway, for all the neighbors to see, were those three female conspirators taking turns sniffing my bathrobe. Not a pretty sight. Someone not privy to the story might have thought those women were abnormal, maybe perverted. So if you run a sniffing experiment, do it in private.

It's a wonder noses aren't better appreciated. Maybe that's because they're not pretty or because they run or get broken or itch or get stopped up or sprout teenage zits. What I like about my nose are its connections. It's hooked through that olfactory nerve to all the right places in my brain. I don't pretend to understand how the whole process works, and I have yet to hear or read an explanation of it.

My sketchy understanding of it goes something like this. I get a whiff of, say, clove—which is what started my sniffing experiment this morning. The sensation passes to the outer layer of my brain's memory where tens of thousands of odors have been tagged and stored. My brain plays back a simple identification message: "What you smell is *clove*, not cinnamon or hot dog or essence of skunk or Brussels sprouts."

What happens next is even more remarkable. Having identified my whiff as clove, my brain, without being asked, checks its deeper layers of memory. It looks for and finds records of my many encounters with clove. Just think, one whiff to activate a host of memories!

I was young again, maybe twelve, hungry as always, having supper at home. It was a ham and yam night, and before Mother started to carve, she told us this was an Arkansas ham, and, as everyone knows, there is none better. I think that was the first time I saw a ham tacked with cloves. Mother was right. That was one fine ham.

Not all my experiences with cloves were so happy. Years ago I had a toothache and couldn't see a dentist right away, so I settled for a home remedy: a drop of oil of cloves on that sore tooth. What ever became of all those natural home remedies we used to have? How many homes would I have to check before finding one with a bottle of oil of cloves?

By sixth grade, several of us boys who walked home together had begun to teach one another all those subjects our teachers and parents said we'd learn about when we were older. The unchallenged expert of our group was Bob Collins. He knew all about what adults did when their kids weren't watching, for instance, or so he claimed, and we believed him.

The afternoon he told us about adults and whiskey made a lasting impression. None of us had ever seen a tipsy adult or had any notion that people could turn into pathetic drunks. Bob said adults are so ashamed of drinking that they do it where no one can see them, and then, so others won't smell whiskey on their breath, they chew cloves. For months after Bob told us that, I used my nose to spot adults who had been drinking. I wonder how often I was wrong. Lots of non-drinking adults chewed clove gum in those days.

There's something else I should mention about noses besides their being well-connected. They're well positioned with the eyes just above, the mouth just below, and the ears just around the corners. This makes for good sensory cooperation. A rose is mighty nice looking, especially when it's just going past the tight-bud stage. It's also nice to sniff. But for best results, it needs to be sniffed *and* looked at. For me, the sight and smell of carnations used to conjure up memories of First Communions and funerals. And then some horticulturist stripped carnations of their perfume. Why?

Most of the time the senses reassure one another. Steaks look good, smell good, and taste good. So do cherry pies with crisscross crust, caramel rolls, curried shrimp, and popcorn. But you can't always count on sensory cooperation. Oysters are great on taste, fair on odor, and awful on looks. Coffee has a wonderful aroma but (to me) a yucky taste. Limburger cheese is foul-smelling and not much to look at, but delicious.

When I began this letter, I meant to list the various items I had sniffed in the previous thirty minutes, and tell you what they made me remember. But I didn't get very far, did I? It's just as well. My memories, after I sniffed the bananas and bleach and all that other stuff this morning, are probably of little interest to you.

And anyway, what I really hope for with this letter is to convert you into a part time sniffer. Just try not to be downhearted because your nose isn't as good as the average Bloodhound's. Bloodhounds have fewer memories than you do. Or so we think.

LETTER 16

You're Not What You Eat

What makes us turn out the way we do? Is it, as some say, strictly hereditary, all in the genetic goo, the genes, the DNA? Such a theory doesn't sit well with those whose DNA makes them "different" in a negative way. Thomas Jefferson wouldn't have liked it either because he'd have had to change that maxim about *all* men (and presumably women) being created equal. With a googol of possible variations in DNA structure, the new maxim should be: *no* men are created equal.

Some folks claim that what really molds us is our environment rather than our heritage. That's the favorite theory of those defense lawyers who want to claim their clients were naughty because they had been mistreated early in life. What I like about this theory is the hope it promises. We can change our environment. Not so with our DNA. If our DNA says we're born to be short, we're never going to play center for an NBA team.

Yet another explanation is that we are what we eat. Now there's a theory for you! If you want a sweet disposition, just load up on pastries and banana splits, and avoid limes and sauerkraut. For a deep, mysterious personality, eat goulash, chow mein and meatloaf. If you want to become a whole new person, try cannibalism.

In the 1930s we had a simple, if shaky, explanation for all this. We were sure that a combination of heredity (10%) and environment (90%) was what made people what they were. With DNA yet to be discovered, we thought of heredity as the unseen force that gave a baby his father's eyes or his mother's chin. When we used the term "environment" we had in mind the present or

the future, not the past. There were very few psychologists around
to scare us with nightmares about early-childhood environments.
What we needed during those depression times was *hope*. We needed
to hope that by changing our present environment, things would
get better for us. What we surely did *not* need was to be told that
because of our heritage and our earlier environment, our future
was all but unchangeable.

It's a shame we couldn't have taken the you-are-what-you-eat
theory seriously. We did have fun eating. The only labels we read
were ones with coupons for free samples. If we ever ran across the
word cholesterol, it must have been during spelling bees. Should I
have come up with a well-balanced personality for having eaten so
many different kinds of food? I'll never know. Exactly *how* Mother's
five children turned out as they did was unimportant to her. What
mattered was that each child was unique, a true individual, and
Mother never let us forget what being an individual was all about.
For me, there were messages such as these: Stand on your own two
feet . . . Create your own set of principles and live by them . . . If
you stray from those principles, don't pretend that what you've
done is OK because others do it . . . Being an individual means
you are better than other individuals in some ways, worse in
others . . . Don't throw up your hands and join a group just because
you lack the courage to stand alone.

A lot of good came out of that bit of philosophy. Best of all, I
think, was the spirit of trust. Since I had my own set of principles
I didn't need a slue of picky rules. I neither needed nor had curfews,
for example. Mother trusted me to be home by what in my
judgment was a decent hour.

Another benefit of this philosophy was the way it got me to
think of others as individuals rather than as members of groups.
Oh, I didn't always blot out thoughts of groups. I just didn't let
groups get top billing the way the public does today. My concerns
were not with Hispanics and Blacks and Whites and Seniors. They
were with *individuals*. James Lee Young, for instance.

He was the richest man aboard our ship (the 393). His money
had come first from a restaurant he owned, and later from a string

of cabs. His wife, judging from the only picture of her he ever showed me, was quite heavy, and clearly upset. Maybe she was angry that the government had drafted her husband, and left her to run the restaurant and cabs. She and James had no children.

With minimal formal education, James Lee Young was an enlisted man, an Officers' Cook. Since I was commissioned and he was not, he was supposed to address me (even on the unorthodox 393) as *Mister* Clark, and I was to address him as *Young.* But he seemed such a nice, friendly guy that I thought we should find a less stuffy solution. The middle ground was initials. I was Mr. W.A., and he was J.L. We kept last names completely out of it.

J.L. had just two moods as near as I could tell: happy (most of the time) and scared. Unlike the rest of us, he was never just miserable. Once, when he heard one of the men complain that the ship had rolled too much in a storm and dumped dishes off tables, J.L. said he reckoned the ship didn't do it on purpose.

He really did get scared, though, when planes dropped bombs at us and tried to strafe us. A fellow crewman claimed he saw J.L. try to crawl under a coat of paint beneath the winch as bombs fell toward us. An exaggeration, of course, but what I saw was real. I saw J.L. get visibly paler during an air raid. What was remarkable to me was that J.L. was black—the only black aboard the 393— and I had never seen a black man's face grow pale.

No one on the ship ever got mad at J.L. Even his blunders were somehow more amusing than annoying. Like the cheese incident. We had been in the war zone several months, and the ship was badly enough battered to rate a trip to Brisbane, Australia, for patching up. While we were there, the captain (John) and I chipped in to buy a big wheel of well aged gorgonzola cheese that we gave to J.L. to store. Gorgonzola is a pungent but very tasty cheese. We hoped that when we got back in the war zone, we would snack on the wonderful cheese in between air raids. So about a month later, when there was a lull in the action, we asked J.L. to fetch the cheese and crackers. He shook his head and explained, "It got to smellin' awful. I had to throw it overboard." He didn't realize that the strong smell was only natural. Maybe we should have told him before we asked him to store it.

I'm glad I got to know J.L., and it's all because Mother taught me to look at people as *individuals* instead of groups.

LETTER 17

Brain Waves

Hypnotists were around when I was little, same as now. So were mind readers and brainwashers, but I didn't find out about them until I was much older. The first hypnotist I watched had a short, pointy beard, a rumpled black suit that was way too big for him, a golden front tooth, and a pocket watch on a chain. Speaking from a stage with a spotlight aimed at his gold tooth, he explained what he was about to do. He would get a volunteer from the audience and put him or her into a deep sleep, a trance, using his secret power of hypnosis. The volunteer, while in the trance, would do whatever the hypnotist commanded.

He got three volunteers to come up, one after another, and he put each of them into a trance just by having him or her stare at his watch as he swung it back and forth on its chain. All these volunteers did some pretty weird things, too, just as he had said they would. They made animal noises, for example, and acted like babies sucking their thumbs, and got down on the floor and rolled over. When the hypnotist clapped his hands the volunteers came out of their trances and claimed they had no idea they'd done anything silly.

Young as I was at the time, I was mystified and scared. I certainly would not have volunteered to go up on that stage. What if he put me in a trance and I didn't come out of it when he clapped his hands? What if he put me in a trance *without* my volunteering and then made me do terrible things and get put in jail? I felt a lot better the next day after some grown-up—I don't even recall his name—told me the whole hypnosis show was a fake. He said the hypnotist and the people who were to be called up as "volunteers" got together ahead of time to practice their act.

In time, I learned the real truth, and it wasn't all that simple. Hypnosis is for real. Doctors use it to get patients to think that they're not in pain, or that cigarettes taste awful, or that liquor upsets their stomachs. But don't ask me how hypnosis works. Since no one has ever explained it to me, I picture brain waves flitting about and homing in on target heads. It's a very handy theory. I use it to explain mind reading, brainwashing, ESP, and something which used to be called female intuition.

Of course, I've not actually seen a brain wave nor met anyone who has. Even so, I'm sure they must flit about like magnetic waves and microwaves, and I don't like it. Having someone else's brain waves come uninvited into my head seems very wrong. And having my own brain waves feel free to take off on their own isn't much better. Somehow my skull should act as a brain wave shield.

For many years now I've been set upon—as have you—by a particular breed of hypnotists, the ones who don't ask for volunteers, don't swing watches back and forth, and don't hypnotize people one at a time. They don't even call themselves hypnotists. Instead, they're known as media people, advertisers, public relations people, and politicians. But whatever their titles, they aim to put you and me into trances so we'll do what they command.

When World War II started, a bunch of us were unfit for combat. We were too civilized; we were law-abiding; we were strangers to violence. According to wizards of war we had to start to behave like near-animals. To do that we'd have to be hypnotized and ordered to feel that *all* Japs—except dead ones—were unspeakably evil, and that *all* Americans were nice as could be. Without hypnosis, I could not have felt that way. I had known a few nasty Americans, and although I had never known any Japanese, I could hardly imagine a whole nation of evil citizens. Come on! Even all the women and kids?

Still, the media did a pretty good job of turning us, under hypnosis, into Jap haters. And would you believe that after the war, the media commanded us to feel that all Japanese were really nice and should not be called by their wartime nickname, Japs?

I wish I could tell you how to keep from coming under the influence of these mass hypnotists. It can't be easy. They're everywhere. Their brain waves reach us via TV, radio, papers, and personal contact. Still, there is one feature of this mass hypnosis that offers us hope. The trances aren't so deep as those produced by the hypnotist who goes one-on-one with his "volunteer." Even though we're mass-hypnotized, we can break out of trances without having to wait for the clapping of hands.

This was easy for me during the War. Like my fellow warriors, I started out (in a trance) thinking all Japs were bad. It was *the* way to think, the *only* way to think. Perhaps the country needed this mass hypnosis just to get through the war. At least I suppose it helps to be mad at an enemy you're about to shoot full of holes. On the other hand, I don't think I became a worse warrior the day something snapped and I came out of my hypnotic trance.

A Jap plane flew over us one morning and drew anti-aircraft fire from every ship in our convoy. None of us hit it, though, at least not enough to bring it down, and the pilot didn't shoot back or drop a bomb. What he did drop came down under a small parachute and stayed afloat until someone finally got up the courage to fish it out of the water. It was a packet of prisoner of war letters. A Jap brave enough and kind enough to risk his life so captured Americans could get word to their families? Incredible! A *good* Jap!

By late afternoon that day, Americans ashore had cornered Japs in small, man-made caves. Most of them were afraid to come out, so bulldozers buried them alive. A few did come out with hands held high, and were drenched with American napalm. A terrible sight, that. A terrible sound, too, with all the screaming. Even a terrible odor despite a hint of barbecue.

Witnessing all that was what brought me out of my trance. The hypnotic message was all wrong. Not *all* Japs were bad, nor *all* Americans good. I hope you come out of your hypnotic trances more easily.

LETTER 18

That Wretched Corsage

I keep meaning to read a book on geriatrics, and keep finding reasons not to: too technical, too depressing, too dull. For you grandchildren too young to know about geriatrics, it's a science about what happens to people as they get old.

Of course, now that I *am* growing old—or older—I really don't need a book to tell me what it's like. I'm learning firsthand, and already I've made discoveries that may not even be in books. For instance, did you know that many old people lie a lot? Oh, I don't mean they lie down—they do that, too, napping like pre-schoolers—I mean they tell fibs, and sometimes whoppers.

If you doubt me, try this experiment. Ask the next six old people you run into what they would do differently if they could start their lives all over again. I'd bet four or five of them will give you an answer like, "Wouldn't change a thing" or "No regrets." That's like saying they made no mistakes; they were perfect, year after year, for decades. Not likely.

What *is* likely is that they once flubbed an exam because they didn't study hard enough for it. Or they made a stupid purchase or banged up a car or lost something valuable or lost a foolish bet or wasted way too much time looking for the right person to marry.

Ask *me* that question about what I'd change, and I won't lie to you. I'll even be quite specific.

I was, I think, about sixteen when Johnny Longmire, a friend from the neighborhood, made me an odd offer. Someone in the top echelon at Johnny's (small) school, having scheduled a dance for early June, worried that too few students show up. In a more-the-merrier-mood, he decided the students should invite outsiders. Accordingly, each student was issued an extra ticket to the dance, and told to give it to a "suitable" friend who could be counted on to bring a "suitable" date. The school, you see, made up in stuffiness what it lacked in size.

Johnny, guessing I might clear the suitability hurdle and bring a date who wasn't riffraff, offered me a ticket.

I think it may have been my first real date. (For *unreal* dates I managed to run into girls inside the local movie house and walk them home). I know it was the first time I ever took a girl to a dance. And I knew, the moment I took the ticket from Johnny, it was trauma in the making.

The girl I planned to take was a virtual stranger, someone I admired from a distance because she looked a lot like a picture of Cleopatra I had seen. Without the snake, of course.

When at last I got brave enough to call her, she was very kind. She pretended to know who I was, and accepted my invitation. The phone, when I set it down, glistened with sweat. I should have felt momentarily relieved, but I was troubled by that nagging thought: What's she going to think when she finds out I'm an absolute klutz on the dance floor? "What kind of corsage are you getting her?" Johnny asked. I had not counted on getting one, didn't know I was supposed to, and knew nothing about the various *kinds* available. When I mentioned this to Johnny, he said I should first find out what color dress my date would be wearing because certain color combinations are ugly. I think he actually thought I'd call and ask her. I'd just as soon have called to remind her to take a shower before going to the dance. So instead of calling her I listened to a friend who was practical about corsage matters. After he said that white flowers were OK with any color dress, I bought my raven-haired beauty a corsage made of three gardenias fringed with fern. I had to mow a pretty big yard to pay for it.

The night of the dance was typical of June: steamy. But who cares about weather when you're having a good time?

My date, when I went to fetch her, looked great in her purple dress, exclaimed over the corsage, and introduced me to her family.

Her older brother had the look of a wrestler willing to crumple any boy who kept his sister out too late.

Off we went to the dance. On the way two facts emerged: (1) We had absolutely nothing in common; and (2) The perfume from those gardenias was so strong it wouldn't have mattered if she *had* forgotten to shower. I tilted my head toward the open window beside me as I drove, and we both struggled to make conversation. By the time we got to the dance, we had said very little. There was no overlap in our circles of friends; we attended different schools, different churches; she liked non-athletic girl activities, which I knew nothing about. We did not discuss my poor foot-ear coordination on the dance floor. She'd soon see that in action.

The dance was held in the school gym—not air conditioned in those days—with music provided by a band that was loud, small, unknown, and destined to stay unknown, and too conscientious to take long or frequent breaks. I glanced around the dance floor. Only three familiar faces: Johnny's, my date's, and one girl whose name I wasn't sure of. My date recognized no one.

So the band played on and on, and body heat from the dancers pushed the temperature and humidity up and up. I kept hoping some young male in that gym would come tap my shoulder and ask to dance with this stranger, this Cleopatra look-alike. It never happened. Hour after hour my date and I moved clumsily about as she oozed perspiration and I oozed sweat. And all the while, almost directly beneath my nose sat that gardenia corsage which, like the band, would not quit. It kept pumping its pungency at me and into my date's hair. By 11:15 I was too sick to go on, and had to excuse myself. I later recovered enough to drive my date home. We never again went out together.

And there you have it. You now know one thing in my life I'd change if I could relive the past. I'd buy something other than gardenias. Roses, maybe, or carnations. What you *don't* know is my date's name. I was afraid if I told you, you might run into her and embarrass her. Her initials were just like your grandmother's: J.W.

LETTER 19

What Happens To Imaginations?

Yesterday, after I walked off the tennis court toward the drinking fountain, I heard a lady say she had no imagination. I wanted to say, "Impossible!" or "You should write to the *Guiness Book of Records*," but she was bigger than I am, and I was in a hurry, so I said nothing to set her straight. She probably wouldn't have listened anyway. Might even have put me down as a batty old man.

I have definite ideas about the human imagination. I'm certain that each of us gets one, either before birth or soon enough after so we can talk to stuffed animals and dolls, and imagine that they hear us. I'm also sure we can no more get rid of our imaginations than we can get rid of our hearts without taking transplants. And I'm at least fairly sure that imaginations improve with age. That's contrary to popular opinion, I admit, because young children *seem* to have the best imaginations, but it could be an illusion.

What happens between us and our imaginations as we plod along through life goes something like this. After our stuffed animals and dolls have started to listen to us, and maybe to talk back, the shadows in our nurseries become fearsome creatures.

When we're a bit older, we invite invisible friends to visit us often. We put on small-scale stage plays in which we imagine ourselves great performers. We daydream our way into the big leagues, into medieval castles and onto TV programs.

Older still, we imagine the future: What it will be like to have lots of money . . . to have as spouses people who today don't even know us . . . to hold down jobs of great responsibility . . . to receive coveted awards. And on the grim side, we imagine failed health or being burgled or going broke or being falsely accused.

And then adults try to spoil our fun. They tell us to stow it, meaning we should treat our imaginations as we treat our underwear—keep them out of sight. Whether we obey this callous command depends on who we are. If we're artists or scientists we don't. But the real point is that, although some of us can be made to *hide* our imaginations, we can't *scrap* them. How could we? How would we take a first step?

Now even if we do hide them or stash them on a shelf deep inside our skulls, they don't stay put. By night they give us dreams: soothing or nightmarish or humorous. By day they take us to vacation spots while our bodies commute or sit at desks.

Lots of us adults do try to keep our imaginations hidden as best we can. It's the custom. It's something we're supposed to do just to show we're grown-up. And some of us, like that big lady beside the tennis court, still try to deny the very existence of their imaginations.

I, on the other hand, think of myself as a champion of the imagination cause. I like my imagination. Although I shelve it some of the time, I think of it as I think of the family sterling silverware. It needs to be brought now and then to be polished and used and cherished.

I also like what I see happening to imaginations, mine included, as they age. We old folks ache. We've slowed down. Our lists of activities keep shrinking. We spend more time alone because our friends are too feeble (or worse) to come calling, and our relatives are too busy. We need to escape a lonely world, to go to a more exciting one. And the older we get, the more frequently we need to escape.

So out comes the imagination, our means of escape. With its help we can go to Shangri-La. We can imagine ourselves young again with lots of friends and no aches. We can relive the past, not exactly as it was but as we like to remember it. We can picture old friends, long gone, sitting with us now, laughing.

I should not have used the first person plural in the two

previous paragraphs. I'm not yet one of those lonely, *really old* guys. I use my imagination in several ways other than escaping to better worlds. But use it I do, at least once or twice a day. As I write, for instance. After I retired, I began to write children's stories because it was fun just to let my imagination go wild. I couldn't do that while I was working; my bosses wanted me to keep my imagination locked up.

Sometimes, just to keep my imagination on its toes, I give it a sentence, and ask it to expand that sentence into a paragraph. If you want to put *your* imagination to work, have it build a paragraph based on this sentence: Several people, not all of whom are relatives, think I'm crazy.

A master woodcarver once taught me another way to set my imagination in motion. He handed me a chunk of basswood. "There's a fish in there," he said. "Just cut away all the wood that isn't fish." He was right. There was a bluegill in there. But it could have been a pike or a shark. It could even have been something other than a fish: a grizzly, a human hand, a 1929 Ford, a spider. To this day, I seldom pick up a nice piece of wood without wondering what's waiting to be liberated by my chisels and knives.

I'm not sure any of you care a whit about carving or writing as hobbies. No matter. You can find your own ways to take your imaginations out of their hiding places, and when you do, you'll be glad. I promise.

LETTER 20

Getting Scared For Fun and For Real

Getting scared can be fun if you go about it right. When you were little, someone put you on a swing and gave you a gentle push, a nudge. With both hands clenching the ropes you were scared, but you came back for more. You were proud of yourself for having been brave. You had gained a smidgeon of self-confidence. On later trips to the playground you swung higher and higher, at first being pushed, and then all on your own. You got scared, too, when you first dove or jumped into deep water, explored haunted houses, and took thrill rides at amusement parks. There's a reason all those experiences were fun. You knew ahead of time what you were about to do, and you were pretty sure you wouldn't get hurt. The scariest scares are the ones you *don't* expect. Some of them are no fun at all.

Come back with me now aboard the 393. It is September or October 1944, and we no longer escort convoys. We now make charts. We are one-third of a group of hydrographic surveyors. The other ships are a minesweeper like the 393, and a slightly larger Australian ship that the Aussies call a sloop even though it has no sails.

Each month the Army decides it wants to make a landing at some Jap-held spot, and asks the Navy for transportation plus some blasting away at the hostile shore. The Navy says, "OK, but first we must make up-to-date charts so that when we carry troops toward shore our landing craft don't get hung up on reefs."

The Navy then tells our little three-ship group to go to the Jap-held spot ahead of time (7-10 days before a landing) and make a chart. To do that, we go ashore, put markers atop hills, return to the ships, and go back and forth over the water we're charting. We move slowly. We record the water depths continuously, and once a minute check our positions relative to those hilltop markers. The Japs don't like what we're doing. They shoot at us as we put up markers and as we go slowly back and forth. If they have a pilot with nothing better to do, they send him out to strafe us. Sometimes they send swimmers out at night to try attaching explosives to the side of the ship.

All this unfriendly activity gets on our nerves, probably because it's repeated month after month with only the location changed. By September 1944, we on the 393 have had to transfer two enlisted men and one officer who had breakdowns. (We had to tie the officer to his bunk). The 393 is undermanned.

We are told to put the ship in shape; something big is about to happen, something *really* big. (I was at this point Executive Officer and Engineering Officer). I set the black gang—the guys who keep the engines running—to work overhauling the main propulsion engines. We must improvise because spare parts are so scarce in New Guinea. We reluctantly put back worn parts that we just removed. But what to do about head gaskets? The old ones can't be used, and there are no new ones to be had. Engines can't run unless tightly sealed with head gaskets. In the end we make gaskets out of chart paper, and hope fervently that our engines won't conk out in the middle of this really big thing about to happen.

Our group of three ships gets underway. For two hours we steer a prescribed course, and only then do we break the seal on our top-secret orders. We are to head for Leyte. We are to get there ten days before a scheduled landing. We are to observe strict radio silence—no calling for help. We are to be the first Americans and Aussies to return to the Philippines. But first we must get from Hollandia, New Guinea, to Leyte. That will take time on a ship as slow as ours, even if no Japs come at us.

Two points about our engines. At standard speed, they will push the ship ahead at about twelve miles an hour on a calm day.

If the propellers break off or if you try to run the engines with the propellers out of water, safety devices (governors) will keep the engines from going wild and flying apart.

We steam ahead, and all goes well. The sea is so calm we don't even have to hold down our plates to keep them from sliding off the table. The chart paper gaskets seem to be holding. The enemy, as best we can tell, either has not spotted us or is waiting to see where we go—and where more ships will join us.

The good times end when we're within a hundred miles of Leyte. It's 10 PM, the sky is starless, and the wind has begun to blow hard. We can't see the waves, but they *feel* huge. Rain hits us, not from above, but full in the face with stinging force. The 393 rolls something awful, and anything not clamped down falls, and slides. Books and dishes and canned goods are not a problem, but suppose something big breaks loose? A sliding refrigerator could poke quite a hole in a wooden ship. No one sleeps; we all wear life jackets; we all stay in out of the weather; we all, I think, say silent prayers.

We are in our first typhoon. What we've read about them tells us they are miles wide . . . they move slowly (maybe only five miles an hour) . . . the winds inside them are phenomenal . . . they are tough to get out of once you've been trapped in them.

At dawn, we face the full fury. The waves, high as a two-story house, lift the stern so far out of the water that the governors kick in to keep the engines from flying apart. The wind blows so hard (over 150 miles an hour) that no one can stand up on deck. The 393, built to sit high in the water, is very tippy. We dare not get sideways to the wind or over we go. But all that can keep us headed into that wind are our not-so-strong engines with their chart paper gaskets. It's panic time! Shortly after 10 AM, we see the other minesweeper in our group get sideways to the wind. It isn't very far from us. We wish we could help. We can't. With our engines ahead standard speed against that wind we are dead in the water. Our friends from the capsized ship all make it over the side in life jackets. They ride roller coaster waves and are wind-blown out of sight.

Although things eventually came out well, including the rescue of the men in the water, we learned a hard lesson: If you want to have *fun* being scared, don't ride a tippy ship into a typhoon. Stick to swings and haunted houses.

LETTER 21

Quirks and Flaws

Here in front of me is a little wooden bud vase I made a couple of years ago. It probably never will have a bud in it because buds like water, and finished wood does not. I keep it around because I like its geometry and its smoothness and its colors and its flaws. It is just three inches high, and most of that is its tapered neck. Down close to the bottom, the vase measures two inches in diameter.

Long before I made the vase, it was hiding inside an Osage Orange log, and the log was on top of a woodpile. Now Osage Orange is fascinating wood. The part just under the bark—the *sapwood*—is bright yellow, and not especially hard. Beneath the sapwood is the extremely hard, reddish-brown *heartwood*. That is where the tree's annual growth rings stand out beautifully.

As the log sat on the woodpile, a wood borer spotted it, attacked it, and found that although he (the borer) could dig holes in the sapwood, he couldn't cope with the heartwood. He simply lacked the proper teeth or drill or whatever borers use when they bore.

Eventually the log was brought indoors and was about to go into a roaring fire when I rescued it. Osage Orange is too pretty to be cremated. Later, when I put the log on the lathe and turned the bud vase, there they were: six small cavities, courtesy of the wood borer. Six interesting flaws. Some folks look at my vase and say, "What a shame the wood had those cavities." Others (and I) think the cavities give the vase character.

My fondness for wood goes back to my boyhood days when we kids begged for scraps of lumber from adults who had some.

My interest in flaws came much later. Until I retired, I either disliked them or ignored them, but I certainly did not think of *good* flaws. During retirement I have learned from experts how to make fine furniture, and, while doing so, how to find and use wood with good flaws.

Boards with *bad* flaws are easy to find. They have splits or large, loose knots; they are warped or cupped or wet or stained by fungi. Boards with *good* flaws have clusters of tiny knots and grain that swirls and twirls instead of just lying straight. These good flaws are Nature's doing. A walnut tree sprouts burls (big wart-like growths) in which grain patterns are spectacular. A mesquite tree lives such a hard life that it must grow slowly. Cattle gnaw on its leaves and branches. Winds flatten it and twist it. Long dry spells force it to modify its cells to hang on to precious water. In the end, the mesquite tree, if it isn't chopped up into chips for barbecuers, becomes lumber with fine flaws: small knots where cattle chewed off branches, wavy grain from the tree's having been windblown, and abnormally high density from having grown so slowly.

When I tried to switch my "flaw" reasoning from wood to people, I failed because all human flaws are considered bad. If I say, "Old Benny's got one flaw in his character," folks just assume it's something bad, not a delightful quirk in Benny's personality. They wonder whether Benny has a terrible mean streak, or is morally loose, or goes around corrupting those who come under his influence. Ah, but you already know about people like that. You've avoided them for years, and rightly so.

Important as it is to spot those really bad flaws and steer clear of their owners, I like to search, too, for something a bit more positive. If English language experts think I shouldn't use the term *good flaws*, so be it. I'll call them *good quirks*, and give you an example in the person of Michael Dvornikoff.

Mike was on the wrong side when the Bolsheviks overthrew the Russian government. He fled the country, suffering great hardship along the way (flu, typhus, hunger, severe cold, rats, lice), and arrived penniless in New York. He explained, as best he could, that he had studied chemistry in Russia, but had no way to prove it. The Bolsheviks were destroying school records and were not forwarding them to escapees. The closest Mike could get to a job as chemist was in a storage battery plant where he had to submerge metal parts in hot sulfuric acid—barehanded!

While in New York, he met a European couple, also chemists, who were headed for St. Louis to work for a newly formed chemical company called Monsanto. He went with them, proved to interviewers that he could answer tough chemical questions, signed on as a researcher, and within months was thought to be a genius. His head was a chemical encyclopedia. Co-workers sought his advice. Always cheerful, he worked long hours—typically from early morning to 9 or 10 PM. His job was to invent practical processes for making various chemicals, and this he did ably.

One night, as this chemical *genius* was in the plant monitoring one of his processes, he decided to weigh himself. As two plant operators watched, Mike climbed onto the scale, removed his overcoat, held the coat at arm's length out past the edge of the scale, weighed himself, got off the scale, and put his coat on again.

When Mike was in his fifties, he bought his first car, and, in a manner of speaking, learned to drive. What he did not learn was how to put on the license plates; plant operators did it for him. Nor did he develop a sense of direction. He went for a drive in Forest Park one Sunday afternoon. It took him four hours to find his way out. He never drove again. He sold the car.

So you see, when it came to things mechanical or directional, Mike was quirky. He's long gone now but still remembered. His friends recall his genius and his cheerfulness, but what really makes them smile is their recollection of the night he weighed himself, and the day he got lost in the park.

Which explains, I hope, why I still look for *good quirks* or *good flaws* in people. They're a lot of what make folks amusing and memorable.

LETTER 22

Marriage and Luck

The day before yesterday, the Olsons, a young couple (in their thirties) dropped by for no special reason, just for a gab. Their visit would have been shorter if Mrs. Olson hadn't asked your grandmother and me how we've managed to stay married for 50+ years. We often get that question these days, and can't seem to come up with a one-sentence answer. Besides, some of the younger folks who ask truly want to hear longer, thoughtful replies—words of wisdom from a couple so old they must have lived through every imaginable marital crisis.

We used to answer that it was all a matter of luck. I think we were afraid of sounding like braggarts if we said anything other than luck. And who can doubt the importance of luck in marital harmony? Your grandmother and I were in our teens when realized we were meant to become husband and wife. Although choosing a mate must be about the biggest decision a person makes, we did no analysis, weighed no pros and cons. We just *knew*. It was a heart decision, not a head decision. And it evidently was a *lucky* decision.

So we told the Olsons to hope for luck but not expect luck alone to carry them along for 50+ years. I then gave them a chance to escape gracefully by saying, "We think we know some of what held our marriage together, but most of it is outdated, out of place in this very different world. Even the very start of marriages has changed. When we exchanged vows, it was for keeps. We meant what we promised: one spouse for life, no changing our minds. Today's couples seem to feel the marriage contract comes with an easy escape clause." The Olson's showed no sign of leaving, so I went on speaking as though I had known for decades all the secrets of happy marriages.

In truth we were, at the start, like most newlyweds: absolutely uninformed. I didn't know how—or whether—I could make enough money to support us after the war, for instance, and your grandmother didn't know how to cook. Both of us wondered what we'd find to talk about after a few months of being together. We were, in those early days, sure that we could learn by trial and error, and that all would be well. In addition to that blind optimism, we had a few pluses going for us. We agreed that our main goal was a big family. We had lots of shared interests and shared friends. We had both had about the same amount of schooling. We would begin our marriage in a city well beyond the reach of our parents.

There were but a few negative forces at work—all of which we were sure we could handle. We were of different religions. We had little money and few material goods other than our clothes. Our families were at two different financial levels, mine being the lower, and my father-in-law was certain his daughter had gotten herself a husband with a bleak future.

After telling the Olsons all that and checking to see that they hadn't gone glassy-eyed, I charged ahead. "Two other factors seem now to have been ever so helpful to our marriage. One is children, and what can I say about children that couples your age could possibly use in the late 1990s? We wanted and got a half-dozen. Having them, watching them grow and succeed and bring spouses and grandchildren into the family was what life was all about. Motherhood was a top-of-the-line career in those days. Most fathers, myself included, viewed their jobs as a means to an end, not an end in itself, just a way to get enough money to support a family properly.

"For whatever reason, the thinking about children changed, and it's not apt to change back. Families are smaller now; mothers go for second careers and delegate motherly jobs to others. Families seldom gather around dining room tables. Married couples pay close attention to trade-offs: another child vs. a new car, a better house, a boat.

"A minute ago I mentioned *two* factors that helped keep us happily married, the first being children. The second is temperance, and I use that word in a broad sense, not simply to mean that we have always stayed sober. Which, by the way, we have.

I don't know how we first got into the temperance mode, but it surely has made for comfortable living. Temperance has meant not overdoing, not going to extremes. We didn't try to keep up with the Joneses, let alone get ahead of them. In disciplining our children, we were neither lax nor overly strict. We kept our moods, except for humor, nearer the mid-points than the tops or bottoms. We struck balances between work and play. I'm sure we were less than temperate in our eating habits, though. Happily, none of us grew a Buddha belly."

After the Olsons thanked us and left, your grandmother turned to me and said, "You should have told them it was pure luck, plain and simple. You just happened to be incredibly lucky over a half-century ago. You discovered the perfect wife. The Olsons would have believed that, and you could have spared them all that talk about what worked for us in ancient times."

She may have been right. Or maybe *she* was the one who was incredibly lucky.

The Olsons? We wish them well. They'll probably do what their friends do: count heavily on luck, have tiny families, and reject the notion of temperance. Will they be among the 50% who split before they find what long, happy marriages are like? I hope not.

LETTER 23

The Toilet Paper Trail

My letters to you have gotten too serious. It's time I gave you something to smile about. Grandfathers are supposed to do that when they write memoirs: tell about a few funny experiences they recall.

My high school was a two-story brick building, ¾ths of a block long with, it seemed, a Jesuit every twenty-five feet. It was an all-boys, no-nonsense school. The Jesuits were there to teach us and to discipline us, and we could never tell which of those jobs they liked better. Their disciplinary system was easy to understand, tough to beat. If you misbehaved and a Jesuit saw you, he said, "You're jugged," and wrote your name and your crime on a card that he later handed to whichever Jesuit was in charge of the Jug Room that day. You then reported to the Jug Room at the end of the school day, learned what your sentence was, and began serving it. There were no juries to hear your pathetic pleas of innocence, no courts of appeal, no pardons.

For minor crimes, such as talking in class or running in the halls, the sentences were mild enough to be worked off in an hour or two. Major crimes were something else. Those could have you return to the Jug Room several days running. You might even have to come in on Saturdays to clean up the campus. The major crimes might not seem major to you, but to the Jesuits they were. Examples: setting off firecrackers in classrooms, putting a dead green frog in a classmate's green soup, climbing out a (ground-floor) window while the teacher is busy writing on the blackboard, playing the *Saint Louis Blues* on the chapel organ, planting stink bombs behind radiators. Crimes worse than those—like stealing or cheating or sassing a teacher—would get a kid expelled, or so we were told.

The halls on each floor of this long, low school were laid out like the lines in this diagram:

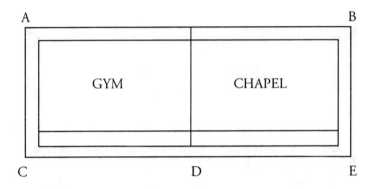

From A to B or from C to D was ¾ths of a block. If you were to walk from C to D you'd pass the chapel and gym on your right, and mostly lockers and classrooms (not shown) on your left. At corners A, C, and D were rest rooms. One of those, the one at C, was the site of a crime never before recorded in the *JESUIT GUIDE TO JUGS.* It was there at Point C that John Carroll put together two known facts and came up with a phenomenon. The first fact was that to flush one of the toilets you had keep the handle pushed down, and as long as you kept it pushed down, the flushing would continue. The second fact was that water came into the toilet with such gusto that you had to wonder whether the school had tapped into a fire hydrant pipe.

"You gotta see this," John told me as I tagged along to find out about his discovery. He peeled off a five-foot length of toilet paper, put one end in the toilet, and let the rest dangle over the side and onto the floor. "Now watch," he said before he pushed down the handle, and held it down. Like a lizard's tongue snapping back after grabbing a bug, that paper scooted across the floor up into the toilet's mouth.

We tried again, this time unfurling enough paper to reach the rest room door. The result was the same. "Amazing, isn't it?" John asked. "You'd think the paper would tear apart being yanked that hard by all that water going down the drain."

I wondered aloud. "Do you think we could . . . ?" and John reckoned we should give it a try. We took a whole roll, or very nearly a whole roll, put one end into the toilet, and ran the rest out the rest room door, down the hall all the way to Point E, and around that corner. John then held down the flusher handle while I held the rest room door open.

Well, that paper whipped around the corner at Point E, and raced down the hall just as we hoped it would, only faster. There was one thing we hadn't expected, though. Following the far end of that paper, all the way from around the corner was Mr. Hindelang, the second toughest Jesuit at the school. He must have been more amused than angry that day because he didn't shove us up against lockers, or shake us, or even grab us. He just whipped out his card, wrote on it, and said, "You're jugged."

Our sentence? I don't remember. It's probably in an up-to-date edition of the *JESUIT GUIDE TO JUGS*.

At my fiftieth high school reunion, one of my classmates claimed to know the meaning of the term *JUG*. (I had always assumed it meant Just Until Graduation). He said it stood for Justice Under God. The rest of us were sure he was wrong. God would never punish boys for creating a water-powered paper trail.

LETTER 24

Laughing Loudly

Our local news commentator must have been hard up for stories this evening. He devoted at least three minutes to a medical study of laughter. It seems researchers up north somewhere claim to have proved for the first time that laughing is good for your health. I wonder what took them so long. I wonder, too, why they even bothered to prove something so obvious. Surely they must know that when a person laughs, he or she blocks out stressful thoughts, gives the heart and lungs a mild workout, and exercises all the right facial muscles.

I figure those researchers should have taken a different tack. They should have asked themselves, "Seeing as how laughter makes people feel great and must be good for their health, why don't we find ways to make them laugh more or harder or both?"

Actually, the problem is a bit more complicated than that. We already have lots of folks trying to make us laugh: comedians, cartoonists, chimpanzee trainers. Some of them are mighty good at what they do, too. The trouble lies within us. We've trained ourselves to wait for just the right time and be in just the right setting before we laugh.

But every now and then we are caught off guard. As we go about our dull routines, something unexpected happens, something hilarious, and we laugh in spite ourselves. It's like being ticklish and being tickled.

I had a green Ford back in the 1950s. It was a two-door. We always bought two-doors so as not to worry about back doors flying open and kids falling out. Seat belts weren't around in the 1950s, or if they were, no one told me. So kids in the back seat were loose, and ours were as frisky as most.

My green Ford was reliable most of the time, thanks in part to me. I was too poor or too stingy to buy complicated cars with all sorts of potentially troublesome extras. Except for its whitewall tires, my Ford was uncomplicated: six cylinders, stick shift, and a heater. We got along fine, that car and I, but any car, however reliable and uncomplicated, will occasionally insist on being treated to a new battery. Cars have their own ways to make their wishes known. When their hearts are set on new batteries, they groan as you try to get them going in the morning, and dim their headlights without being told to do so.

My Ford was sending me those messages. Instead of rushing out to buy a new battery, I tried to prolong the life of the old one by giving it nightly transfusions from a battery charger I had hooked up in the garage. Before many weeks had passed I faced reality. I would have to pull the plug on the life support system. I would have to bury the old battery, buy a new one, and get on with my life. My friends, many of whom also had to pinch pennies, assured me that *the* place to buy batteries was Sears. The price is right, they said, and if a battery conks out before its guaranteed life is up, you get paid for the months it failed to live.

I chose a Saturday morning to go to Sears even though the store was apt to be crowded. I grabbed the keys, the checkbook, and our three oldest children (Ken, Josie, Steve), and away we went. The kids used to like going with me in that Ford. Whether they expected adventure or liked my company or were half-sure they'd get a treat, I don't know. I suspect the latter.

Not until I drove into the Sears basement garage did I discover what my friends had failed to mention. Buying a Sears battery was no snap—not then anyway—a bit like adopting a child. I could not simply hand the garage boss my keys and say, "Please take out my old battery and put in a new one the same size." The garage boss would let me leave my Ford with him, he told me, but he would do nothing until I went up into the store, got all the right pieces of paper, and brought them back. I figured five minutes, ten or fifteen tops. The kids could amuse themselves that long looking at Sears goodies. Ken and Josie were old enough to be trusted. Steve, at age three, and by nature inquisitive, could be a problem. Oh well, if he gets into trouble, it would be Sears's fault for making such a big deal out of buying a battery.

The only two battery salesmen upstairs were busy with customers and forms. I waited. The kids roamed, and by the time my turn came to deal with a salesman, I could get only occasional glimpses of the kids in the crowded store. Hoping for the best while trying to be patient, I rocked back and forth as the salesman lectured me on the good and evil inside each of several models of batteries. He then heaped upon me various forms I was to read and sign. He did not require my thumb print. I wrote him a check, and he sent for someone who apparently could simply look me over and decide whether I was the sort who wrote rubber checks. Once I had passed inspection, the salesman handed me the papers to take to the garage boss. It was too late. Not by much, but late.

I caught sight of Steve, maybe forty feet away. He was standing in front of a toilet in a display bathroom. His pants were down by his ankles. He hadn't noticed that the bathroom had neither walls nor pipes. How could he be expected to at age three? Oddly enough, in this crowded store, only two people seemed to have noticed what was going on. One was wizened old woman looking quite shocked. The other was a fat man whose considerable tummy shook as he enjoyed the comedy before him. He didn't make a sound but he was laughing hard, and I'm sure he laughed out loud later when he told friends of the incident. I know I did.

When I began this letter, it was to say I wish people hadn't changed my laughing habits. I used to laugh a lot and enjoy it. In the grown-up world, folks want me to be serious. I can be that way some of the time but I'd still like to laugh often, and hard. I promise not to laugh out loud in really wrong places, like symphony halls and funeral parlors. Meanwhile I need to figure out ways to make myself laugh. Tickling myself doesn't work, and Steve is no longer three years old.

LETTER 25

Mother's More Personable Dogs

One day your biographer will ask, "What individual was most responsible for making you what you are today?" My advice is: Don't answer. If you're a whopping success, lots of folks will want full credit. Name one of them, and the rest will be sore at you. If you haven't succeeded, no one will appreciate your naming him or her as the person responsible for your failure. Even if you're just average, mid-way between success and failure, your answer could get you into trouble. Name a parent, for instance, and your spouse, if you have one, will give you a bad time.

It's that term *"most* responsible" that makes the question so tough. How do we even measure "*most* responsible," knowing that several people were so important in shaping us? For me, one of those people was Mother, your great-grandmother, whom few of you ever met, and fewer remember. Which is too bad, because you'd have liked her.

I'll tell you a bit about her now, and more in later letters. Some you already know. Early on, she helped Uncle Walter adjust to deafness. By her mid-thirties she had had all five of us kids and had been widowed. Thereafter, she single-handedly raised us, put us through college, kept the house in Webster Groves, and bought us a small second home in Michigan. From those facts alone, you can guess correctly that she was most unselfish. Whatever we kids needed, plus a lot of what we just wanted, we got. Mother, without saying so, did without. Her new clothes could wait for another day in another month.

She had strong convictions, one of which went like this: For one adult and five children to live together happily they must have morals, senses of humor, music, dogs, and yummy meals.

Her love of dogs went way back to her childhood, to a pair of fox terriers named Teasel and Tax. Home for her was a boxy old brick house. A cobblestone alley ran along the back of the property, and on that alley were the garage and a trash pit. In big cities where houses were close to one another, each house had a trash pit out back. I don't know why they called it a pit. It was above ground, a 6 x 6 foot plot surrounded by brick walls maybe 5 feet high. Each homeowner heaped trash into his or her pit, and usually set it afire. When the heap was high enough, a trash man shoveled it into his truck and drove on down the alley. Such was life before garbage disposals and trash bags.

The aroma from these pits, especially on warm days, appealed more to rats than to people, and that's where Teasel and Tax came in. They were ratters, trained I believe, by my grandfather Pop. Teasel, once lifted into a pit, dug around until he found a rat, but instead of trying to kill it in the midst of all that trash, he flipped it high in the air in the general direction of Tax, who stood in the alley beside the pit. Tax was quick, had strong jaws and sharp teeth, and never fumbled.

Those rat hunts got to be a regular Saturday sporting event in Mother's neighborhood as the dogs attracted quite an audience by working over trash pits along a two-block length of alley. Mother sure did like those dogs. Never forgot them, even when she was pushing ninety years old.

While I was growing up, we always had dogs, usually two. Mother welcomed dogs of all sizes and most breeds, (except Chows and Dobermans, which frightened her). She didn't always wait for us to bring home strays. One day, she went grocery shopping at a Piggly Wiggly store, came back with an abandoned, bedraggled, curly-haired female mutt, named her Rags, and kept her for nearly eleven years. Rags was a fine, good-natured little dog whose only fault was her urge to chase cars. I think she must have felt it kept her young to sprint after cars at 30 m.p.h. Only once did she get hit. Got her tail run over and had to have it amputated.

Rags was impatient with dogs who didn't live in the same house with her. She seemed especially hostile to strange male dogs that came calling from time to time, and after that hostility had lasted several years, Mother concluded that Rags's previous owners must have had her "fixed." Not true! Very late in life, Rags crawled into my closet and gave birth to three pups. Mother would let us keep only the one called Chubby, but we found good homes for the others.

Until I got married and went off to war, Mother let me keep big dogs (the biggest being Great Danes Horace and Boris) while she kept small ones. She favored Scotties, particularly a female named Tammy, who, Mother said, often smiled. We kids found the idea of a smiling dog preposterous, and said so. My sister Mary once asked Mother, "If Tammy can smile, she must be able to laugh. How come we never hear her laugh?" But Mother was right. Tammy *could* smile. I finally saw her crinkle her upper lip while wagging her tail at a drum roll rate.

In her sixties, Mother got an Irish Setter named Rufus. Not everyone agreed with me that Rufus would be good for her, but he was. Mother had liked the way Tammy, with just a smile, showed she had emotions, personality. And here came Rufus, who, without cracking a smile, revealed his personality in more detail than Tammy could. Rufus was, to be sure, an Irish imp. Although he meant no harm and was non-violent, he was addicted to teasing.

Picture the scene. Mother is downstairs in the sun room knitting and half-listening to recorded music. The telephone is on the table beside her. Her feet are up. She is comfortable. She pays no attention to Rufus, who thinks she should. He trots upstairs to rummage, finds a shoe (or a piece of underwear or a pillow or a sock), and carries it downstairs to show Mother what he has stolen. That done, he carries the shoe (or whatever) to the northeast corner of the living room, under the grand piano. He lies there with the shoe, and waits for Mother to get down on all fours to come retrieve it. By the time she does that and takes the shoe back upstairs, she'll have had a bit of exercise. She'll also have one more dog story to tell.

I don't think Mother cared much for the other kinds of pets we had: white rats, fish, guinea pigs, and turtles. I'm pretty sure none of them smiled, but with turtles it's hard to tell.

LETTER 26

Mistreated People and a Mis-made Pie

These letters, though written to you, add to my peace of mind. I get a worthwhile thought once in awhile, and were it not for writing you about it, I'd drop it into a dusty, musty patch of my brain. Later I'd try to retrieve it, fail, and get all upset with myself.

Today I have two thoughts to write about. The first one is serious, if not downright scary. The second is about, of all things, the making of a pie. Since the two thoughts have absolutely nothing in common, this should be the strangest of letters.

Men and women, once they have a little power and get to huddling in groups of one kind or another, have a nasty habit. They change their definition of "*human being*" whenever using the old definition would cost them money. They've been at it for quite a spell. The thing is, until recently, I never dreamed they'd hang a "*sub-human being*" tag on people like me. Now I fear they will.

When Europeans, with greed in their hearts, came to America, they found Indians in their way. No problem, they decided. Call them savages—meaning animal-like, not exactly human—and treat them accordingly. Drive them from their land, seize their minerals and furs, make them as submissive as you'd make your dogs, and if they resist, kill them.

Once rid of the Indians, many of the settlers down South figured they could make scads of money farming. All they'd need was a slue of new savages who could be made to do grubby work for free or close to it. African slaves. They could be bought like cattle, whip-trained like mules, slop-fed like hogs. They were, some people thought, not exactly human. Like the Indians, they were colored and ignorant, and they smelled different.

European Jews during World War II were declared inferior for economic reasons. Jews had money; Hitler wanted it. So why not make them out to be inferior? Why not jam them into cattle cars and gas them the way dogcatchers gas unclaimed strays? After all, many Germans thought, they were hardly human in the German sense.

Notice how, over the years, the numbers of people in each sub-human group grew, reaching several million in the case of the Jews. Although the people in all these groups were indeed human, having all the right genes, it apparently was easier for the public to accept Indians and Africans as sub-human. The Jews weren't colored. They *looked* human, and a lot of the world outside Germany felt they *were* human.

The next group to be tagged sub-human were the yet-to-be-born, the fetuses. They, like the Jews, had all the right genetic stuff to make them human, and no one doubted that they, like month-old babies, were destined, with a little help, to grow up to be human beings, not chimps. Each was an individual, too, distinctly different from either parent. But these fetuses, as a group, involved lots of money. Allowed to live, they'd have to be fed, clothed, educated, and medically attended to. Which would mean less for those already born. So why not call them sub-human and get rid of them the way you would rats?

And this brings me to the scary part. We older people involve *really big* money. There are lots of us, we take more medical care than younger folks, we withdraw Social Security money, and we no longer earn money by working. Suppose some enterprising abortionist or neo-Nazi were to say, "I know how the country can balance the budget. We can just redefine 'human being' to mean someone who is, or can become, a *productive* worker, and we'll just get rid of all the *non-human* critters in a humane way."

*   *   *

Enough of that! On to a happier subject: pie making. This was a happening from the 1960s in our home in Kirkwood, when your parents, aunts, and uncles were in school. The main characters were your grandmother, your Uncle Steve, and two of his friends—Terry and Polly. But to understand this story, you need to first know about three things. The first was our 3-bite rule: if your grandmother served some food we didn't like, such as peas or cauliflower, we still had to eat at least three bites of it, no matter what. Second, your grandmother often experimented with strange desserts like Apple Brown Betty, a peculiar brown mush that looked awful, but actually was kind of tasty. Sometimes the 3-bite rule helped us appreciate foods that we otherwise wouldn't have wanted to even taste. The third thing you need to know about is an earlier story concerning Uncle Steve (who was then about ten years old) and your grandmother's father (he would be your great-grandfather, Ralph Watt—we called him Granddaddy). We were all having dinner at the Shorewood house in Michigan. For dessert, your great-grandmother, Gars, passed around pieces of coconut cream pie from the Lloyd J. Harris Pie Company in Saugutuck. Although this was the first time any of us had had such a pie, no one needed to be reminded of the 3-bite rule because the pie looked delicious with all that fluffy stuff on top. Granddaddy, who was sitting next to Uncle Steve, picked up his piece and said it smelled wonderful, then he held it in front of Steve to sniff. When Steve put his nose close to the pie, Granddaddy, as a joke, pushed it into Steve's face, and Steve got whipped cream all over his nose. We all had a good laugh, including Steve (all, that is, except Gars, who was the epitome of decorum and good table manners—I think she walked out in protest).

So now that you know the background, I'll go back to pie-making in Kirkwood. Grandma Jo started it all by putting together from scratch her first key lime pie. She made the crust, baked it, mixed, and poured in the tangy filling, which she tinted light green, and put the pie in the fridge (or ice box as we always called it). There it was to sit and chill all afternoon, and be just right for dessert that evening.

At mid-afternoon, Steve returned from school with his best friend, Terry, and they went directly to the ice box for stomach stuffers. Seeing the pastel green pie with its DO NOT TOUCH sign, they helped themselves instead to some ice cream. When they went back into the ice box for soda, Terry said to Steve: "You know, the color of that pie looks familiar. You know what it looks like? Aero Shave Cream."

If they hurried, there'd be enough time. After phoning ahead, they went, shaving cream in hand, to Polly's house. She was Terry's girlfriend, and was famous for baking cookies. Many a boy her age had found her chocolate chip cookies and toffee squares way more alluring than any cologne she might have worn.

Well, Polly baked a pie crust, but they all thought the pie would need more weight than just shaving cream, so they first filled the crust with vanilla pudding that they colored green. Then they put the green shaving cream on top that. The green from the shaving cream didn't exactly match the green of the pudding, but the colors were close. Steve then took the pie back home, and put it in the ice box. He hid the real pie in the basement.

At dessert time that evening, your grandmother said she'd come up with a brand new kind of pie that everyone was sure to like. Amid mumblings of "I bet!" and "Yeah, sure!" she cut the first piece. When she held it up, she saw the two shades of green. "Hmm," she said, "the eggs must have separated." And of course, there were more grumblings. She passed out the first piece, which was supposed to come to me at the other end of the table. But your Uncle David took a fingerful as it was going by, and popped it into his mouth. "Yuck!" he said, "I'm not going to eat that. It tastes like soap." Grandma Jo said, "You know the rule: three bites." All the rest of us remembered the coconut cream pie story and thought that David was just trying to get us to smell the pie; no one wanted to risk getting a nose in this pie. So everyone ignored David, and each of us ate a piece of shaving cream pie. Each of us, that is, except Steve, who started to laugh. Ken, who was sitting next to him, realized who the perpetrator was, picked up his pie and gave Steve a face-full. We then had a good-natured pie fight before the real pie was served. The eggs on the real pie hadn't separated, and no one needed to be told the 3-bite rule. The real pie was delicious.

LETTER 27

What's the Very Best Time of Life?

If you've looked at recent pictures of Grandma Jo and me, you know that we're wrinkly, of average height, but shrinking, we're reasonably fit for old folks, casually clothed, fairly free of blubber, and not strait-jacketed. We both have light-colored hair, mine an earned gray, Grandma Jo's a bought blond.

If you've read these letters, you know more about me, and to a degree about us, than our pictures show. The pictures merely show how we'd *look* if we were flattened into two dimensions. These letters were written (in part) to show the inner me, the stuff that has no dimensions. Here are some salient messages I may have hidden too well in those letters:

- Most of my heroes and heroines were folks who met hardship head on and tamed it.

- The years of discipline—in grade school and high school, in the navy, at home, and via my conscience—seem to have left no ugly psychological scars.

- I've always felt free to laugh, to acquire new skills, to dream, to explore, and to mingle with fascinating folks.

- Having right attitudes, like having enough oxygen, struck me as mighty important.

- Using my imagination, never denying it or locking it away, was certainly the thing to do.

- Having been temperate in the broadest sense didn't seem to cause me grief or cut into my joy.

- I liked having dogs until society wanted them chained, penned, neutered, quieted, and kept out of classrooms.

- Family life, even without today's gadgets, wasn't half bad.

- I learned early and never forgot how to be scared. At age nine I was scared to face the world without a father. In my twenties I feared typhoons. In my seventies I dreaded strangers who might do away with people like me to save money.

- Being allowed to be a kid, to roam, and to play games with no adults hanging around, was just fine.

- Sense of humor was attractive in others and essential to my own well-being.

- My brain was often pleased when I told it to cast out drab thoughts and worries for an hour or two, and concentrate on hobbies and dreams.

- Several friends made what I thought was a mistake. They were too acquisitive to be inquisitive. They were so busy buying, they had no time to wonder.

- Being grateful for such gifts as the five senses was not enough. I needed to *use* them often, and in caring ways.

- To search for good in people and in things seemed proper

to me. But I learned that some things (such as war) and some people (such as corruptors) are best avoided because they contain only an ounce of good per ton of evil.

That rehash of past letters took so much space, there's barely enough for today's thought. It's about a question I overheard one woman ask another: "What was your favorite age?" I was in the check-out line at the library, and didn't hear Woman #2 give an answer, but on my ride home I realized how tough the question really was. So many of my ages have been great that it's hard to choose a favorite. There were the ages at which I got married . . . became a father . . . got home from the war . . . finished getting all six children through college . . . became a grandfather . . . retired.

In the end I chose age fourteen. For all the boys I grew up with, being fourteen was mighty nice. We had not begun to shave or use deodorant. Our greatest worries, if you could call them that, were about questions on up-coming quizzes. We were not yet involved with girls and the complications that would entail later on. We spent more time outdoors than indoors. We were treated by parents as more than halfway to adulthood. We had real adventures. We needed no pills, only food, huge helpings of food. And for me, age fourteen brought two bonuses. That's when, as part of a group of Boy Scouts, I went to Europe. It was also at that age that I began to play tennis.

If, after you've lived a few decades, you've had so many good ages you're hard put to choose a favorite, be grateful. What you're having is a good *life*.

LETTER 28

My Grandfather Pop

It's high time I told you about *my* grandfather, Pop. He was a great guy—although he wouldn't have liked my calling him a *guy*. For many years he ran the St. Louis branch of the Western Newspaper Union, which was a company, not a labor union. A good thing, too, because at the mere mention of unions, Pop got all flushed, and his voice grew louder. He believed that people who joined unions would never get past St. Peter, having already sold their souls to communist organizers.

Except for the word "union," nothing got Pop all riled up. You could even tell from his face he was mild-mannered and bemused. His eyes were twinkly and a trifle squinty, and his mouth was set in a half smile. Just a glance at him and you got the feeling he was about to tell you one of the hundreds of funny stories tucked in his head. The humor in those stories was low-key, never blatant or off-color. As you listened, you smiled rather than laughed out loud.

Pop liked to tell about the time his brother Ed's wife brought home a cat she planned to keep. Ed, being a dog lover and cat hater, was sure the cat would have to live elsewhere if at all. The question was how to make that happen. If he arranged a fatal accident or mailed the cat to Zaire, his wife was sure to find out and make him regret his deed. No, he'd have to come up with a way to make his wife *want* that cat back out of the house.

Whenever Ed was alone in the house with that cat, he secretly trained it to bite any human thrust at it. He even trained it to make ugly cat faces and ugly cat noises before biting. Pop said his brother Ed must have been mighty patient and very lucky because cats are almost impossible to train. Pop told me I shouldn't believe those lies people tell about how cats are smart but too independent to let themselves be trained. They're just not very bright, he said. If you put all the Earth's creatures on a tall ladder with the smart ones up top and the stupid ones at the bottom, cats would be one rung above garden slugs and one rung below chickens.

Ed's wife got rid of the cat all right. After she and two of her friends had been nipped. She figured the cat had gone insane, and she knew why. It couldn't bear to live in the same house with anyone who hated cats the way Ed did. And that made Ed very happy. She'd never again bring home a cat and risk having it go stark raving mad.

Pop was a lot like the *typical* grandfather of the times. He had a gray moustache, a four-inch circular bald spot, and enough excess weight to leave no doubt that he was well-fed. He smoked fat cigars, drank in moderation, wore loose-fitting clothes, and was sedentary rather than off-and-running. He was a good listener: to kids and adults and radio episodes of One Man's Family (a radio soap opera). He was self-educated and never got around to dropping out. Instead, he kept on reading, usually while sitting in the rocking chair I still use.

He reckoned that the finest book written in English was *Huckleberry Finn.* I think he was right. When I was very young, he put me on the arm of his rocking chair and read me the whole book. I don't recall how many sessions it took. A lot, I suppose, because Pop often had to rephrase grown-up sentences for me. It's a very happy memory now, riding that raft with Huck and Jim. It's just as well Tom Sawyer didn't tag along. He was getting too civilized, using way more soap than a boy ought to and foolin' around with that fool girl, Becky.

Pop once took me by bus to Huck's home town, Hannibal, where we ate catfish as he told me how bad life must have been for slaves like Jim.

Then one day Pop showed me a pair of tickets he had, one for me and one for him, to ride a riverboat steamer, a stern wheeler, the Golden Eagle, all the way to Cape Girardeau and back. Going downstream would take the better part of day. Coming back against the current would take two days and nights. What a trip! We saw gravel bars Huck and Jim may have camped on, landings they may have used, swampy spots where they might have hid, boats old enough to have been around as the boys drifted by. We also saw something much newer, a state penitentiary. Pop's explanation of what went on inside there made a lasting impression.

We were met in Cape Girardeau by a friend of Pop's who owned a farm close by, and who was about to have a well drilled. But first he needed to pick the right spot to drill. A four-year-old farm girl would show him where. Her name was Janet. Well, I couldn't see how a girl that young would know where there was water underground. Pop's friend said she had been born with a rare talent. She could dowse. She was a genuine dowser, the only one for miles around. She could walk along holding a forked peach branch, and once that branch started to twitch and point downward, you could be sure you'd get water by drilling. It all sounded crazy to me, kinda like witchcraft, but I watched Janet in action, and sure enough, that peach branch shook and pointed, and that's where the drilling started. Pop heard later that they struck water not very far down.

From the time my father died until I was about through high school, Pop lived close to us, a mile away at first, then a block away. He filled my head with dreams and gentle humor, and a few principles about how to live life well. And all at a time when I really needed it. Our great times together went beyond the stern wheeler and the rocker. We fished together, drifting and casting into lily pads in the Kalamazoo River, each of us using the same lure, a Heddon Queen with a weedless hook. He always caught more bass than I did, and always lectured me about the evils of using any lure with more than one hook. You have to give the fish a sporting chance.

Mother and my grandmother, Mom, and I were all set to drive Pop to the hospital when his liver cancer got real bad. We were all in the car, engine running, and I was about to put the car in gear when Pop said, "Wait up. I want to have one more look around the house." And he did.

LETTER 29

Careers and Office Pranks

Do you feel, as you read these letters, that I try too hard and too often to escape the "real" world? You could be right. Seldom does a whole day go by without my wanting to escape a world that worries me or scares me or puzzles me or annoys me. Little wonder that I have found so many ways to escape. I use my imagination. I let the intensity of a tennis game block all else from my brain. I dip into my collection of memories to live once more in the rather different world of the past. I read novels in which the people and places are not like those around me. I throw myself into hobbies: woodworking, writing, computer stuff. I remind myself that since the world is a wonderful place, I should take time to wonder about the things and creatures in it.

I can't tell whether others feel as intensely as I do this need to escape. Probably not. I got an earlier start than most. When I heard my father had died, I must have felt an overpowering need to escape. And later on, as I watched shipmates on the 393 go to pieces mentally, I wished they could have understood the calming effects of escape.

Fifteen minutes ago, I discovered something about myself. This escape habit of mine may explain why my career went the way it did. Instead of sticking to a single specialty (like accounting) I had to "escape" to another, then another, and another. This worked out just fine for me. I liked the challenge of having to learn a new specialty every two or three years: chemical research, technical selling, corporate planning, applied mathematics, corporate economics, marketing research, and so on.

What shall I tell you about my career? It lasted forty-one years, counting my time in the navy. I worked for just two companies (Monsanto and Gulf), both of them large, both in the chemical business. Most of my bosses were either great or pretty good; only two of them belonged in psychiatric wards. I earned a fairly decent income, was active in outside professional groups, won a few honors, authored 30-40 articles and 3 textbooks, traveled quite a bit (Europe, Asia, U.S.), and helped a few young folks along their career paths. So all in all, my career rates a grade of B. It suited me well. It gave me the variety I wanted, the money I needed to raise a family, and a bit time to enjoy life. It was, however, decidedly inferior to my second career, Retirement, which rates a grade of A+.

During my first career, I took a continuing education course on Corporate Culture. An interesting word: culture. When we say a person is cultured, we mean he or she is well-educated, well-mannered. I don't think corporate culture is like that. I think it's more like a culture of fungus growing in a petri dish. Even so, watching it was sometimes fun, often amazing.

Our top managers clung to high school habits. They thought that slogans, like football cheers, would promote team spirit. They wore certain styles of clothes and made fun of those who didn't. They formed cliques. They did homework. They went to classes (called meetings) where they asked and answered questions. They talked a lot to one another by phone. They ate lunch together, met socially on week-ends, and they played games. Ah! the games. Some were great, especially when underdogs won.

Charlie, one of our top managers, would try just about anything, provided a competitor tried it first. When someone told him *three* competitors were intent on making their companies more creative, there was no stopping him. What we need to do, he said, is identify our creative employees and give them enough freedom and money to bring out that creativity. They'll come up with new products and processes. Profits will rise. Management will look good. He was too excited to hear a staff man's questions: How will we identify *creative* people? How do we know their ideas will be practical, let alone profitable?

And thus did a new game begin. Several bright young men saw an opportunity. It paid to be creative, and no one could tell whether you were or weren't. *Ergo*, fake it. (It was commonly thought that creativity was most obvious in the art world). So these bright lads became what they imagined the typical artist to be. They got shaggy and wore loose-fitting clothes and cheap jewelry. They spoke to their bosses in brusque, almost rude tones. Two of them went barefoot.

Whether the company profited from the creativity scheme is uncertain. The bright young men did, though. They were tagged "creative" and were better paid.

Some of the games were quickies—practical jokes designed to amuse hundreds of employees. Jack M. had just finished a wretched assignment. For nine months, he had taken care of the detailed work needed to close a string of retail outlets. He had let people go, recovered cars and office furniture, disposed of inventory, paid creditors, and terminated leases. It had all meant long hours for Jack, and a very large stack of columnar paper. In those pre-computer days, accountants kept track of details with sharp pencils and columnar paper.

With that messy assignment behind him, Jack felt much better. He had been back two weeks, doing something interesting for a change, when he happened to glance at an item on the bulletin board. Washington decided to tell the company not to get out of the retail business. Jack smiled. The Feds were a little late. Jack returned to his office as the phone rang.

"Jack, this is Ed [a company lawyer]. We need to talk. We've got trouble."

"Yeah, I saw the notice. But what's the problem?"

"You don't understand. When I say *we're* in trouble, I mean *you're* in trouble, and *I'm* in trouble."

"How so? I've done nothing wrong. How can I be in trouble?"

"Let me put it this way, Jack. How long will it take you to undo what you did?"

Jack whipped out those columnar sheets, and for ten minutes had very dark thoughts. How do I rehire people, buy back desks and cars, re-lease offices? And then the phone rang.

"Ed here. Gotcha!"

LETTER 30

Attitudes Toward Learning

Remember my writing you about getting yourselves some good mini-attitudes? Let's try one on learning. I'll tell you mine. You come up with one you can live with. Okay?

I was pretty young when I started to hate learning, and I kept on hating it for more years than I remember. It always interfered with having fun. Learning usually meant being indoors, which is not right for a normal boy, and I had to sit quietly on a hard wooden seat, which is likewise unnatural. On top of that, my teachers expected me to turn in *neat* papers. Ha!

Summer was the best time of all, and on the day after Labor Day, when school started up, I might as well have been going to a funeral for all the joy I felt.

Maybe if learning hadn't been forced on me I'd have felt more kindly toward it. Adults were always saying stuff like, "You have to study to amount to anything when you grow up."

In time I got to like a few subjects. Arithmetic was tolerably good because it was a boys' subject, and I wanted to be one of the boys. Girls in those days didn't fancy Arithmetic or nightcrawlers. I also had two other reasons for thinking Arithmetic was OK. Answers were clearly right or wrong, not "sort of"; and except for multiplication tables, I had nothing to memorize. I hated to memorize what was already in print.

History, with all those silly dates, was awful. Besides, I got to where I knew how the history stories would turn out. English composition was bad for another reason. Our teachers always gave us lousy subjects to write about. Penmanship was no better with those endless exercises and all that ink-smudged paper.

Had I known about Monarch butterflies I'd have envied them. They're born with all the learning they'll ever need. They can start out for a place a thousand miles away, a place they've never been, ask no directions along the way, look at no map, accept no rides, and get there. Can you do that? I can't.

For too much of my life, my attitude toward learning was none too good. I should have been quicker to outgrow some of my early ideas. Instead, I went on feeling that learning was all work and no fun. And I clung to my biases, favoring mathematics and the sciences while detesting subjects that had no right or wrong answers. By the time I arrived at these five convictions, I had probably grown a few gray hairs (prematurely):

1. Learning is a lot like eating. You have to do it. You have to have a balanced diet. You can take in just so much at a single sitting. You enjoy it most when the "meals" are well-seasoned, well-served, and unrushed. You're bound to like some parts of your meals better than others.

2. Mother Nature seems to have goofed. She shouldn't have made us peak so early. We learn most easily while we're very young—which is why adults bombard us with knowledge at that stage. But it is then that we are most easily distracted. We have so many better things to do, so many games to play.

3. Beginner courses are seldom any good. There's a reason for that. Before you can get familiar with a new subject, you must master the jargon. That means *memorization*—and certain boredom. You'll memorize vocabulary words for foreign language courses, formulas for chemistry, names of species for biology. The trick is to *endure* those drab beginner courses so you can enjoy the more advanced ones.

4. Learning is addictive. The longer you do it, the larger your daily shots of learning, the tougher it will be for you to cut back. And quitting altogether will be fatal. I've heard certain

retirees say they're too old to learn. They sat before TV sets and at bingo tables waiting to be entertained. In no time they were brain dead.

5. The *act* of learning seems more important than the subjects learned. We study so-called *practical* subjects to fatten our wallets, and *impractical* ones (my favorites) because we're curious. Both do wonders for our brains. The real sense of accomplishment, though, comes when at last the *act* of learning becomes fun, not work.

Lewis Thomas, whom I never met but wish I had, was a most enthusiastic learner. He'd get curious about something in Nature, like warts, as most of us do. Unlike us, though, he was not content to say, "That's interesting," and let it go at that. He had to find out all about warts. He had to read about them, and talk to wart experts, and folks who had warts. Once he had learned enough, he wrote a short plain-English essay on warts. Did you know that when you get a wart, your skin isn't puffing up to try to get rid of the wart-causing virus? Actually, your body is offering the virus just what it wants for food. You probably know that warts often disappear overnight. But did you know that people have gotten rid of warts simply by making up their minds that it was time for the warts to go? Real mind over matter!

The Dr. Thomas mini-essays cover scads of other biological marvels: snails, ants, jellyfish, ponds, and embryos, to name a few. Although all these essays fascinated and enlightened me, what I liked best was the way the author's enthusiasm shone through. In the wart essay he wished he had a wart. He wanted to see whether, using only his brain, he could make that wart disappear.

But then he wondered: suppose it isn't brain waves that do the job, after all—suppose there's a mysterious predator out there, an invisible wart-eater lurking about, just waiting to swoop down.

Makes you wonder, doesn't it? Makes you want to learn more.

LETTER 31

Big Changes esp. in Females

Have you figured out why, in none of the first thirty letters, did I make one of your parents the main topic? I'll tell you. It's partly because I want y'all to find out about your parents from your parents. And it's partly because I'm not looking for trouble.

Suppose I were to write a letter about one of my daughters, a mother to some of you. Suppose also that into that letter I put an innocent sentence like: Everyone thought she was a beautiful baby. The English Language being what it is, that sentence would cause great stress. My daughter would have dark thoughts about me: Does he think I got ugly when I grew up? How come he didn't write about how smart I am and about my incredible athletic skills? And the rest of my children would assume I remembered their having been grotesque babies.

Two questions often asked of old people are: What's your secret to living a long life? and What's been the biggest change in the world since you were a kid? I answer the first question by saying I've lived this long because I had good genes and good luck, and because I kept my head down low during the war. I've toyed with the idea of giving credit to some hoked-up health food, like stir-fried caterpillars, but haven't tried it.

Choosing the biggest change that I have witnessed is tough. There have been so many. Good changes like no longer putting a quarantine sign on the front door whenever a kid gets a contagious disease . . . bad changes like no longer being able to get up kids-only games on vacant lots . . . and mysterious changes, those changes that got made, and you can't tell why.

When we think someone or some group has been mean to us, we find ways to get even. Or ahead. Sometimes we do that physically, as when we wage war. Other times, we go at our enemies mentally, as when we hold mob demonstrations. We bait them, scare them, get them so hopping mad they can't think straight. You might say that war is like driving cattle into a slaughterhouse, and mob demonstrations are like what goes on in the bullring.

There weren't many mobs around until I was well into my forties, or if there were I didn't notice them. Later on, they cropped up like mushrooms on a damp summer night. Their members all felt they had been shortchanged, and aimed to get the shortchangers to settle up. The mobs liked the word "discrimination," applied it to lots of biases (color, age, sex, religion, physical condition, mental condition, politics), and made out pretty well. They didn't call themselves mobs, that name having already been taken. Names like Movement, Union, Association, and Lobby were preferred.

Most of these Movements were easy to understand because their members seemed to have been very obvious victims. The blacks, for instance. A *mysterious* change was the one wrought by the women's movement. At least it was mysterious to me.

Whereas the blacks could complain about being poor, the nation's women had more money than the men did. Blacks could complain about how their living conditions made them die younger than whites. Women, by contrast, outlived men. Blacks contended that because they amounted to only 10-11% of the population, whites had an unfair size advantage. But women outnumbered men, then as now.

I guess what puzzled me was that females of all ages seemed to have the best of just about everything. Early on I was told about how girls were to get extra nice treatment. "Mustn't sock 'em," some adult told me. "Mustn't even cork 'em on the arm or Dutch rub their hair."

Other messages of male inferiority kept coming my way. If you decide to walk one of those girls home, you gotta carry her books; she won't carry yours. And don't forget to walk on the outside next to the street, so if a car comes by and hits a puddle, you're the one who gets wet and muddy. If you're ever in a place without enough chairs, you have to stand up and let girls sit. You must always open doors for girls, and never ever cuss when girls are around, or even talk about disgusting things like chicken guts. And don't expect teachers to be on your side; teachers think *all* girls are better behaved than *any* boy.

Things will get worse when you're older. Car insurance companies will charge girls less just because they are girls. If you want to go out with a girl, you'll have to call her, not vice versa, and you'll pay for everything, even if she's richer than you are. The average girl will have lots more clothes than you do; at some point, she'll have more shoes in her closet than you'll own in a lifetime.

As adults, many, if not most, females were treated royally. They had what was regarded as the noblest of careers: raising proper families. They were not forced to go scratch out a living. Although husbands said their homes were their castles, they still had to report to their queens, their wives. Husbands only *made* money; wives *spent* it, and ran the castle.

So what happened? Someone set out to "improve" women's lot in life using logic like this: Have fewer kids so you'll have more to spend on yourself. Get a job so you'll have still more money— unless it all goes for transportation, work clothes, lunches out, taxes, and what you pay someone else to raise your kids. Behave the way you *think* men behave, drinking, cussing, and fooling around, but speak as though everyone had just been neutered. No such thing as men and women, only people.

And that, I suppose, was the biggest change I witnessed during the first seventy-odd years of my life. It was sad for me. I hated to see family life head toward oblivion. I also hated to see women turn into persons. They were better when they were soft and gentle, and had female intuition. Happy to report, there are still some male-female differences. When men shop, it's because they need to buy something. When women shop, it's to see what there is to see.

LETTER 32

Water and I

Rarely do I get around to pitching those old papers stacked in, on, and around my desk. When I do, I marvel at my persistence in writing never-to-be-published essays and stories. Just yesterday, I ran across a book-length gem with a 1960s date. I had written it the hard way, on a manual typewriter, and given it a strange title: *Education Need Not Be a Hindrance*. It's my thoughts about how to be a fit father. Since we hadn't finished raising the children, I don't know why I felt qualified to write such a book. But write it I did, and now I can't bring myself to pitch it. Not yet anyway. Not until I swipe a few items from it to put in these letters.

Even back in the 1960s, I evidently went around telling folks they should look closely at things, use their imaginations, and call forth memories. Water, for instance.

Water is a magical element in a child's wonderland. Add dirt to it, mix thoroughly, and you get a smooth, squishy mud that is good for molding and sun-drying, or for oozing between tiny toes. Water with just a touch of soap can become an iridescent web between the fingers. Blended with flour, it becomes a fairly decent paste, though it lacks the tangy taste of library paste. Blended with flour and sugar, it becomes sparkling snow on a cardboard roof.

Nothing does quite the job that water does when you want to make drippy pinnacles of sand. Water is where you find tadpoles. It comes out of maple squirts, and out of hoses throttled by inexpert little thumbs. When it comes out of the sky, it makes collecting earthworms easier. It forms rivulets that can be dammed to create waffle-sized lakes.

Water floats things: snapping turtles, beach balls, canoes, people (once they learn the secret), jellyfish, bobbers on fishing lines, toy boats, dragonflies, pirate ships, sea gulls.

Unlike wood or metal or cloth, water is easy to change. With a drop of the right dye, you can make it turn just about any color you can think of. If you want water to be something other than a liquid, boil it or freeze it. If you want to change its taste, add sugar and lemon juice, or put it in that special earthenware crock with some sugar, yeast, and root beer extract.

Water is what makes watermelon refreshing, and icicles glitter. It sizzles when poured on hot coals, gurgles in drainpipes, whistles from tea kettles, roars beside a coastline. On a washcloth, it cools a feverish forehead; in a hot water bottle, it stops shivers. It is a friend to children except when it is misused on necks and behind ears.

To jar my memory, I just fetched myself a glass of water and set it here on a coaster. Because it has three ice cubes in it, I expect more water to bead up on the glass like dew on a lawn. I'm not thirsty. I don't want to drink this water—not yet anyway. Right now, I just want to look at it.

There! It worked! I now see the water of Missouri's Current River. We're on a float trip, my sons and I. They're only partly grown up, big enough to handle canoes and swim if they have to, but not big enough to go make their ways in the world. We are inexperienced floaters. Except for a short stint on a sluggish stretch of the Meramec, we haven't floated at all. On the advice of a friend, we have opted for a one-day float of twenty-odd miles beginning where the Current River begins, at Big Spring. It is good advice. The river gets us off to a gentle start. The water there is hardly deep enough to keep our canoes up off the rocky river bed. We are surprised that the Current is so narrow here, more like a golf course creek than a river.

But with each passing mile the river widens, and its volume grows. Springs all along its twisting route pour in clear, cold water— and give us the excitement we had hoped for. Every half hour or so we paddle along a stretch of calm, deep water, come to a bend in the river, and hear the roar of white water ahead. We can't see what's in store because the bank is high, and the turn is sharp. Only briefly do we wonder what dangers await us. Drop offs? Fallen trees? Rocks in all the wrong places? Narrow channels where white water rushes with enough force to tip a canoeist who swerves sideways?

We round the turn. Anticipation ends. Reality takes over. We must choose quickly and well which paths to take. The river's choices won't always be right for us. If the river wants to send most of its water under a tree trunk that's only inches above the surface, we dare not go there. So we choose a safer path (we hope), and paddle like crazy to take it.

Throughout the day, each run of white water is livelier than the one before it, again because springs along the way keep adding new water. Most of them sit back well away from the river, and send their water via creeks, but one is smack dab on the edge of the river inside a cave. We paddle right into that cave. It's small, hardly enough room for two canoes. The water in there is deep and frigid—fine for drinking out of a cupped hand, but you need to be quick about scooping it up. If you're not, your fingers will ache from the cold.

We stop at gravel bars along the way whenever we're tired or hungry. We don't stop long. We can't tell how many of those twenty-odd miles are behind us, and we dare not try to shoot those later, livelier rapids after dark. We've kept our food in plastic bags, knowing that water, for all its charms, can be mean. It can burn the inside of your nose, stop up your ears, and turn your sandwiches into sodden messes.

Years after that day on the Current, it dawned on me. A float trip is a little like growing up. As children, we pass one test, add a tad of self-confidence, rest a while in calm water, then start to worry about what life has in store for us around that next bend. As the cycle is repeated, and the tests get tougher, our ever-expanding self-confidence makes us more decisive. We choose promising paths in a hurry, and head for them, knowing that just to sit there with paddles across our knees, and let the river take charge of our lives would invite disaster. And that's partly what growing up is about.

LETTER 33

Those Foxy Folks

Humpty Dumpty must have been very careless the day he fell. With so fragile a body, he should never have climbed that wall in the first place and then leaned too far forward. He wasn't dim-witted, you know. He was able to come up with profound thoughts. Like what he told Lewis Carroll: "I use words to mean what I *want* them to mean." That was his way of poking fun at the English Language because so many of its words have multiple definitions. Most of us, like Humpty, use words to mean what we want them to mean.

Take the word *commit*, and its close relatives *committed* and *commitment*. A man commits a crime. Society then has him committed—put in jail if he's sane or in a mental lock-up if he's daft. An unwed couple say they've made a commitment. What they mean is that they plan to live together under a non-binding agreement that can easily be broken. A woman commits to the purchase of a house; a man commits to a hitch in the navy; a couple commits to a till-death-do-us-part marriage.

I'm happy to report that there are some words no one, except maybe Humpty Dumpty, can define any old way. Occasionally I think of human behavior as somewhat animal-like, and when I want to tell someone about it, I can find good words in the dictionary: "porcine" (pig-like) to describe dedicated overeaters; "feline" (cat-like) for sneaky people who attack without warning; "ovine" (sheep-like) for those who mindlessly go along with the flock ; "bovine" (cow-like) for top-heavy women . . . vulpine (fox-like) for the crafty, cunning people of the world.

Of those words, the one I like best is "vulpine," maybe because my life has been affected by so may vulpine characters. They're everywhere, or so it seems, the worst species being the "promoters of change."

To understand how these folks think and act, pretend to be one. Close your eyes and imagine your job requires you to serve customers. Let's say you run a post office, and one day you decide to become vulpine. You talk to yourself. "Taking care of these customers sure keeps me busy. It would be mighty nice if I could get them to do some of my work for me. How to do it? I can't just order them to help out. That would get them sore at me. No, I need to be foxy. I need to get them to *like* the idea or at least to accept it as an inevitable change, a step along the path of progress."

Back in the 1930s, our mailman (first Mr. Merz, and later Mr. Warren) came calling twice a day during the week and once on Saturday. He was usually escorted by four or five neighborhood dogs, and sometimes by one or more neighborhood kids. He'd pause long enough for a short chat or to sell us stamps, and once in a while to have a glass of lemonade.

About the only time we visited the post office was to mail a big package or put money into our postal savings account. We dropped our outgoing letters into corner mailboxes, which were emptied three times during the day, and once at night. There were plenty of those mail boxes around. Nowhere in Webster Groves could you be more than three blocks away from one.

And along came those vulpine postal people—not Mr. Merz or Mr. Warren—who told us how streamlined and efficient things would get, and how patriotic folks like us would be delighted to help move the country to this better world. As you know, the foxes won. Our mail deliveries were cut in half, the corner mail boxes all but disappeared, and the price of stamps went up, up, up. We had to shoulder some of the mail-sorting burden by putting ZIP codes on letters. We had to go to the post office more often because mail carriers no longer certified mail or wrote up money orders. When we got to the post office, we now had to queue up and then be told to do what clerks had always done for us: fill out post office forms.

And did all this "progress" result in shorter delivery times? Not yet.

Whoa! I told myself, as I began to write these letters, that I wouldn't carry on about how much better the world used to be. But I've gone and done it. Sorry about that. I actually just meant to warn you about vulpine creatures, and tell you how they victimized my generation. Whether you can stand up to them remains to be seen. They're all around you, so keep alert.

Without meaning to glorify the past, let me tick off three more examples to show how these creatures got the better of us.

Our grocer used to take orders by phone, gather up what we ordered, bring it to the house, put it into cupboards and into the ice box, and send us a bill at the end of the month. Grocery shopping has since become a do-it-yourself operation.

In the '30s and '40s, we drove into filling stations where attendants washed our windshields and checked our tires, radiators, batteries, and oil levels. Later, these filling stations were renamed service stations. A bad choice of words. All the free service disappeared. Attendants wouldn't even fill the gas tank except for an added fee.

When we used the telephone, we spoke to a lady operator with a real first name and a pleasant voice. She was very helpful. We gave her a number if we knew it. If not, we gave her a name and an (approximate) address. Whenever we had trouble with the phone itself or with a phone bill, we told her about it, and she got the right person to call us or visit us. If we placed a long-distance call that didn't go through right away, she took charge and called us back once all the lines were clear. Today, we punch buttons, listen to drab tunes, and let ourselves be shoved along a network of dead-end paths. And we wait. My, how we wait.

Will those vulpine creatures outfox you, too? I bet they will.

I began this letter with comments about words in the English Language. I have one more word for you: transmogrify. It's a verb. When you transmogrify something you change it into something ugly or ridiculous. It's what vulpine people do to keep busy.

LETTER 34

Our Cottage's Door Panels

I've just taken a short course on how to write about my memories. The teacher, a Hope College English professor, had each of us in the class write four essays, one about a memorable *person*, one about a *place*, one about a *happening*, and one about a *tradition*. I chose, as my *place* to write about, the Shorewood cottage. Your grandmother said she liked what I wrote, but I was all wrong about that colored stew. Maybe one of you knows the *real* story. If so, pass it along. Anyway, this is what I wrote:

We've had a slue of visitors to our cottage during the last decade, and every last one of them has complimented us on our door panels. They say, "What a neat idea!" or "What are you going to do when you run out of panels?" or simply "Wow!"

Some of those same visitors enthuse over our view of the lake out front or our beach or the woods out back, but all believe that what really makes our cottage unique are those door panels.

Ours is a boxy brown cottage, creakier than I am but less wrinkled, a frame house whose nails, after ninety four years, must surely have rusted away, leaving the entire structure held together by paint. When grandchildren visit, and a storm comes at us across that ninety miles of water, and the cottage shudders in the wind, and lightning draws tree patterns in the night sky, I say, "Don't be scared. This cottage has stood up against storms for nearly a century." Still, I'd bet that at least one grandchild says to himself or herself, "Yeah, and maybe all those storms have made the cottage so weak it'll just collapse."

There are a dozen rooms, all small, all with walls of unpainted pine bead board, a screened-in front porch, a deck, and a septic tank. Because all members of the family want the cottage to be one of the few things in life kept unchanged, tradition wins out over convenience every time. We have room for the old pump organ but not for a dishwasher. Our peak capacity for overnight guests is twenty, provided the group is made up of the proper genders, ages, and legal relationships. I'd like to say the cottage can sleep twenty *comfortably*. It can't. No house I've ever been in can. In any group of twenty there's sure to be someone who, during the night, is bothered by the odor of mothballs in the blankets or a sound like a swooping bat, or a mattress molded to the wrong-shaped body, or the terrifying thought that the bathroom might be occupied when Nature's call is loud and clear.

Nearly a half-century ago, someone in the family decided to record on a door panel the happenings of that summer. The idea seemed good enough for us to go on like born-again cave people recording our history that way. We have lots of doors, each with five rectangular panels front and back. At the end of each summer, someone takes pen in hand to draw little pictures, and to print phrases and words chosen because they just might trigger memories later on.

The 1966 panel says we set a dishwashing record: ninety-eight pieces were washed and dried after a single meal. In 1974, Grandma Jo served her first—and probably last—blue stew. At some tot's request, she added blue food coloring to a pot of ugly brown stew. That same summer, our dog had his rear end operated on. To keep him from biting the stitches, we made him wear a bottomless bucket over his head. There's a sketch of him on the door panel in this condition, along with the phrase, "Bucket-head Wolf."

The 1979 panel shows sketches of Andy and David, two grandsons born that year. Miss South Carolina, who was a house guest that summer, didn't rate a sketch, only a mention.

Printed above a drawing of a hump-top chest on the 1984 panel are the words, "Pirate Treasure Hunt." To understand what that was all about, you must first be aware that the woods behind the cottage are enchanted. Whenever there are three rings around the moon, the wee folk go to any of several clearings in the forest where they dance and plan a treasure hunt for the next day. These wee folk are mostly elves and fairies, although there has been one unconfirmed sighting of a gnome.

Three rings appeared around the full moon one night in 1994. Three-year-old Emily found the first clue the next morning. It was in the myrtle, a note on ragged-edged tissue paper, large print, dreadful spelling. (Elves don't go to regular schools). After a half-dozen more clues, the grandchildren were on the beach following a mile-long path of bright blue hand-painted stones. The path snaked into and out of the woods. It ended with a clue about where to dig in the sand for that hump-top chest filled with presents for all.

I've heard folks in other houses exclaim, "If these walls could talk, oh the stories they could tell!" Our cottage has no talking walls, just the next best thing: talking panels.

LETTER 35

To-Do Lists, Not Got-Done Lists

I have a to-do list of sorts. Doesn't everyone? Mine is in the computer, out of sight. I used to keep the list in my head until I found that having it there made me sleep fitfully. I also went through a period when I kept it on odd-sized scraps of paper, which worked pretty well. I still slept soundly after scribbling tasks to be done, and then not being able to read my scribbles. Best of all, I lost some of my to-do lists, and laundered others inside the pockets of shirts and pants.

Have you sometimes wondered why people even bother to make to-do lists? I think it has to do with conscience. Folks feel less guilty when they jot down a task to do. It shows intent, even though deep down there is no intent. I like to think I'm different in that I actually intend to do what's on my list. I mean to paint the garage, let's say, and I put it on my list, but I'm careful not to add a starting date.

One of the older items on my list is: *Do a piece on safety*. The term "piece" means an essay or maybe a video tape, and the reason I intended to do one was simple enough. Parents were trying to teach their kids safety using what I thought was a wrong approach. And I should know, because I had used that very same approach on our kids. I had let them learn safety on an incident-by-incident basis.

Here's how it worked. Let's say daughter Chris at age four was standing too close to a barbecue grill full of red coals. We told her to step back to avoid being burned. From that incident, she learned to keep her distance from barbecue grills in use, but nothing about the dangers of being burned by boiling water, curling irons, or the sun. To learn about those took three more "incident" lessons. And since burning was only one kind of danger to be covered in a course on safety, the number of incidents needed would have to be very large.

And then I had this idea—probably because my brain wasn't cluttered with to-do lists—that safety should be taught as an *attitude* rather than as a bunch of rules. Until a child is old enough for a safety attitude, he or she must of course be kept from harm's way by whatever means. Often a shriek or a stern "No!" will do. If not, grab the scissors before the baby shoves the points into a wall socket.

The attitude I have in mind is one of sensible caution. If you have it, you are unafraid to act, but first you want a minute to consider the risks. You may want a second minute to choose ways to protect yourself. Maybe an example would help. You're about to cut the grass. You've done it before, and you know what *could* hurt you: gasoline and a rotating blade. You also know ways to protect yourself. You wear safety glasses (in case the mower throws a stick or stone); you go outdoors to pour the gasoline into a cool mower; and of course you remind yourself to keep hand and feet away from the blade.

The risks a kid needs to recognize are from sources such as these:

> sharp objects; spinning things; poisons; fire; big moving things (like cars); small moving things (like grains of sand); water; explosives; wind; unseen forces (like electricity, and gravity, and invisible gases).

So a parent takes up the sources one at a time with his kids. Let's say it's spinning things: mixers in the kitchen, bicycle wheels outdoors, power tools in the work shop. And what's the risk with spinning things? That given the chance, they'll grab you. Therefore, you don't give them anything to get hold of. You remove your watch and rings. You roll up your sleeves. You put your hair under a hat. And you pay attention to where your fingers are.

But what's most important is that attitude of caution. You can't memorize all that might possibly go wrong. You can be the sort of person who stops long enough to think before acting.

It's time I got this to-do list of mine off the computer screen. That *piece on safety* won't be done very soon. Nor will most of the other eighteen items on the list, and yet I feel just fine about having so many good intentions. Maybe I'll start a second to-do list.

LETTER 36

The Soaps of My Boyhood

This will be about soap. I got the idea last night when I ran across a quotation attributed to W. H. Davies: "What is this life if, full of care, we have no time to stand and stare?" Even though the thought didn't make me toss and turn all night, it must have bothered me some, because it was still in my head this morning. I was ready to stand and stare at something—anything—so as to behold the beauty Davies thought I was missing.

I stared first at a bar of soap by the bathroom sink. Nothing obviously beautiful about that. White except for traces of grime from a child's (?) dirty hands, a dark hair barnacled to the surface, an underside with the feel of fresh-cooked oatmeal. Davies must have meant for me to stare with my mind, not merely with my eyes.

When I was a wee lad, and times were tough, folks bragged about how thrifty they were. That's when I first heard someone say he used every part of a hog except the oink. Besides ham and bacon and chops and loin, people ate jowls and feet and assorted innards. Hog bones went into soup; skin became leather; lard went onto bread and into pie crust; hog blood and scraps were turned into sausage. And some of the fat, the lard, became soap. To make soap you cook up a mixture of fat and lye, but go easy on the lye. Excess lye is tough on skin.

Although in those days Mother cooked up all sorts of things, soap was not one of them. She left that to hog-raising farmers, preferring instead to stock Ivory soap. She bought it by the case to get a good price, removed the wrappers, broke each bar in half, and spread the halves on closet shelves where they dried, some for months, so they'd last longer. The bars, before Mother broke them, were thick, and about six inches long. They were 99.97% pure, or so the ads said, and they contained no lotions, dyes, anti-perspirants, or sissy perfumes. Still, there must have been some sort of perfume in that soap. Mother often told us how clean we smelled after showering, and no one ever told me that I smelled like hog fat after an Ivory shower. Maybe before my shower, not after.

Until we were old enough to shower, Ivory floated in our tub baths and left rings around the tub walls. The dirtier we were, the darker the rings, and I don't recall ever having seen a whitish ring. We washed our hands with Ivory before every meal—a rule strictly enforced. And we scrubbed our hair with it whenever we failed Mother's head check-ups.

Because regular soap didn't lather in hard water, many folks—and Mother was one-set rain barrels under the downspouts from roofs. It sure seemed out of character for Mother to ladle stagnant hair-washing water from a barrel lined with green slime.

I once tried storing my minnows in our barrel. It didn't work out. The barrel was too dark and too deep, and the wrong shape for me to recapture those minnows. I'm sure Mother never captured any either. If she had, I'd have heard about it.

Ivory was our unisex soap. It cleansed males and females alike, human and canine. Eventually it became more a hand soap than a bath soap. That was because, at some point in our teen years, we began to want proper gender scents. We boys showered with Lifebuoy, which made us smell like the disinfectant used at the time on hospital floors. My sisters would have nothing to do with Lifebuoy, and made nasty faces whenever Lifebuoy was mentioned. They demanded a feminine soap. They demanded Lux. It would soften their skin. It would clothe them in a flowery vapor. It would have them looking like Loretta Young. (Loretta appeared in magazine ads for decades. She never changed, never wrinkled anywhere. My theory was that all pictures of her were taken when she was nineteen, and the prints dribbled out over many years).

Fels Naphtha was another well-known soap in our house. It was neither white nor 99.97% pure, and it didn't float. It wasn't for bathing or shampooing. It was for laundry, and for washing out the mouths of any of us kids who used a four-letter word or sassed Mother or uttered some outlawed word. Fels-Naphtha, even a smidgen of it on the teeth, is mighty uncomfortable. Today's no-discipline advocates would scream, "Child abuse!" at such treatment, and be disappointed to know that (a) we survived; (b) we needed very few treatments to get the message; and (c) we didn't later develop foul mouths.

When it comes to soap, you're going to be lots better off than we were. Most of what you think of as soap is really synthetic detergent, not hog fat and lye, so it will lather in hard water. (I wonder where you'll try to keep your minnows). Your so-called soap won't make ugly rings on the tub, but then you don't get very dirty anyway because kids these days don't even have mud-ball fights. You won't have to flake your Fels Naphtha the way Mother did because now the soap comes all flaked or ground up in a box. And chances are you'll never feel the bite of Fels Naphtha on the tongue.

On the other hand, maybe you're not entirely luckier than I am. You have too many kinds of soaps in too many forms with too many perfumes and colors and anti-perspirants and lotions guaranteed to turn prunes back into plums. No single soap will give you the memories I have of, say, Ivory. Too bad! If you're going to follow the Davies advice to stand and stare, you're going to have to look beyond the soap dish. Where will you find your memories?

LETTER 37

Medicine Cabinets and Sick Beds

You're bound to like this. I'll tell you about a place that's *better* now than it used to be. It's where I stared at that bar of soap before writing you about Ivory. It's the bathroom.

Earlier bathrooms were smaller than today's. They had doors, not picture windows, and they were built for single occupancy. The typical bathroom was all white and had one sink, one toilet, and either a tub or a shower stall. With so few bathroom products available, there was no need for counter space. No need for electrical outlets either, since folks dried their hair with towels, shaved with soap and razor, and brushed their teeth the old-fashioned way. Tubs were without whirlpools, and showers without pulsating sprayers.

Floors were not carpeted (unsanitary) or even covered with vinyl tile (uninvented). In our main bathroom, the floor was ceramic tile, thousands of tiny flat hexagons grouted together. That meant trouble, and not just because the floor had to be scrubbed weekly by a young boy. The tumblers and the bottles in the medicine cabinet were made of glass, there being no plastic back then, and they always broke when dropped on that cold hard floor. Have you ever pulled glass shards from your toes?

Our bathroom doubled as a first-aid station. It's where we took our cuts and scrapes to be scrubbed and daubed with iodine. We knew iodine killed germs by the millions on account of the way it stung so much. Since medical science wasn't very far along, our medicine cabinet was small and strangely stocked by today's standards. We had no antibiotics or antihistamines or Band-Aids or Tylenol or even Kleenex to sop up our tears of pain.

How can I tell you what it was like to get sick or wounded in those days? Without wonder drugs, we counted on psychology. We convinced ourselves that we'd get well. We believed Dr. Bleyer was rooting for us, and would somehow pull us through. But the psychology of illness went beyond feelings of faith and hope. There was fear—profound fear.

We were deathly afraid of lockjaw (tetanus). If you got it, it got you, for there was no cure. The lockjaw germ, we were told, was spread by horses. It then stayed in the ground for ages, so it was easy enough to pick up just by getting dirt in a cut. It might then lie quietly inside you indefinitely as it waited for you to get the sort of wound that kills off a bunch of your tissue. A wound from an exploding firecracker might do it, or a jagged wound from a rusty nail. If something like that happened to you, the tetanus germ moved to the dead tissue, multiplied and put out a terrible poison which could paralyze one muscle after another. Before long you were stiff all over. In the final stages, your jaw muscles locked your mouth shut.

Today, people can ward off tetanus for years with a mild injection. During my childhood that was not an option. All we had was a very potent injection which *could* be given (if you were brave enough) after one of those nasty accidents with a firecracker or a rusty nail or whatever. You had to be quick to decide on taking the shot, though. If you waited, say, a week, and let the tetanus germ get a good head start, you were a goner. The shot, when taken promptly, was supposed to give you a *mild* case of tetanus and short term protection. The trouble was, some people were made deathly ill by the shot itself, and a few died. My brother Q.U. used to get rigid all over from those shots. So after every damaging wound there was that huge decision to make: to chance *not* taking the shot or to chance *taking* it.

Be happy that you can get lasting protection with little discomfort. Maybe you should also be happy you have fewer horses around to spread the germs. Horses pulled milk wagons and ice wagons past our house, and people put horse manure on their gardens. Nowadays, folks fetch their milk, make their ice, and put synthetic fertilizer on their flower beds.

There were other diseases we couldn't treat with things in the bathroom medicine cabinet or the linen closet. Lots of folks, but mostly grown-ups, died of pneumonia. A pale, frail girl in my eighth grade class got sent off to the mountains because she had TB. We all got mumps and chickenpox and measles and whooping cough. Some of those (I don't recall which) caused the public health people to come paste a quarantine sign on our front door. What good that did I don't know. Everyone except dressed-up company used the back door.

Scarlet fever was rough. My sister Alice and I got it at the same time. Even with ice packs on our heads, we got so hot we went a bit bonkers, hollering, and talking nonsense. And when we finally got well again Mother had to burn all our toys and books.

Most of the time, our cuts and germs were more a nuisance than a threat. Our treatments were often do-it-yourself with directions from Dr. Bleyer. We prayed a lot, and tried to think positively. In some cases we had pat treatments. Head/chest stopped up? Fill the sickroom with a vapor of steam and tincture of benzoin. Stomach queasy? Drink water plus baking soda; keep a basin close by, just in case; eat chipped ice. Constipated? Milk of magnesia from the medicine cabinet, and if that doesn't work, out comes the enema bag. Impetigo? Let Dr. Bleyer scrub it with silver nitrate, but bring a rag to bite on because you're in for some pain. A knee cut that needs only about three stitches? Better bring that rag along again. There'll be no anaesthetic for a measly three stitches.

LETTER 38

How Female Logic Was Destroyed

The day after I wrote that last letter about how bathrooms and medicine have gotten *better* over the years, a tennis buddy asked me, "What's the *worst* change during your lifetime?" That was his way to get me to lose my concentration on the game. We were tied at 4-4.

Knowing he really didn't care what I thought, I answered, "The change in women. They used to be great." It was the right thing to say. My off-the-top-of-the-head answer wrecked *his* concentration. I won 6-4, 6-1. The truth is, I'm not sure what the very worst change has been. It was probably the decline in morality, and the messes caused by that decline. Still, the change in women was pretty bad. Worse than the disappearance of the 5-cent double-dip cone or the way radio stations switched from jazz to noise.

I already wrote you, a dozen or more letters ago, to tell you how I hated to see women change. I should have told you why. It had nothing to do with economics. I didn't resent women's controlling way more money than men did. Nor did I want to stand in the way of those who sought "fulfillment" in the workplace—though I doubted they'd be any more fulfilled than are most men who have to scratch out a living.

No, I just felt it was a shame to uglify what was pretty. The world needed all the touches of beauty it could get. There was more than enough ugly stuff to go around. Why would anyone want to transform bluebirds into sharp-clawed hawks?

This beauty in women wasn't altogether obvious. A lot of it, unlike bluebird feathers, was well hidden, and finding it became the basis of an ages-old game. Men went looking for this beauty while women enjoyed watching them search. And all too often, once a man found some of this inner beauty, he really could not understand it.

One of the gems men found was *female logic*. All women seem to have it. No men do. It may even be beyond male comprehension, like an exquisite painting whose beauty cannot be explained.

And you, my grandchildren, who were not around before women were liberated, may never have watched female logic in action, so I'll give you an example. This really happened to a guy named Jack who was in a car pool with me during the 1960s.

Jack's wife, Rosemary, and her mother, who was in town for a week's visit, had just finished grocery shopping. They had parked the car in the driveway, and had gone into the house where Rosemary asked or ordered Jack to fetch the sacks from the car. Being an unliberated female, she thought it proper for husbands to tote bags on command. Jack obeyed. He almost always did, even when Rosemary's mother wasn't there. He had learned, early on, that disobedience begets cold stares, cold shoulders, and cold suppers.

When he brought the first two sacks into the kitchen, he was clearly upset. "Rosemary, that isn't our car," he announced. "You've taken someone else's car."

"Don't be ridiculous. Of course it's our car. Now get me the rest of the groceries before the ice cream turns to soup."

"I'm telling you," Jack repeated, "that is *not* our car. We have to get it back right away before the police come after us."

"And I'm telling you I have better things to do than stand here arguing about anything so stupid. I drove *our* car to the store, and I drove it back. It's a green Ford; it has four doors; it started when I used *my* key in the ignition. That car in the driveway is *ours*, so just get the rest of *our* groceries out of it."

Jack, now sputtering, said, "Rosemary, listen to me. The car in the driveway has a radio. Ours doesn't."

"That has nothing to do with it," was Rosemary's response, her female logic going full tilt, her stare beginning to frost.

This was one of the few times Rosemary's female logic let her down. The car was not theirs. Theirs was in the supermarket parking lot. Alongside it stood a puzzled, middle-aged man who was relieved to see Jack drive up in the radio-equipped model. The incident had been one of those statistical quirks: interchangeable ignition keys for nearly identical cars parked at a single point in time beside the same supermarket.

Rosemary was never liberated. If she had been, who knows whether she'd have gotten a male haircut, worn male clothing, taken up cussing, got tattooed, and put a hog ring in her nose or navel. Worst of all, once she had hung around the business world awhile, she might have changed the gender of her logic from female to male. What a loss that would have been. Certainly to Jack.

LETTER 39

Those Once-only Encounters

Have you ever run across someone just once and then remembered him or her for a very long time? I have, though not often. To this day I remember four people I met like that. Well, three I actually talked to, the fourth I barely saw.

First there was Mr. McWay, one of those desperate men who came knocking on our back door looking for work during the Depression. He was fairly thin, tall, and bony, with eyes sunk deep in their sockets, and a scary scar that went from the right side of his mouth to what would have been the bottom of his ear, only lots of his ear was gone. His clothes were a sight. I've seen better in rag bags. You'd have thought he'd have acted sad or worried, but he didn't. He spoke in a happy, booming voice, and he smiled so much you'd have thought he wanted you to see he was missing a front tooth.

Mother had no yard work for Mr. McWay that day, the grass being too scorched to grow, but perhaps Mr. McWay would care to stop long enough on his journey to have a glass of lemonade and a sandwich. He told Mother that would be ever so nice, and when she went to the kitchen, he and I sat in the shade on the back stoop. I purposely sat on his left side so I wouldn't seem to be staring at his scar. I knew it was all wrong to stare at anyone's deformity, but when you're young, it's hard not to.

Mr. McWay asked me all about myself—the games I played, the things I collected, what I thought about school—and he seemed really interested in my answers. Most grown-ups didn't care what I thought or did in those days unless it meant trouble. Once we had our lemonade and sandwiches, Mr. McWay told me about himself. He had lived on a Kansas farm that bankers had taken away from him because he couldn't pay the mortgage money. The ground on his farm had turned to dust and had been blown away by the wind. When he could find no work in Kansas, he left his wife and three daughters with his in-laws and hopped a freight train headed for St. Louis. There, he was sure, he would find some sort of city job and send money to his family so they could come join him. Meanwhile, when the freight train slowed on that hill coming into Webster Groves, and he saw the houses with big yards, he hopped off to see whether he could get temporary work.

"But enough of that," he said. "What most folks want to know about me is how I got this scar. They don't say so 'cause they're afraid to hurt my feelings. I don't mind. I was camping alone in north Wisconsin, and just sitting on a log like we're sitting here, and I was cutting slices of a pear with my hunting knife when out of the woods comes a bear. He came at me so fast I didn't have time to get up and run or even toss him the pear and tell him he was welcome to it. If he'd been a grizzly, I wouldn't be here, but he was just a black bear, and I managed to stick him good with my hunting knife. Neither one of us won that day. He went back in the woods bleeding, and I went to a hospital bleeding, and the pear just stayed on the ground."

Before Mr. McWay left, I gave him my address so he could send me a postcard some day. He told me to study hard but not to become a banker because they're about the meanest people around. I never again heard from him. Maybe he couldn't afford a penny postcard.

I was younger when I met Mr. Blackstone. He was a magician. My grandfather, Pop, took me to the Schubert Theater to watch him perform. I think Pop must have known him because Mr. Blackstone rode back home with us and continued to do tricks right there in our living room. He was the first real magician I had ever watched. But that isn't why I remember him after just one encounter. Mr. Blackstone pulled a canary out of my ear, a real canary that my grandmother kept in a cage for months until her cat killed it. Until Mr. Blackstone did that, hardly anything had ever come out of my ears. A little wax now and then, or blood when I had to have an eardrum punctured, but never a bird.

Once, when I boarded a train in Philadelphia, I was told I'd have to stay for awhile in a club car at the end of the train. It seems the car I was supposed to be on was yet to be picked up. To my surprise, there were just three of us on that special club car, two of us ordinary folks, and former President Harry Truman. We chatted for two hours or more, though never about political matters. It was a pleasant enough encounter, and one I could later brag about, but it wasn't all that interesting. What I did learn was that President Truman and I agreed on only one thing: *Huckleberry Finn* is the finest book written in English. I lent him a book, and enclosed my business card hoping he'd return it with a note. I never heard back. Surely he was better fixed for postage money than Mr. McWay had been.

My fourth just-once encounter was with a Jap pilot. If I ever actually saw him, it was for a tiny fraction of a second. Our ship was at Morotai, a place in between New Guinea and Leyte, a place where Americans were surprised to find there were very few Japs. The cruisers and destroyers in our task group were together in one part of the harbor, and we were by ourselves, a half-mile away. A couple of Jap planes flew over, dropped bombs on the big ships, and drew lots of anti-aircraft fire. One of the planes, badly hit and trailing smoke, was not going to make it back home. Apparently, the pilot figured that instead of just crashing into the water or jungle, he'd aim at our little minesweeper. His aim was pretty good, too. He almost got us. He flew just over our bow and crashed so close to us that the fire atop the water scorched our paint. Except for the gasoline, the only thing from that plane that rose to the surface was one of the pilot's sandals. It was made of dried grass.

LETTER 40

Rules, Rules, Rules

What shall we do about all these rules? The list is awfully long, and it keeps growing, and I know why but I don't know how to solve the problem. Too many people are too fond of rule-making. For some it's a sort of hobby. For others, it's an addiction that could drive them to such extreme actions as running for Congress or donning judges' robes.

But these addicts may not be the worst offenders. Folks in business and government and private institutions make up rules which they call policies, procedures, or regulations. Tiny clubs need—or *think* they need—bylaws. Condo associations write unenforceable rules. Athletic groups put together booklets and whole books of rules. I was reminded of that as I watched this afternoon's football game on TV. The Dolphins broke three rules on a single down: illegal motion, delay of game, and holding.

Where is all this rule-making headed? I wish I knew. I try to be optimistic only to find that logic wins out. There are already way more rules than I could possibly memorize. (I can't even memorize the ones put out by a single government agency, the IRS). And once a rule has been made, it's almost indestructible. Its maker wants it to live on and on, and it may be a source of income to that great swarm of people who defend rules, interpret rules, enforce rules or contest rules. So you see, what we have is a whole *rules industry*, which creates nothing tangible to enhance our lives but puts cash in the pockets of "rules industry" employees.

Sixty-odd years ago our list of rules was, of course, much shorter than today's. Still, there were those, some only children, who felt the urge to make up rules. Example: our game of marbles, a simple enough game until newly made rules permitted a player to yell certain phrases at his opponent. If you were my opponent and you yelled, "Knucks down!" at the right moment, I had to shoot awkwardly with four knuckles flat against the ground. Unless, just before you yelled, "Knucks down!" I had yelled, "Vent fore and after!" That would have kept you from putting any sort of hex on me as I was about to shoot.

To be honest, I must admit the weird rules made for marble games didn't really lessen our fun. I doubt that they added much, though.

Our family's rules during my marble-shooting days and for some years thereafter were of three types:

MORAL RULES. These were the biggies, by far the most important: the Ten Commandments, the Church Laws, and such derivatives as the Golden Rule.

These MORAL RULES were broadly stated, and we were expected to let our consciences tell us whether a specific act was right or wrong. Thus, the broad rule was "Thou Shalt Not Steal," and conscience was to decide, for example, whether it was O.K. to swipe a loaf of bread to feed a starving family.

For other classes of rules to be worth their salt, they could not be at odds with any MORAL RULE.

PARENTAL RULES were more explicit. In our house, Mother counted on MORAL RULES and our consciences to take care of truly important matters. She imposed no curfew rules, but instead trusted us to come home at a reasonable hour. Her PARENTAL RULES dealt mainly with peace at home, responsibility outside the home (including school), and what Mother called "cultured courteous behavior." In that last category were rules about table manners (no chewing with an open mouth, elbows off the table, no hats, no leaving the table until finished eating). Mother had no rule that said, "Don't wear roller skates while delivering lemon meringue pie to the table." My sister Mary tried that. She never was very good on skates.

To the outside world, I was to appear refined, which was well nigh impossible for a regular boy. Refined was what sissies were. I had to speak proper grammar, avoid gutter language, and never hurt an adult's feelings. On top of that, I was to treat all females as though they were frail queens and princesses, too weak to open doors, and so "special" they were always to have first choice.

If some of these PARENTAL RULES strike you as quaint, there's something you should know. We did not challenge Mother's rules. We did not demand to know why Mother set down any particular rule. She was in charge. She was our mother. And we were bound by one of those powerful MORAL RULES: Honor Thy Father and Thy Mother. Ours was not to reason why.

LEGAL RULES, those man-made rules enforced by police, didn't affect us much. Although we heard stories about kids being sent to reform schools, we figured we were safe as long as we lived by the MORAL and PARENTAL rules. Anyway, we wouldn't displease Chief McDonald (Our Chief of Police) for anything. He was every kids' friend. He stood up for kids, no matter what. He said he was once a kid himself, and we believed him even though it was hard to imagine anyone that big and round and bald ever having been a kid. He also stood up for dogs, although he never claimed he had once been a dog.

LETTER 41

Our Non-Dog Pets

Now about those animals, other than dogs, of my childhood days. You already know that dogs were far and away the top choice of critters in our house. We always had at least one, usually two, and occasionally a litter.

When it came to other animals, we were never without opinions, sometimes strong opinions. Mother didn't like snakes in the house. My sister Alice didn't care for white rats, especially those we put in her dresser drawer. I think we all hated cats. We didn't believe those who told us that cats were smart but too stuck-up to do anything nice for people. To us, cats were lazy, sneaky, effeminate, and too ignorant to let us know when it was time for them to go make a mess outdoors. Most of them couldn't even recognize their own names. None we ever heard of could learn such simple tricks as fetching the newspaper although an average cat could "play dead" for hours without ever being told to do so. Cats were mean to birds, as afraid of water as the Wicked Witch of the West, and too stupid to climb down out of trees. They were cruel hunters, teasing their terrified prey, and they dumped small corpses into such inappropriate places as beds and laps.

So we hated cats. Even so, they were safe around us because of a code we lived by, a code that said we must never mistreat animals. Only once did I violate that code. Johnny L. and I were talking one day about how we knew that when you scare a cow she squirts sour milk, but we had never seen it happen. In the block east of our house was a field of grass and weeds where a Jersey cow grazed. Well, Johnny and I tried everything to scare her. We ran up behind her and yelled, "Boo!" We popped paper bags near her ear. We even set off a firecracker near her. That Jersey never squirted a drop, sweet or sour. We must not have done something right.

Twice we had chickens, a pair at a time. The first pair were Mary's, chicks when she got them, and only one lasted long enough to grow real chicken feathers. When he or she got big enough, Mary decided it was time that chicken learned to walk on a leash, so she made one out of string. Off they went down the sidewalk, north toward Lewis's. Minutes later they were back, the chicken now in Mary's arms. She ran to Mother to report, "My chicken looks very dead." Mary was no better at tying knots than she was at roller skating with a pie in her hand.

The second pair were Banty roosters, one of which was killed, early on, by a stray cat. They belonged to my younger brother, Fat (Fat's given name was Walter, but no one called a kid "Walter" in those days, so we called him "Fat" because he was chunky). Fat took extra good care of his surviving rooster. Fat even took the rooster all the way to Michigan with us one summer, and fixed him a ladder to roost on under the eaves. We stayed in our little house in Saugatuck in those days, right across the street from Miss Laura. Things went well for a week or so before getting tense.

And all because Fat's Banty learned, all on his own, to crow. It didn't amount to much—a puny crow really—hardly the kind to send sound sleepers tumbling out of bed at sunrise, but it got Miss Laura all worked up. She had a shack full of hens that kept her in eggs plus a few more to sell, and those hens were itching to have a man-chicken around the house. They had sat around too long just listening to one another cluck. Their eggs weren't turning into chicks. They were ready for the patter of tiny feet.

When Miss Laura told Mother about how she thought this Banty was going to shake up things in the chicken shack, Mother smiled and said she thought it unlikely. "Even if that Banty knew how to go about it," she explained, "it would be like a hummingbird mating with an ostrich." I'm not sure what finally happened. The Banty disappeared one day, Mother and Miss Laura went on being friends, and we kept getting free fresh eggs. I wonder whether there's a Banty skeleton out back of Miss Laura's.

As for animals in the wild, we were very selective. We penned up a few box tortoises that dug their ways to freedom when we weren't looking. The snapping turtles we captured from the shallows of Lake Kalamazoo were poor travelers. They got out of their box in the car on the way back home from Michigan, and nipped at our feet and fingers. Worse still, they got at Mother's ankles as she drove along the highway. She didn't like that, but later she laughed about it.

We gave first aid to injured and fallen birds. From Algonquin Creek we scooped tadpoles, hoping to see them become frogs; one did. But mostly we let wild animals be. Rabbits made nests in our vacant-lot ball fields, but we knew better than to touch those baby bunnies. Their mothers would pick up our scent and abandon their families. We also left squirrels alone, and coons and possums and chipmunks. We joked some about how to catch and tame a skunk but never had the nerve to try.

LETTER 42

That Busy Old Kitchen

I never know, as I write you about memories from way back, what your reaction is apt to be. Will you pity me because I lacked so much of what you take for granted? Some of what you now have had not been invented; some we couldn't afford. Or will you envy me because my life was simpler, and I was freer to move about in a safer world? Or maybe you'll conclude that both you and I got what was just right for each of us, so it's good we don't have to swap childhoods.

Meanwhile, return with me to the home I grew up in. We're in the dining room, facing east, about to open the swinging door that leads to the kitchen. It's an oak door, solid, not one of those flimsy hollow panels. I'm not sure how to choose which room in a house is the most important. Today it's probably the family room or whatever other room has the best collection of electronic gear. In my childhood, the dining room and kitchen were just about tied for first place.

Maybe you find it hard to imagine a kitchen's being that high in the rankings. Virtually everything served at every meal was put together in our kitchen, often from scratch. TV dinners? We didn't even have TV sets. Packages to heat in the microwave? No microwaves. Sacks of fast foods? Nowhere to buy them. Frozen juices or vegetables? No freezer space in which to store them. We *could* get baked goods and canned goods—though not canned soft drinks. And we could get ice cream if we were ready to eat it at one sitting, which we always were. The ice cream came packed in dry ice.

It was in this kitchen, you may recall my telling you, that on Sunday nights we kids ate suppers of our own choosing: doughnuts, popovers, waffles, apple fritters. On Mondays through Saturdays the suppers were better balanced, usually meat, potato, green vegetable, milk, and dessert.

There was an advantage to having a kitchen where Mother had to cook from basic raw materials. Here she was challenged. She took pride in what she did. It took more talent than melting frozen blobs of pre-cooked meals. She varied the menu so we never had the same meal twice in ten days. And best of all, she got very good at cooking all sorts of dishes. I wish we had told her that. She probably knew how we felt anyway because we ate a ton in those days. The truth is, we may not even have known how splendid our meals were. We'd find that out later in life when we ate mass-produced meals at schools, aboard ships, and in restaurants.

For eating those grand meals we paid a price. We had to learn certain lessons about food and eating. Examples:

- Meat should be well-done. Blood, especially pig blood, is apt to teem with germs. If folks tell you well-done meat has to be tough or dry, tell them they're wrong. Tell them to look into searing, basting, and marinating.

- Don't drink unpasteurized milk. Mr. Schmid did, and look what happened to him. He was a neighbor, a banker who had a farm on the side. He was very sure his cow was healthy, so he drank her milk raw, said it tasted great, and got undulant fever.

- Always think of dessert as the prize you get for eating the rest of your meal. Eat at least three bites of everything or no dessert. That will be good practice for when you're invited out, and your hostess serves something you hate but which you have to eat just to be polite.

- Make sure you have a *healthy* diet most of the time. (Sunday suppers didn't count). There are five essentials: protein, fat, carbohydrate, vitamins, and minerals. At times the only way you'll get some of these is from foods you won't like. Too bad! Think of it as medicine. It may taste awful but if it makes you healthy, swallow it, and rinse the bad taste from your mouth.

After all these years, I still like my meat well done, I still don't drink raw milk, and I'm absolutely convinced that I eat all that meat and those vegetables so I can win that prize: DESSERT!

And was Mother ever good at making desserts! Apricot pies, cream puffs, peach upside-down cakes, taffy, chocolate eclairs, apple dumplings, caramel custard, hand-dipped chocolate candies, cookies square and round, thick and thin, assorted flavors. And on my birthday, every year for more years than I can remember, she always made sponge cake with chocolate icing, served on a turquoise glass plate with silver handles.

If the memory of those desserts is vivid, so too is the memory of those "medicinal" foods we were served. Back then folks believed (a) that something gobbled up kids' red blood cells during winter when the sun wasn't out enough; and (b) that about the only way a kid could grow new red cells was by eating (ugh!) liver. Liver was known to be full of iron. I have no idea how iron was supposed to have been related to sunlight. The point is, Mother dosed us periodically with liver. That's the only animal innard she ever made us eat unless you count tongue, which is maybe as much out as in. Mother was pretty understanding about liver. She served it with bacon. I used to take a piece of liver the size of your pinky fingernail and wrap it in a full slice of bacon. It didn't quite kill the taste of the liver, but it helped.

LETTER 43

Life in Stages

Murray, that young vice president at our bank, asked me what I thought had been the best time of my life. I smiled and said I couldn't answer that question. "It's too soon to tell, Murray. I'm still alive. I'm waiting to see how the years ahead turn out."

The truth is, I don't know which of the years I've already lived were the best. How do you tell? Maybe you'd better think about it. Someone's sure to ask you. Whether your answer will help anyone is doubtful. The time of life that's great for one person may be miserable for another. For example, I had a super childhood, but I know people whose childhoods were drab or downright scary.

Mostly, though, I've had lots of happy periods, and therein lies the problem. Too many good ones, each for different reasons. How can I choose the best?

The very early years were probably so-so. I don't remember being an infant. Who does? I must have been well taken care of: fed, bathed, burped, changed, and cooed at. The bad parts must have been eating bland food, getting diaper rash, being put in solitary confinement behind crib bars, and having nothing better to do than stare at brightly colored shapes.

The time between infancy and kindergarten was, I suppose, better if also blurry in my memory. The best part must have been learning to do things that upset grown-ups. Your parents' cousin Tim was good at that. At age three, Tim noticed that his baby sister and her crib were off-white, and wondered whether that was their best color. In the basement, he found black enamel and a brush, carried them to where Karen was napping, and painted quietly so as not to waken her. That had to have been fun. And if some of the paint got on the bed clothes and the carpet and the stairs, well, it couldn't be helped.

The years between ages five and fourteen were good except for when my father died. It was during that time that I developed athletic skills and friendships, and I roamed further and further from home in search of caves and swimming holes and dark woods. At twelve, I passed the age barrier for joining the Boy Scouts. The camping trips more than made up for those dreary weekly meetings. At age fourteen, I went with nineteen other scouts from the St. Louis area to a World Jamboree outside Budapest, Hungary. We were away from home two months that summer, touring nine European countries including Hungary. It was some adventure! We visited castles whose dungeons had all sorts of torture devices. We saw King George, Queen Mary, and Mussolini. We rode steamships and trains and gondolas and alpine cable cars. We saw famous paintings, graves of famous people, crown jewels, gargoyles atop Notre Dame, and the axe and block used to behead one of Henry VIII's wives. That block had two gashes in it. I wonder why. A practice swing?

My high school and college years get high marks from me, higher for sure than the ones on my report cards. It was then that I discovered girls and learned to put up with the joy and anguish that go along with such discovery. I learned to drive, got my first jalopy (a $35 Model A), and could now roam further than my bike had taken me. I landed my first real summertime job, and several more after that. My confidence grew, I got better at tennis, and my head took in lots of knowledge plus maybe a smidgeon of wisdom. I slept like a log, ate like a hog, and being carefree, I smiled a lot. It was grand to be that age, in good health, and with no serious responsibility. What really put this period of my life in contention for top honors, though, was the big decision I made, the biggest and best of my life: the decision to marry Grandma Jo.

The next period, one with way more ups than downs, ran from college graduation to retirement. It's the period most folks would grade tops in importance. Not necessarily the happiest, though. For me it worked out very well. Marriage . . . kids getting educated and staying out of trouble, and making fine additions to the family . . . good health . . . plenty to do and learn . . . a respectable career. Still, in any period that long, there are bound to be low points. Getting shot at and bombed was no fun. Nor was losing my mother, my sister Mary, my brother Q.U., and several friends.

The present period, retirement, is now in its fifteenth year. And a delightful period it is. You see, early in life I let others seize control of my time. They were people with such titles as teacher, boss, customer, and co-worker. They told me what to do and where to be. Usually I obeyed. But those people are gone. They wandered off when I retired. I am now in command of my own time. What I do now are things *I* want to do, not what someone else wants done by me. I always have a backlog, so I'm never idle, and I make sure there's variety in that backlog: furniture to be made, stories to be written, financial models to be built, wood to be carved, tennis strokes to be improved. Now this will amuse you. I was happily retired, and with firm control of my time when The Conference Board asked me to write an article on retirement. And I took time to do it! I must remember to include a copy with these letters.

Of course, the retirement years aren't flawless. More friends are ailing or worse. My win/loss ratio on the tennis court goes down; my doctor bills go up. And I sometimes have more fun remembering than doing.

What's the best time of life so far? I still don't know.

LETTER 44

House Maids

Two letters ago, I took you through that swinging door into the kitchen. I meant to tell you about the room itself and the rooms attached to it. Instead, my mind wandered, as it often does, and I wrote about food. Well, let's return to the kitchen. We're standing on linoleum because that's what kitchen floors were made of.

Straight ahead is the four-legged stove, not a built-in one, complete with oven. To the right of it was what Mother thought was the one appliance to be treasured above all others. It was her KitchenAid, the last present she got from my father, and it did all sorts of food preparation tasks. It mixed, of course, and squeezed orange juice, kneaded bread dough, ground coffee beans (every morning), shredded lettuce, and ground meat into hamburger. It also sliced potatoes paper thin (to cook potato chips), flaked ice, turned the ice cream freezer, and polished silver.

There is a lot of cabinet space in this kitchen, but the only good work space is an enameled metal table. Every autumn, Mother used to fill an empty sugar sack with grapes and hang it over a crock beneath that table. Next day: grape juice!

We now walk almost due east past the stove. In so doing, we pass (on our left) the four-legged sink, a radiator, and an incinerator. That's where burnable trash went. It dropped to a fire chamber in the basement.

Once you're past the incinerator you can turn right or left or go straight ahead. If you turn right you can go up what we called the back stairs. If you turn left you'll be in a small area that houses the old ice box and leads out the back door. You've never seen such a door. It has a built-in cabinet with its own little doors, one outside, one inside. The milkman used to open the little outside cabinet door every morning and deposit bottles of milk. Later, someone inside the house opened the inside door and transferred the bottles to the ice box.

Now let's back up a couple of paces, face east again, and walk straight ahead. We are now in the maid's room. "THE MAID'S ROOM?" you shout. "Do you mean to say you had maids?" That's the reaction some of you older grandchildren had when you first heard that indeed we *did* have maids. I suspect that some of you have been taught in school that having a maid was a terrible thing to have done, almost like having slaves. Well I aim, right now, to tell it like it was.

During the Depression, unemployment was at a crisis level. Over 25% of the work force could find no job. The jobless were desperate to get work, any sort of work. They were too honest to steal, too proud to beg except to be fed and bedded down, usually in church buildings. There were no government handouts such as unemployment insurance. Families who could possibly afford to hire these unfortunates, even for an hour, were urged to do so. One of these unfortunates was a girl named Bernetta, who came to Mother hoping for a job doing housework. She was from a poor Ozark farm, and had never worked for anyone.

Mother, by no means rich, was faced with a workload that you'd be hard-put to picture. A single parent, five children, a large house, and except for her KitchenAid, none of the appliances that make your lives a whole lot easier today. Take any of your household chores and make a comparison.

Laundry? Some of it you by-pass altogether. You use paper diapers, paper towels, Kleenex, paper napkins. Mother had to deal with the cloth versions. As for the laundry process itself, you dump the dirty stuff in a washing machine, add detergent, turn a dial, and go away until it's time to move things to the dryer. At the time Bernetta came to our house, what Mother had to do was this: flake the Fels Naphtha soap into one of two tubs in the basement, run in the water, and add the dirty clothes, towels, etc., scrub laundry by hand on a corrugated metal scrubbing board, rinse clothes in second tub, wring out water using a hand-operated wringer, hang clothes to dry, (outdoors if possible, otherwise in the basement), take dry clothes off the line, iron everything except bath towels (because no-iron fabrics didn't exist), sort everything, and put it all away. If only there had been laundromats!

Meals? I've already told you how meals used to take more effort than folks put forth today. I should have added that paper and plastic had nothing to do with our meals. We ate off china, used silver-plated or sterling utensils, and wiped our mouths with cloth napkins. There was no dishwasher or garbage disposal.

And then there were chores you don't even have. Mending, for instance, darning socks, sewing patches onto the elbows of sweaters and the knees of pants. Mother made things of cloth and yarn and such, too: sweaters, mittens, socks, skirts.

Get the picture? Mother was one busy woman. Impossibly busy. And along came Bernetta, young, strong, in real need of income. She moved in with us and helped out with all sorts of work. She was happy to have the income, the food, and lodging, the experience of learning how to cook, and, I think, the company. We must have done something right, because when she got married, she brought us her younger sister, Eve, to take over her position.

LETTER 45

First Impressions

That red-headed nurse who spoke at my pre-retirement seminar fifteen years ago was as sharp as an oak sliver. She had worked in what used to be called old folks' homes before someone gave them names with more of a Shangri La ring. She was upbeat. What she gave us was a pep talk. We were not to worry about our health, she said; we'd be physically, mentally, and sexually active for years. She said nothing about the likelihood that some of her audience would soon be back in diapers.

Senility? It's rarer than you think, she assured us. When a senior can remember events from way back but not from yesterday, he probably hasn't gone batty. He can't recall yesterday because it was just like the day before and the day before that. He's in a rut. Nothing exciting happens *any* day. His brain, instead of feeling bored, brings forth from the distant past what really was worth remembering.

Our redhead said nothing about how we might go bi-polar. Some seniors do that, you know. They switch back and forth uncontrollably between deep depression and giddy joy. Not I! I control that switch. I neither fly too high nor dive too low. Let's say I want to feel humble—as we all should now and then. One good way to do this is to 'fess up to my shortcomings, question my worth. So I consider my career years. What did I really accomplish? What major changes in the company did I make, changes that would stay in effect for even a decade? If I were to wander back into my office and give people my name, would anyone cite a single example of the difference my presence had made?

Depressing? Yes. But hold on. I did a bit of good for the people I hired and brought along. And by bringing home paychecks, I did pretty well by my family. I even did myself some good as I let my career teach me about the corporate world and its dwellers.

Most white-collar dwellers, I found, were amateur actors. They put on their costumes, their coats and ties, went onto stages set up with office-type props, spoke in stilted tones, and pretended to be fictional characters. A tough setting in which to make good friends because friendship is based on honesty, not pretense. But every so often along came a white-collar dweller who couldn't act.

Howard was like that. He was a vice-president of Research. In that company at that time, vice-presidents were well-behaved, if not a bit on the prim side. At least they *seemed* that way. Their mischief was kept hidden. Their on-the-job behavior was businesslike, humorless. Even their memos were deadly serious and short on active verbs.

Howard got one of those dreary memos from the company's medical department. He was to show up the following Wednesday for his annual physical exam. He was to prepare for this by all but emptying his digestive tract top to bottom. The memo didn't say why. It didn't have to. Howard knew that at his age, he was to suffer the indignity of a proctoscopic look-see.

He showed up on time, evidently less concerned than most of us would be on the days of our physical exams. For openers, a medical aide with a clipboard quizzed him. When she asked about whether he had emptied himself properly, he offered to shine a flashlight inside his mouth and project a beam for her to see on the floor. She was not amused.

The doctor (male) saved the biggie test for last. First he had Howard bled, poked, shut into a sound chamber, fed chalky barium liquids, X-rayed, wired for an EKG, and put on a treadmill. That done, Howard was tipped upside down in a chair designed to mortify patients and give doctors a sense of power, a sense of being in command. The doctor fetched and greased his proctoscope, a length of chrome-plated drain pipe with a built-in light. He looked like a bullfighter with sword in hand, moving in for the kill.

But Howard was no ordinary bull. At the moment of truth, with the doctor's sword inside him, though not to fatal depth, Howard blew on a duck call he had hidden in his fist. Well, that doctor must have jumped three feet, luckily backwards and up. And for the rest of the day, the phone line to the medical department was extra busy. The word had spread—everywhere. Time and again the medical aide picked up the phone only to hear, "Quack!" She still was not amused. No sense of humor, that one. She probably wasn't even ticklish, but I can't swear to that.

Rarely have I run into someone like Howard. The more common species is the masked play-actor, so whenever I meet someone new, I do not judge him or her quickly, but wait instead for the mask to come off. It works. I have good friends who at first appeared conceited or crude or dull.

The moral, if there is one, is: Always double-check first impressions.

LETTER 46

Hanging Onto Intangibles

In an earlier letter I wrote of my habit of hanging onto things, all sorts of things. I may not have told you how much I've gathered. You'll find out. Once Charon drags me onto that boat of his and ferries me across the river Styx, you'll find my many collections. You'll ask yourselves, "Why would anyone save all these rusty old paper clips? These odd scraps of wood? These papers that mean more to silverfish than to people? These clothes that could be worn only on Halloween?"

Just remember this. The tendency to gather is an inherited trait. *You* might have gotten that marvelous gene from me or from Grandma Jo. She too saves things, but unlike me she can get rid of such items as *my* clothing, *my* easy chair, *my* pillow. If you are lucky enough to have this super gene, your life will be greatly enhanced. You'll never have to put on yard sales, only attend them. Your trash can will not runneth over. You will be a true friend of vermin. Occasionally, with a bit of work you will convert a piece of junk into a restored piece of junk. Perhaps twice in your lifetime you will find, in your mountain of collectibles, that carriage bolt or toggle switch you once stashed because you were sure you would one day need it.

What I have in mind as I write this letter is hanging onto, not material things, but intangibles. They're quite nice. They don't take up space or rot or attract rodents. You're already hanging onto the intangibles I'm thinking of. You just don't often get them out and look at them. You may even have forgotten where you stored them. Well, now, I urge you to find them.

There was a splendid movie, made years ago, called *Citizen Kane*. It was a biography. It began with pictures of a small boy playing happily in the snow, coasting on his little sled. Suddenly he is grabbed by adults and sent off to be schooled. During most of the movie, he grows up to be very rich, very mean, and so alone that when he at last dies, only his servants are near him. As his worldly goods are later sorted, many are simply burned. The movie ends as his little sled goes up in flames. The sled has a name on it—it's called "Rosebud."

Citizen Kane was, I suppose, an exaggerated biography of us all. We don't get as rich as Kane or as mean or as lonely. We *do* get yanked from our childhood playgrounds. We are forced to grow up, and we are not allowed to return to our toys. I don't know. Maybe we do get at least a streak of meanness from having been treated like that.

What Kane left behind and later missed was not a mere sled. He got that back when he was too big and fat to ride it. What he really longed for was one of those intangibles I mentioned. As a tot, he could be happy with very simple toys. It was easy for him then. He had the knack. For each of you, there was a time when you, too, had the knack. Kane stored that knack in his memory, and for reasons unknown to me, he never tried recalling it. Instead, he sought happiness by buying fancier and fancier toys, grown-up toys like yachts. It was all in vain. His joy never came close to what it had been when he had coasted on that sled.

What do you suppose would have happened if Kane, the adult, had deliberately tried playing with a *simple* toy? Would he have recaptured his youthful joy? It works for me, at least to a degree. I don't get out my Flexible Flyer anymore—there's no snow around here—but give me a knife and a chunk of walnut, and I'll sure enough be happy. As for fancier grown-up toys, well, they're okay but worrisome. They're always getting scratched or banged up or out of adjustment.

There's another intangible for you to fetch from your memory banks. Early in life you learned to trust people, and you felt good about it. Oh, you were warned to steer clear of strangers who offered candy and free rides, but you trusted most other people. As the years passed, your knack for trusting everyone got tucked deep in your brain. You grew more cynical, more suspicious of your fellow men and women. That must not have made you a happier person.

So how about trying an experiment? Choose five people: friends or just folks you know from schools or stores or wherever. Trust them completely for a month (except by lending them scads of money). Trust them to keep secrets, or to be truthful about what they tell you, or to do you no harm, or to make good on promises. Try it. You'll like it.

LETTER 47

The "Why" of Love

Twice a year I go, as I did last night, to a meeting of the local Writers' Club. I'd go more often except that I'm not fond of meetings, and I don't fit in. Ninety-five percent of the members are female. Some write poems that I can't comprehend (come to think of it, I can't even tell a poem from a non-poem anymore); others write steamy stories too easy to comprehend. Most of the group pretend they're professionals, not hobbyists. Although the money doesn't roll in, they're cheerful and hopeful. They don't really expect publishers' checks to put food on the table.

Ms. A told the club how she got relatives to write out for her whatever family stories they could recall. She then edited and compiled what they sent her. It took some doing. Nine cousins sent her the same story about Aunt Eunice's getting sat on by that hog and pinned to the mud for two hours. Some relatives had to be prodded to write anything. Others fumed when the ten pages they had sent in got pared to three paragraphs. Eventually, though, Ms. A had her collection printed and bound.

Thanks to Ms. A, the people at last night's meeting had family matters on their minds. Ms. B spoke up. "On Thanksgiving, while I had my family together in one room, I tried something new. I told them I was sure we all loved one another and that some of us even say so at times. But we never say *why*. Then I said to each of them, 'Tell the person on your right *why* you love him or her.' There was a lot of stammering, but all in all it worked out real well."

I'm glad I wasn't in that room. I'd have stammered all right. Answering that "*why*" question is no snap. When you love someone—or even just like someone—it's not because of a single trait. It's because that person has a neat *mixture* of traits.

Late one evening back in 1957, Grandma Jo and I were at the dining room table. Our kids (your parents) were tucked in bed. As Grandma Jo read her *Ladies Home Journal,* she spotted an announcement of an essay contest. Subject: Why I love my spouse in 500 words or less: the top ten essays would be published. Grandma Jo tossed me the magazine and dared me to write 500 printable words about her. Which I did, and got it published. You may find the original somewhere but I might as well type it out here and save you a search. Notice that although I stressed only one of Grandma Jo's traits, I hinted at more. Here it is:

When the roof is leaking and the car fender has been crumpled, when carpet beetles have chewed one corner of the living-room rug and the dog another, when the hot-water heater has succumbed to a perforated ulcer and the children have been so ornery that I'm ready to knock their heads together, Josie remains calm—wonderfully, miraculously calm.

Often during the fourteen years that Josie and I have been married, I have tried to analyze her calmness to see whence it originates and how it has affected our six children and me. I have asked such questions as: What is it in her make-up which enables her to laugh when one of the children cooks a sliver of soap in the toaster? How can she talk so hypnotically to a child with a severed scalp artery? Or how can she bring about a swift, friendly cease-fire between two boys who are bent on bludgeoning each other?

An inner calm such as Josie's doesn't come from barbiturates or tranquillizers, but from a deep-seated virtue which is given to few of us, the virtue of *contentment.* Josie is completely content. With the material things that she has, with the way her children are turning out, with herself, even with me.

Because of this contentment, my task of earning a living is made easier, for I can set my own pace, going about my work unharassed by the demands of a wife intent on keeping up with the Joneses. Josie enthuses over my promotions, but is never discouraged when they do not come as promptly as they might. By not longing constantly for new clothes or a new car, she makes it possible for us to have a savings program, since there is not an incessant demand for whatever funds are left after we have paid for life's essentials.

At parties, she is friendly but never flirtatious. At bridge, she can make about two more tricks than I could with the same hand, yet she never replays a hand either during the game or on the way home. Business associates find her charming, a good hostess, and surprisingly youthful for the mother of so formidable a family. To her children she is an A-1 parent because she finds time to read to them, shoot baskets with them, build them model planes and cars, stretch out with them for a nap or take them on in a game of Monopoly. She can handle a Pogo stick with the best of them, catch a curve ball if it isn't thrown too hard, be runner-up in a three-handed game of jacks, and swim 300 yards or so in Lake Michigan. She can draw pictures, fold paper boats, and make funny faces. She makes yummy birthday cakes—with lavender icing if so specified.

And how would I improve her if I could? I'd teach her to share a closet on a 50-50 basis instead of a 90-10. I'd also put an end to her kibitzing when I repair a screen or an extension cord, and I'd regrow the beautiful long hair she cut off. Mostly, though, I guess I'd leave well enough alone. Maybe her contentment is contagious.

LETTER 48

The Sidewalk at 405

Here I go again, lopping off the years. I'm young again, though I can't tell you exactly how young. I'm on the sidewalk that runs beside and in front of the house at 405. Between adjacent slabs in the sidewalk are spaces that we call cracks. Step on one of those cracks and you break your mother's back, they say. Bill Riesmeyer did that on purpose quite a while ago, and we waited and waited for the ambulance to come cart his mom to the hospital. When it finally came, she didn't have her back operated on. She got to the hospital to have a new baby. So now I wonder whether stepping on a crack doesn't just get your mother a new baby instead of breaking her back.

It's summer now, and grass grows in these cracks. I don't mind. I get a penny a crack to dig out that grass, using a dull old table knife. Johnny Longmire's Dad says it will be so hot this afternoon you can fry an egg on the sidewalk. He should know. He's smart. He had to be to get so rich. Has the second biggest house in the neighborhood. Drives a seven-passenger Packard with spare tires sunk into both front fenders. It even has little glass vases for Mrs. Longmire's flowers, but most of the time she forgets, and the vases stay empty.

Johnny and I take two eggs, some bacon grease, and a spatula to a sunny section of the sidewalk where at 3 PM the pavement would blister bare feet. Even so, it doesn't make our bacon grease sizzle. We break our eggs and watch them "cook" for a good ten minutes. They don't look anything like fried eggs, more like raw eggs, so we go play catch in the yard and let them cook on their own. A bad decision. Curly, my Chesapeake pup, is not finicky. When it comes to eggs, he is happy just to find them within reach, no matter whether they are nicely fried and served in his bowl or raw and on the sidewalk. Our experiment is a failure. Still, the end-result is not all bad. I don't have to clean up the mess on the sidewalk.

Hot days are right for spitting contests on this same stretch of sidewalk. The rules are few and simple: take turns, don't step over the starting crack, run or jump to the crack if you like, mark the spit-spot farthest from the crack with chalk, keep playing until interest in the game wanes. Our parents find these contests disgusting, yet they don't actually forbid us to compete. Better just to lecture us on spit-germs and wait for us to outgrow the game. We go on spitting frothy dimes on the sidewalk, and the germs get what they deserve: death by boiling. As our dimes dry quickly, we see no little potholes in the sidewalk, so what's the harm? We kids can justify whatever we have fun doing.

It is cooler now, and I am, I think, two years older. On the sidewalk, four of us neighborhood boys vie for the top-spinning championship, a title none of us will hold for more than a week because luck is what counts, not skill. The tops we spin are cones of painted wood with sharp steel points. The tops are easy enough to spin, once you get the hang of it. The object of the game is not to see whose top will spin longest. If it were, we would use those fancy nickel-apiece tops with ball bearing tips rather than these two-centers with the spike tips. In our game, the lead-off player spins a "target" top; those who follow try to hit that target. The winner is the one who drives his spike into the target. We play lots of rounds and have lots of near misses before a winner is crowned. Almost never do we hit the target top solidly enough to split it. That would be a disaster for the owner of the target top because two cents is tidy sum.

It's downright cold now. I'm indoors because this snow is worthless: too light for sledding, too dry for snowballs; worthless. My only hope is for the Curran pond to freeze so I can skate. Mother is in the breakfast room sipping steamy coffee and watching the new snow swirl. There's hardly any on the ground. She lets out a low-volume shriek followed by, "Bill, hurry up. Look at this!" I do, and am not disappointed. It is my first time ever to see a hog trot along our sidewalk, a whopping pink cylinder whose color stands out against a background of brown and white and gray. He or she reaches the corner, turns right, down the front sidewalk, and is out of sight in seconds. We wonder, though not for long, whose hog it is. Here comes Mr. Lewis (actually, Reverend Lewis), also trotting, switch in hand.

There's something I must explain. Once you cross Rock Hill, you're out of Sherwood Forest and can keep farm animals, like the cow Johnny and I tried to scare. But on our side of Rock Hill, that's a no-no—with exceptions. Keeping a *small* farm animal such as a bunny or chicken is okay, and if your house happens to have a proper stable, you may keep a riding horse. But you may not give bed and board to other farm animals—cows, goats, pigs, sheep, mules.

Why would Mr. Lewis have a hog? He must know he's not supposed to, and he's a stickler for doing what's right, especially since he's a minister. You should see how strict he is with his kids. Won't let them read the Sunday funnies on Sunday. Won't allow cards in the house even to play Old Maid or Go Fish. Arnie Lewis sets me straight. When his Dad got a pig from a parishioner, he kept it in the basement garage until he could figure out what to do with it. Well, the pig grew so big Mr. Lewis couldn't get it into the car to take it away. Pretty soon, the car wouldn't fit in the garage, and hog stink got all through the house.

Here comes Mr. Lewis back around the corner switching that hog's rump. I think the whole Lewis family wants that hog to find another home.

LETTER 49

What Games Do for Folks

You get—or *should* get—to make three big decisions on your own: whom to marry, what line of work to pursue, and what game(s) to play most fervently (also true when deciding on a hobby; but I've already told you that). Others may advise you, but should not coerce you as you make those choices. If you choose well, it will be because you spotted good match-ups. You will find a spouse who complements you in many ways. You will find a career to match your skills, personality, and needs, and you will find games that suit your head and your physique. As important as those choices are, you probably will make them based on your instincts and your hunches. Years later, you may pretend you had initially given lots of thought to each decision, but we all know better.

This letter is about games, not spouses or jobs. Although I will use my favorite game, tennis, as an example, please don't think I'm pushing you in that direction. As I now describe the five stages of my tennis experience, you'll find things that apply to *your* favorite games as well.

STAGE ONE. I am thirteen. I know nothing about the game, but I have a friend, Ken Becker from Chicago, who does. He has had lessons, and he owns an extra racquet. He says, "C'mon," and I do. We go to a public court, where I show no signs of having been born with tennis skills. Still, we have fun, enough fun that we go back again and again. Little by little my game improves. The summer ends, and we both go back to school, and I get caught up in other sports because in St. Louis, tennis is a summer-only sport except during breaks in the Spring and Autumn weather.

The following summer, Ken and I take up where we left off. He continues to whop me, but that's okay. What has happened is that Ken has become my best friend, and I am beginning to think of tennis as the game I like best. I'm too short for basketball, not rugged enough for football, and too impatient to enjoy standing around waiting for my turn at bat. Soccer is okay except that it takes too much running for so few scores.

STAGE TWO. I'm fifteen now. I've put behind me that period when being on a tennis court meant just having relaxed fun with a friend. I now want pressure. I want competition. I don't even have to play against a friend to enjoy myself. A stranger will do. I play a few minor tournaments with some success. Too bad I can't get lessons to improve my strokes. In all of Greater St. Louis, there is only one teaching pro, and he's way up north. Besides, we can't afford lessons. So I practice against a wall in the school gym.

And in summer I play Ken Becker—every day the court is dry. He still beats me. In the tournaments we enter, he wins, and I'm sometimes runner-up to him. We win the doubles.

STAGE THREE. I'm seventeen as I begin this, the longest stage of my tennis experience. I think I play pretty well: I'm on the school tennis team, I become a State semi-finalist, and I win a few medals and trophies. The thing is, I'm only now discovering what most players learn early on—namely, that it's important to *think* about how I will play each game. It's not enough just to have great strokes. I need to think about *strategy*. During warm-up before a match, I hit my opponent a variety of shots (long, short, top-spin, flat, etc.), and watch how he handles each. I find, say, that he has trouble returning deep top-spin shots to his backhand. So as part of my initial strategy, I'll hit him shots like that, and go to the net to put away his weak returns.

But STAGE THREE goes sour on me. Ken Becker dies suddenly, and I all but stop playing. I go off to war, return, and still don't pick up a racquet.

STAGE FOUR. After eleven years off the court, I start all over. I find new friends, but it's not the same. Married and pushing thirty, I can no longer build the strong friendships I could as a boy. Nor could I bring my game back to what it had been. I go on playing, though, and thrive on the competition. I even discover yet another dimension of tennis. I can analyze an opponent's character right there on the court. Not really thoroughly, you understand, but well enough to be fun. Apparently, when players are absorbed in the game, they don't think about hiding their traits.

I can tell whether an opponent is patient, whether he's honest, whether he stays calm in crises and laughs at awkward shots, whether he's a good sport, whether he's a gracious winner, whether he's more concerned with clothes and equipment than with the game itself, whether he blames the weather and his racquet for his goofs, and whether he'll quote the fine print in the rules just to win a point.

STAGE FIVE. I'm old now with weaker arms and slower reflexes. In some ways, I'm back near STAGE ONE. I play just for the relaxed fun and to be with friends. Tournaments? Just a few senior ones.

So you see, tennis has treated me well over the years. As a boy, I made a sound but lucky decision, and you will, too, whatever your game. Just remember, if you want a game that will last you a lifetime, choose one that features no more than four players at a time. It's tough to get two teams of seniors to suit up for football.

LETTER 50

Fiddling with Strange Headlines

Last night on TV, a gaunt guy spoke about depression. Not the biggie of the 1930s, with the capital D. No, his subject was the sort of depression that can fester inside a person's head—even the head of someone young, rich, and good-looking. The TV guy was a good choice to scare the public with his grim forecast of the spread of depression. He had the look: morning fog complexion, eyes made huge by thick lenses, an icy expression that showed no signs of an early thaw. His name was hard to pronounce and impossible (for me) to spell. It sounded like the name of a Polish sausage on a stick.

He didn't say so, but I reckon depression is one of those diseases that is easier to prevent than to cure. Which is why I cram my head full of non-depressing thoughts, leaving no room for darker ones. Non-depressing thoughts are easy to find, even in newspapers. Every now and then a headline tweaks my imagination. I clip it and try to dream up a good story behind it.

Above the Miss Manners column in a recent *Houston Chronicle* was the headline: SHOULD WOMAN EAT MICE HER CAT KILLS FOR HER? The woman who asked Miss Manners that question explained her perplexity. She was sure her cat felt obligated to repay the woman for all the free cat food it had been served, and did so by bringing in dead mice. Should the woman eat these mice so as not to hurt the cat's feelings, and if so, should she dine alone or share the mice with the cat?

So what do you suppose really went on in that household? The column doesn't say, but given the time, I can make up a pretty good story. I can pretend I'm the woman. I make the cat a neutered male, and name him Killer. At first I balk at eating dead mice at all. I think if I eat even one, and act as if I like it, Killer will want to bring me more, many more. I'll be eating mouse meat every night for supper. Not a very exciting diet, probably not even a healthy one. Still, if I don't eat at least one, there's no telling how Killer will react. Maybe he'll just sulk, or maybe he'll start bringing me bunnies and sparrows and really BIG mice. I guess I'd better try this one small mouse he dropped in my lap.

How to fix it? Well, first I'd better get the scissors to snip off its head. I wonder why its beady little eyes are wide open. Shouldn't they be closed now that it's dead? I might as well snip off the tail, too. Not much meat in that. My! what's left is pretty small. I can't use these big scissors to slit this mouse's front so I can clean out the innards. Fingernail scissors should work. I sure hope Killer wants to snack on these innards; I know I don't.

Skinning that mouse torso is trickier than I thought it would be. I need my biology dissection kit. The pelt, now that I have it off, is tiny. To make even a fur cape would take a thousand pelts this size.

What meat there is has good color, light gray with streaks of pink, and I can see Killer's tooth marks on the rib cage. I realize that most meat has to be hung and aged before it's eaten, but mouse meat? I think not. The only cold spot I have is the fridge. I could bend a paper clip into a hook easily enough, and hang the mouse carcass in there but I don't like to see dead things swinging every time I open the fridge door. Besides, Killer wouldn't understand why I'd get his mouse all ready to cook (or eat raw?) and then just put it away. Killer wants me to think he's smart. He's not, you know. Can't even remember his name most of the time, so he'd never understand the aging of meat.

Now, let's see. How to prepare this little fellow? Raw mouse meat sounds yucky. I need to cook it, but how? I check the cookbook. Either the author can't spell or there aren't any recipes for mouse roasts or mouse steaks. The closest thing is chocolate mousse (French for mouse?) which I rule out because I'd rather put my chocolate chips into cookies than use them to coat a mouse torso.

I consider various possibilities: barbecue on a paper clip skewer, bread and fry, smoke, poach. In the end I make mouse chili, which is easy to divide between Killer and me. Being a good sport, I eat mine. Killer just watches and waits. He's holding out for good old canned cat food.

Other headlines have filled my head with story ideas and blocked out depressing thoughts. Three from the old *Houston Post* for instance. WORMS WITH ALTERED GENES LIVE LONGER, SCIENTIST SAYS. They also *grow* longer. By the time they're eighty, they're as long as a garden hose, and grumpy to boot. MAN CONVICTED OF KILLING OFFICER TO GET NEW TRIAL. Why couldn't he just have asked nicely for a new trial? Killing a cop to get one is uncalled for. MULE SHOE KEY CLUE IN SNIPING. Did the sniper throw mule shoes at his victims instead of shooting them? Or did he plant a mule shoe hoping to incriminate the poor mule?

If you don't like my headline approach to avoiding depression, do what Mother did. She got convinced that faith and hope are virtues to hang onto no matter what. Which is why, late in life, after having lost her husband and two of her children, she could say, "Aren't we a lucky family? We were able to stay together here in this house."

LETTER 51

Fascination with Crimes

Peggy S__ says I have an unhealthy attitude toward crime and criminals. I don't think so. What I have is a *selective* attitude. There are just certain types of crime that fascinate me, and when I find a good one to ponder I don't feel at all unhealthy. I feel fit, comfortable, excited, and safe. It's as though I were watching a football game on TV, well away from the violence, and in no way wishing to be a player.

I don't bother with murders by political fanatics, child molesters, drug dealers, rapists, drive-by shooters, or mercy killers. What I look for are distinctive crimes committed by criminals who show touches of genius, for instance, or who just count on luck and still succeed. I favor brave criminals, and those slippery enough to escape punishment. I also like my criminals to show signs of being human, even humane, not like hired killers.

And how, you may ask, did I develop this healthy attitude? I got it as a lad the same way lots of guys my age got theirs: by reading *True Detective Magazine* in dim light.

1930s-style censorship was what made it possible. Back then, parents did the censoring—no need for government to mess with it—and they kept it simple. Of course there were fewer "evil influences" then: no TV or computer networks or 900-number phone calls or really raunchy printed matter. Even the radio programs were harmless. So what parents censored were movies, magazines (plus a few books), and friends with a reform-school look about them.

To keep kids away from improper movies was a snap. Where I grew up, parents simply conspired with the manager of the Ozark theater. They'd let their kids go to the Ozark on Friday nights, and the Ozark would show only suitable movies on those nights. I must say that it all worked out quite well, at least for us boys. On Friday nights, the Ozark was wall-to-wall kids, and it always showed two full-length feature films plus "selected short subjects." The features were westerns, comedies, and every now and then, a really scary film—the kind that made little girls cover their eyes with jackets or scarves or hands. Karloff as Frankenstein, Lon Chaney as the Phantom, Lugosi as Dracula. The "selected short subjects" were a mixed bag: cartoons, and comedy skits that were applauded, and travel films that were not.

Keeping kids away from improper magazines was something else. Conspiracy was impractical. The magazines were at too many locations just waiting to be found by curious boys, and that was 99% of the boys I knew.

Mother was far from dictatorial about the magazines we read. She approved of and subscribed to *Saturday Evening Post, Collier's, American Boy,* and, before it went for an "R" rating, *New Yorker.* She regarded most comic books as "trash," and *True Detective* as "not very nice," but I don't think she ever actually forbade our reading any specific magazine. She may have understood, better than we imagined, what went on inside small boys' heads. She probably knew that by putting *True Detective* on her "not very nice" list, I would (a) search all the harder for copies; (b) relish reading them all the more because they were vaguely taboo; and (c) shun the criminal life because I was made of good stuff.

She was right. At the magazine rack in Kaegle's Drug Store, I raised my reading speed. In Rexall's, I was even quicker because clerks there gave kids no more than five-minute-parking by the magazine rack. My barber gave me tattered *True Detectives* to hide in my closet, read in bed, and eventually swap. At the library, Miss Sanders issued *True Detective* only to those with adult cards, so I had to wait for adults to leave copies lying on the tables. Miss Sanders was hard to figure out. She hogged those copies of *True*

Detective but let boys have *National Geographic,* from which they learned about overdeveloped females in underdeveloped countries.

What most parents failed to see was *why* the boys my age were eager to find out about crime and criminals, and it was ever so simple. We were used to a make-believe world filled with violence. We had been expert swordsmen. We had run lances through black-plumed knights. We had used knives on grizzlies, and ducked flying tomahawks. As members of Robin Hood's band, we pinned sheriffs' men to trees with arrows. As cowboys, we used pistols and rifles as our Indian opponents drew bows. When we played cops and robbers, it was all guns. Although we outgrew these games, we never quite lost the fascination with the notion of what it must be like to be part of some violent action—without getting hurt.

So we needed up-to-date action scenes with modern good guys and bad guys, and who should come along but some colorful bad guys who played a strong but losing game against The Law. It was cops and robbers all over, but with new words (like "gat" and "heater" for guns), and strange nicknames for bad guys: Scarface, Machine Gun (Kelly), and Greasy Thumb (Guzik). We followed the bloody trails of Dillinger, Bonnie and Clyde, and Pretty Boy Floyd. We knew how the stories would end. It would be just like the movies. The good guys were bound to win. Still, it was fun to watch the stories unfold, and to wonder what it must be like to live each day in mortal fear. We may at times have cheered the hunted animal, but we never truly envied him.

LETTER 52

The Color Gray

When a wonderful day comes along, a day like today, I'm apt to pause to wonder what I should wonder about. *Colors* should be good choice right now. I'll wonder about a couple of colors and jot down what comes to mind.

Now you'll probably think I've gone about this all wrong, and you could be right. Most folks think first about an object, and then about its various properties, including its color. They think first of a cloud, and then of how it looks like something popped from a gigantic kernel of corn. Its whiteness is but one of its properties. What I'm going to do is think about a color, and see what it conjures up. I might think pink, for example, a color I hate, and pretty soon wonder how sick I'd get if I were to eat pink pork.

No color is either all good or, for that matter, all bad. Even that wretched pink is okay when it's on a flamingo or a boiled shrimp. Red is fine for sports cars and slinky dresses, but red spurting from a wound is not. Even black, though not really a color, has a split personality. Mourners wear black. So do bad guys in cowboy movies. But when wives want to show off their husbands, what do they dress them in? Black tuxedos.

I begin this experiment with gray. Drab, you say? Well, yes. What jumps to mind are November skies, clothes that once were white but are no longer, and people who either are dead or could be tomorrow. The friends I've polled give gray a grade of D-. They say it's dull or depressing, which is why so many old folks dye their gray hair. Chances are, these friends missed having any *good* experiences with gray.

During those summers when I was still a pre-teen, my grandfather Pop sometimes let me tag along while he and Dick—whose last name I never learned—fished the Kalamazoo River. (I mentioned this about twenty letters ago but I reckon you don't remember that). It was a clean stream then, with bass among the lily pads near shore and walleyes down deep along the edges of the channel. There were bluegills, too, and channel catfish, and snapping turtles, but the goal was to catch bass by casting toward lily pads as we drifted slowly downstream.

It was good fun, for me at least, but all too infrequent. We had to wait for Dick's day off from work because he was the only one of us who owned a boat. Then one morning Pop said, "I've been thinking. Maybe it's time you and I chipped in and bought us a boat. How much money have you got?" I told him I had a dollar and a quarter in a can in my closet. "That should just about do it," he said. "We won't be able to get a round-bottom, but a flat-bottom's better for float fishing anyway."

Well, let me tell you, I was mighty excited about becoming half-owner of a flat-bottom rowboat, and Pop could tell I was. Of course I thought he meant to buy a used boat, but no, he had found a guy who would custom-make us one. We even got to watch it being made, which took lots longer than I had hoped it would. When it was just about ready, Pop said, "Seeing as how you put up a dollar and a quarter, I figure you get to choose the color," and he handed me a booklet with sample strips of paint. Whoever put the booklet together hadn't used ordinary names like blue and green for the colors. The names were aquamarine and emerald, and my choice: *Battleship Gray*. A perfect color for a boat that I just knew would look and be awesome, and invulnerable. Pop got to choose the trim color: ruby. A nice touch. Like narrow streaks of blood on the deck of a battleship.

Our first time out happened to be Dick's day off, so we picked him up, got our tow upstream, and began casting. On just my third cast, a small-mouth bass hit my lure and took off. When I finally landed him, with plenty of coaching, Pop said. "Looks like we have us a lucky boat." I agreed. So did Dick, who couldn't understand how we ever got a boat like that for $2.50.

Green, like gray, is easy on the eyes, and is regarded by most as a calming color. Which strikes me as odd. There's nothing calming about being green with seasickness or envy. Green scum on an otherwise nice pond doesn't calm me. Nor does the sight of green Brussels sprouts on my plate.

To be calmed by green, I need a proper setting. Forests work well for me, provided I'm amply coated with bug lotion and can find a mossy stump to sit on. Years ago I used to hear the wee folks in the woods. Never did see them, though, so I don't know whether they were elves or fairies or what. One thing's for sure, though: they were fine friends to have around. They never scolded me or hit me or called me bad names. Not out loud anyway.

The last time I went into a forest I listened for them. It's a habit I guess. I heard a rustling sound, too, just like I used to hear, but it turned out to be a squirrel. I think my ears must have been much better when I was young.

LETTER 53

Old Customs, Old Toys, Old Folks

What do baggy pants, old shoes, and certain customs have in common? They're comfortable. They're also sure to disappear, and to be missed, acutely for a while, and then all but forgotten.

Where I grew up we had a rather nice custom. We whistled a lot. It was a male thing. Except for two tomboys, I knew no girls who were good whistlers, but boys pretty much had to be. Whistling was one of several measures of a boy's real worth. He had to be handy with a ball, glove, bat, agate, knife, bike, and slingshot. He also had to show he could climb a tree and a rope, spit a fair distance, belch loudly, recite a few boys-only words, and whistle. As you'd expect, our neighborhood, with such talented boys, was bound to have a few skillful grown-ups as well. Within a block and a half of our house lived a Congressman, a Nobel Prize winner, and an FBI Director.

To earn our stripes as whistlers, we had to show we could whistle loudly, and in several ways: cupped hands, thumb-and-finger, straight whistle, tongue-inside-top-lip, through-the-teeth, and flapping tongue.

The straight whistle and the flapping tongue were for tunes. The through-the-teeth whistle was very quiet, and was used in classrooms and libraries. The loudest whistles were used to summon friends and dogs. It was a sort of sound signature. When I wanted Johnny to come out and play, I went to his back yard and blew my loud two-noter. Not only could he hear me, wherever he was in the house; he knew it was I outside.

Even grown-ups whistled tunes back then. I'd hear men at work do it, clerks in stores, mailmen, builders, guys climbing telephone poles. It was a sign of happiness. So why did this whistling custom disappear? Was it because tunes grew less melodious? Composers of old thought more of *notes* than *words*. Today's music lovers want to hear vocalists tell stories, and that doesn't make for good whistling.

Another fine custom from the olden days was fixing things. We didn't always like doing it. We felt they shouldn't have broken or worn out. We cussed their makers for not having made them right in the first place. In the end, though, we fixed them or, if we weren't able, had it done. In our house, all that got pitched was what Mother proclaimed couldn't be restored by any mortal on earth. The slogan, "Waste not. Want not," should have been framed and hung on one of our walls. We didn't discard socks because of toe holes or pants because of rips.

When I got my first car, a Model A Ford, I had to promise to fix whatever went wrong with it. That was quite bold of me, because I knew nothing about engines and had no money to spare for repairs. Fortunately, I found a good adviser, Walter Weir, who owned the filling station on Big Bend. When I told him my radiator leaked more every day than a mastiff did, he said, "That's no problem in the summer. Keep filling it from a hose or bucket. Winter's different. You'll have alcohol in the radiator, and you'll have to drain it each night, and pour it back in in the morning."

I asked him what it would cost to plug up the leaks. "Hard to say," he replied, "probably more than you paid for the car. Tell you what, though. Go over there to Al Kaegle's (he pointed to the drug store) and buy a nickel's worth of flax seed. A tablespoon of that will stop leaks for a few days. The seeds get stuck in the radiator holes and swell up. I think drug stores sell seeds to people who have the trots and need plugging up."

Before I got my Model A, I had a bike I kept fixing. It leaked air rather than water so I learned to fix flat tires, a skill I later used on car tires. It was a *Rugby* bike, maroon, sturdy, 26-inch, coaster break, single-speed (actually, it was a single *gear*—my legs controlled the speed). There were no "extras" on it until I added a siren and an odometer, which I got from Mr. Locke, who had a bicycle shop in a little shed behind his house on Swon Avenue.

Mr. Locke was one of those men you admire a lot but don't envy. He knew everything there was to know about every brand of bike. He claimed he never saw a bike in such bad shape he couldn't fix it. (It's a good thing Bob Collins never took his bike to be fixed after he left it on the train tracks). Mr. Locke smiled a lot, told funny jokes and wild stories, and whistled happy tunes. There was just one thing wrong with him. He had lost both legs, all the way up to his hips, in the First World War. He moved around his shop on a board with skate wheels, using his fists, which were padded.

One rainy afternoon I skidded my bike into a maple tree close to home, ruining my front wheel. I couldn't ride the bike or even walk it without holding up the front wheel. So there I was, at home, a mile from Mr. Locke's, with the rain pouring pretty hard. I asked Mother whether she'd transport the bike and me. She said I'd have to wait, maybe until the next day. I fussed, and then she said, "All right. I'll drive you there if you promise to look down at Mr. Locke, look him straight in the eye, and tell him your mother brought you because you didn't feel like walking."

I couldn't make that promise. I got soaked.

LETTER 54

On Being a "Different" Sort of Father

When I awoke this morning I had a good idea. Which almost never happens. Usually, when I first open my eyes I am nearly comatose. My thoughts, if any, are questions. Where am I? Must I get up? If I do get up, will all my moving parts move? What's for breakfast?

For years, I've kept paper and pencil in the drawer of my bedside table hoping to record thoughts that came in the night. It hasn't worked. I sleep too soundly. On those rare nights that thoughts *did* disturb me, I was clumsy about recording them. I fumbled with the lamp, fumbled with the drawer, and wrote words that looked like tilted sanskrit, and might well have been.

My good idea of early this morning was that high schools should offer their male seniors a course entitled, *"What's a Father to Be?"* We males get hardly any pre-fatherhood training. We're expected to learn on the job and on our own, and it's partly our own fault. We figure it will all come easily and naturally. We'll just have to go to Little League games and PTA meetings, serve proper helpings of praise and discipline, drive non-profit cabs, and make enough money to feed, shoe, and school our kids.

Before I had had a decade's experience as a father, I made a decision. I would be unorthodox—*different*. Instead of obeying those rules of fatherhood that nearly everyone held in high regard, I would break them. "Read to your young children," one of those rules said. How could I possibly obey it? When I read *Chicken Little*, it was as though I were sitting too comfortably in a symphony hall. I nodded, and sometimes my head didn't bounce back up for quite a spell. My kids could tell that I really didn't care whether Turkey Lurky was in front of Ducky Lucky or behind him. The truth be known, I thought Chicken Little was daft to think the sky was falling. Reading *The Gingerbread Man* was no better. That fleet-footed brown guy couldn't challenge groups of people, only individuals. Over and over he shouted, "Run, run, as fast as you can. You can't catch me. I'm the Gingerbread Man." Too bad a cookie-eating jack rabbit didn't hear him.

So when our kids were little, I seldom read to them. Instead, I made up stories: continuing stories that came to stopping points each night with the good guys and girls in grave danger. We had the tiny people, the Argophytes, notably Homer and Penelope, and the enormous people, the Argophobes. All the people in our stories, large and small, were friendly. Although the Argophytes, who loved adventure, had nothing to fear from other people, they had to cope with animals, insects, and the elements. Imagine yourself an Argophyte. You are seated with three other Argophytes in a boat you have made from half a walnut shell. As you drift lazily, you see a fish streak toward you. Can it be a large-mouth bass with a big appetite? Or maybe as you drift lazily, the wind kicks up and starts to blow acorns off the oaks. What if an acorn were to fall on four Argophytes in a walnut-shell boat?

Another of those rules-for-fathers that I absolutely rejected was: "When you put kids to bed, get them calmed down." Whoever came up with that one was dead wrong. Normal kids don't like being packed off to bed against their will. Nor do they like being calmed down. So it's better, I'm sure, for kids to go to bed excited, preferably laughing, and just drop off to sleep with that wonderful suddenness that only the young and the very old can manage.

It was easy, I found, to prepare kids properly for bed. In the tub, you don't always scrub them with soap. Now and then you use an ice cube. When I dried them, I didn't just blot them with a towel. I put knee to tummy and shined them as though they were shoes. Once I put scarlet nail polish on the middle toenail of each child's left foot. It was time we honored the *middle* toe, I explained. Whenever folks talk of toes, it's always the *big* toe or the *piggy* toe, never the *middle* toe.

The excitement continued. With the kids in bed and fully alert, we had that night's episode of the Argophyte saga. Penelope was left impossibly caught in a spider's web, for example, and no one, not even Homer, knew where she was. Only the spider knew.

The evening's finale was always the same—in a manner of speaking. It was a test of one's ability to refrain from laughing, no matter what. To take the test, each child lay supine, hands beneath head, and pajama top hiked high enough to expose plenty of tickle space. Anticipation showed on every face. The kids knew they'd be tickled, mostly by very light touching. What they didn't know was where those light touches would fall. We had what we called tickle bugs. For the centipede I had to use all one hundred of my fingers to run lightly across tummies, up into armpits, and alongside necks. We had spiders that jumped a lot, and such rare species as the dress bug that could run zippers up and down rib cages.

One memorable night I surprised the kids. "Instead of giving you a bug, we'll play a game," I told them. "I'll fill your tummy buttons with peanut butter and build towers of toothpicks. Whoever lies still enough for me to put on the most toothpicks wins." The kids giggled longer than usual before falling asleep, but I learned something that night: It's better to have a little peanut butter on sheets than tear stains on pillowcases.

LETTER 55

Emotions

You have them. I have them. Emotions. You don't know how many, nor do I. We know about the ten commandments, the seven wonders of the world, the three little pigs, even the seven dwarfs, but we can't say how many emotions there are. Isn't that strange?

Emotions are like ocean waves. They keep coming at you, some gently, some not. You learn to get along with them. When they knock you down you get back up. When you find friendly waves, you ride them. You cope with hostile waves by swimming away or accepting help, and your frequent visits to the emotional sea do wonders for your self-confidence.

Coming home from the Big War in 1945, I was awash with emotions. The first really big wave to hit me was *relief*. I got those long-hoped-for orders to go home as soon as my replacement showed up. *Relief!* You bet! What the orders didn't say, what I just read into them was: "You've won. Leave all the sights and sounds and stench of war behind you. Go home. Live."

The second emotional wave was *anticipation*. While in the war zone I had got used to thinking an hour ahead or a day ahead (except for slogans about getting home in one piece). Now, my dreams of the future would cover months, years. I was about to see your grandmother after nearly two years, and Ken, our first-born, who, while I had been gone, had learned to walk and talk. I would see Mother and stay in my old room in Sherwood Forest. I would hear no explosions, see no blood, and in time, I would find a job, raise a family, and live happily.

Other waves that swept over me were more like sins than emotions. I was *proud* of what I thought had been a job well done. I was *angry* at politicians and military leaders who had recklessly ruined or ended so many lives, and I *envied* those who stayed out of the war by being "essential" in their jobs.

Things went well after I landed in San Francisco. Your grandmother had come west to greet me, though not to the dock. Ken didn't know who I was but decided I was OK. My brothers and most of my friends survived the war. I had trouble for a while riding in cars. I was too used to riding slow-motion on a ship with no brakes. I had trouble with breezes, too. Whenever one came up I got this uneasy feeling that it was the front end of a typhoon. But mostly, all was fine. I got a job, starting at $240 a month, sold my car, bought a bicycle and a house, and began to raise a family. My self-confidence was awesome. I could be anything, do anything.

But the real world soon showed me what realism really was. I kept running into folks who outdid me. Some were younger than I and richer than I'd ever be. Others were wiser than I, physically stronger, more agile, even on the tennis court. I didn't stand on the top rung of any ladder. Even so, I thought I could overcome any obstacle.

It wasn't all that easy. Before I could begin a career, I was hit by a weird ailment that I at first mistook for stomach flu. As the months passed, it struck repeatedly. What was weird was that it only struck when I dined with a few (non-family) folks. To have even the most informal supper with one or two couples was impossible. I felt too ill to take one bite or one sip. Yet I was all right with large groups.

The months grew into years. "There's nothing organically wrong with you," the doctors said, and they had all sorts of test results to back their opinions. They prescribed pills and liquids of many colors, none of which worked. I turned down promotions and offers of jobs that would require my having people out to lunch or dinner. I made excuses not to dine with friends, even in our own house. I was a social cripple.

It must be in my head, the doctors decided, and they were quick to add that it was in my *subconscious*. I wasn't going bonkers; I just had some crossed wires between my head and stomach. I resolved to fight back, to have my head tell my stomach not to get sick, no matter what. I got worse.

What finally worked was my following the advice of a doctor who said, "Stop fighting it. Admit to yourself, *really admit*, that there's something wrong with you." It was a hard lesson to learn but one worth remembering: *Self-confidence is essential most of the time, humility some of the time.*

LETTER 56

What To Do About Your Mind

There's a guy who comes onto my TV screen now and then to say, "A mind is a terrible thing to waste." He does it to raise money to support colleges, and his message is, I suppose, about 98% correct. Only 2% of the minds I've run across should be buried at toxic dump sites.

When I pay attention to TV commercials (usually because I'm slow to hit the "Mute" button) I look for hidden meanings, inferences, subliminal messages. This TV guy wants me to believe that only colleges with big bank accounts can make sure that minds are not wasted. Rubbish! Some minds that never go to college get along just fine. He would also have me believe that what colleges do to minds, namely keep them busy memorizing and figuring is the *only* way to keep them from being wasted. Also rubbish!

Perhaps the problem is with two words: *mind* and *waste*. I think the TV guy means *brain* rather than *mind*. For all I know, he may want to see brains cultivated even though they've already had lots of furrows dug into them, and I assume he thinks brains are wasted when not constantly put to work.

In my book, mind and brain are not synonyms. The mind uses the brain but is far more powerful, not just a tangle of nerves. I can let my mind wander, but my brain must stay cooped up in its little skull-closet.

I like to *change* my mind. I would not like to change my brain. That would require a costly operation, plus pain and worry. By contrast, changing my mind can, and often does, give me pleasure. Although I don't recall the first time, as a tot, I changed my mind, it must have been about food. Ice cream most likely. Vanilla, chocolate or strawberry? That was before the days of 50-flavors, including such taste treats as Burgundy Cherry, Mackinac Fudge, Bear Tracks, and French Silk.

The joy of changing my mind is that I get to experience all the choices open to me, not just one. I can taste each flavor as surely as I could by putting ice cream on my tongue. I can feel tiny strawberry seeds crunch between molars, lick my lips clean of imaginary chocolate, put my ice cream into any of several cones or into a sundae bowl, and add toppings.

If the early incidents of mind-changing were about food, later ones ran the gamut: which girl to ask out on a date, what camera to buy, where to go to school, whether to take a trip, and if so, where to go; and in each instance the fun came from pretending to opt for one alternative after another.

Then, before I was even old enough to vote, the world closed in on me. "You can't keep changing your mind," people said. They knew it was grim advice. They wore the unhappy expressions of children about to be served Brussels sprouts. "You have to choose. You have to make up your mind. You have to be decisive. You have to plan and stick by what you plan."

I should have fought back. I didn't. Instead, I became a closet mind-changer. Whenever I wasn't absolutely forced to make immediate decisions (as during multiple-choice exams), I quietly and happily kept changing my mind.

On a fuzzily remembered date later in life, I found that making up my mind could actually be pleasant, given the right conditions. I needed absolute freedom with no one "suggesting" how I should decide, and no one insisting that I make up my mind by a certain time. Ideally, the decision would involve only happy-sounding choices: raspberry shortcake or chocolate eclair.

The lessons I eventually learned were these. Keep changing your mind for as long as it's fun. There will come a time when the fun stops. You will fret about how indecisive you have become, a procrastinator or worse. You will hope that something or someone will come along to remove the need for you to act. At that point, make up your mind. You'll like yourself for having done so. You'll be proud you didn't stall by saying (untruthfully) that you needed more information. Proud, too, that you didn't seek "cheap courage" by making others party to your decision and thus partially liable in case of a bad outcome.

Sometimes it's really hard *not* to keep changing your mind. About what to pitch as you clean out a desk or closet, for instance. Or about something really big and with long-lasting effects, like which house to buy or when to get married. But once you've made up your mind and felt that surge of pride, don't torture yourself. Don't look back. Don't say, "If only I had decided differently."

This letter sounds too serious, too preachy. Maybe I should scrap it. No, I've made up my mind. I will add it to the stack.

Just remember those differences between minds and brains. Minds, like beds, can be made up and, like sheets, can be changed. Brains cannot unless you are mighty handy with protoplasm. Minds can be read. Brains, clean or dirty, can only be washed. Minds can roam, but you'd best not lose yours.

A final thought: Livers are a terrible thing to waste, too, unless they're from animals, and cooked, and put on my plate.

LETTER 57

Cars, Now and Then

While sorting junk* in my old gray sea chest in the garage, I came across a clamp I'd clean forgotten I had. For some reason, I thought I must have pitched it years ago or, more likely, that Gommie had pitched it for me. As clamps go, this one is palm-sized, sturdily made of forged steel, obsolete, and odd. Its name, in raised metal letters, is "5-minute Vulcanizer." From the side it looks vaguely like a deep-throated C-clamp. Of the two surfaces that come together to hold a clamped object, the top one is a flat circle fully an inch and a half in diameter. The lower one could pass for the flattened foot of a five-toed crow.

Throughout the time that I had my 1931 $35 Model A Ford, I used this clamp perhaps four times a week to hold tire patches in place while the glue set. Tires, you see, were pretty bad back then, even the new ones, and I either bought used tires or had my old ones recapped. But mostly I just kept patching. Of course it was inner tubes rather than tires that sprang leaks. This meant taking the wheel off the car, then the tire off the wheel, removing the inner tube to patch it, then reassembling everything and pumping up the tire. To find all the leaks, I patted soapy water all over the inner tube and looked for bubbles.

As I thought about this clamp and those many flat tires, it occurred to me that I've not yet told you much about those 1930s cars. I'll do that now. You can decide whether to pity us for having to put up with our primitive machines.

Compared to your cars, ours were lots cheaper. You'd expect that because they lacked so much that your cars have: automatic shift, air conditioners, tape players, defrosters, air bags, computer chips, and power everything (steering, windows, seats, locks, and brakes). You'd think that with all those extras your cars would need more frequent repairs than ours did. Not so. We had lots of breakdowns. On the other hand, because ours were such simple machines, repairs were also so simple that we often made them ourselves.

Believe it or not, some of what we had wasn't half bad. Although our cars were gas guzzlers compared to yours, we paid only about a dime a gallon to have our gas delivered with a flair, usually by two attendants. One pumped the gas and handled the money while the other checked the oil, tires, and battery, cleaned the windshield, and brushed out the inside.

My Model A came with a hand crank to be used whenever the battery was too weak to run the starter. I never used that crank. I was afraid to. One slight mishandling, and that crank could kick back and break your arm. What I did when I knew my battery was low was park on a hill. To start the car, I released the brake, pushed in the clutch, put the gearshift in 2nd, turned on the ignition, coasted, and said a short prayer. Once the car got rolling well enough, I let out the clutch and pulled out the hand choke. If my prayer was answered, the engine came alive, and I kept it that way by pulling the hand throttle to a "fast idle" position.

On those many days that I forgot to park on a hill, I got a push, either from another car or from friends on foot. We got pretty good at pushing cars on foot and jumping on running boards (narrow outdoor platforms on the sides of cars). What we did was no doubt dangerous—we sometimes *rode* short distances while standing on those running boards—but no one I ever knew got hurt. People in those days were not very safety conscious. Seat belts and bicycle helmets were yet to be invented.

The police were friends, not foes. They wanted us to be careful but were not about to bother us about diddly stuff. To become a driver, all a person had to do was have a sixteenth birthday (or a fourteenth in some states). There were no driving classes, no drivers' licenses. The theory was that it was silly to give a person a test on one day when he might be reckless the rest of the year. There were no parking meters and no law ordering people to carry insurance. New license plates came out each year. They were made by convicts, sold for about $3, and mailed to drivers, many of whom saved the old ones to hang on their garage walls.

On most counts, your cars are much better than ours were. They're roomier and more powerful. The seats are softer, the brakes more reliable, the steering wheel easier to turn. All of which may explain the disappearance of those once famous brand names: Franklin, Overland, Essex, Deusenburg, Auburn, Cord, Packard, Hudson, LaSalle, Stutz, Hupmobile, Studebaker, Pierce Arrow.

If you compare your cars to those like my Model A, please ponder two thoughts. First, when you get behind the wheel, you just *know* your car will take you where you want to go. I always had the excitement of guessing. Would it start? Would it konk out along the way? What would I do if it let me down? Second, you have to lock your car and worry, lest it be stolen. Those cars of yesteryear were almost never stolen. They were too slow and too unreliable to attract a thief with an IQ of 50+

---

* A WIFELY NOUN; THE HUSBANDLY EQUIVALENT IS *TREASURE*.

LETTER 58

My Chemistry Set

One Christmas in the 1930s, I got a Gilbert chemistry set, which made its mark on me—and I don't mean a scar from an acid burn. Santa and parents used to give lots of sets to young boys, especially to boys who hated to sit around reading or playing the piano. There were tinker toy sets, train sets, tool sets, erector sets, and many more. There were no plastics then, and hence no Lego sets, which was too bad, but we built grand little metal structures held together with nuts and bolts.

We boys were given these sets at Christmas, not to make us smarter or to hone our fine motor skills, but to keep us from teasing our sisters. During the winter, there were always a few days when nothing outdoors was quite right. The snow was slushy, the ice on the ponds too thin, the vacant lots too muddy. On such days, sisters indoors were at risk.

Well, my sisters must have been delighted when I got that chemistry set. I was fascinated. I had no need to pick on a sister in order to feel powerful. I had power at my fingertips. I could make brilliant colors in test tubes: copper salts for blue, nickel salts for green, cochineal for purple. I could generate gases, even one that smelled like rotten eggs. I could even mix (tiny) batches of gunpowder and dip string into a nitrate solution to make fuses. I could formulate invisible ink, mix pairs of liquids to form solids, and turn a colorless liquid into a red one. The little alcohol lamp in my chemistry set might once have been Aladdin's.

Still, the mark my chemistry set made on me had nothing to do with feelings of power. Rather, it shaped my attitude toward various school subjects and indirectly toward various people. I'd best explain. The appeal of chemistry (as of math, which I also liked) was that answers were unequivocal: right or wrong, not the wishy-washy in-between answers heard in, say, classes on history or law. If I mixed chemical A with chemical B, I either got C or I did not, and if I did, I could count on getting C the next day or the next year. It was like adding 3 to 2 and getting 5. It was a sort of pure, precise knowledge. It was not like an historian's knowledge of, say, Hitler's regime, which would have little value dealing with North Korea, Vietnam, or Iraq.

As time passed, my pro-chemistry bias broadened to include other hard sciences such as physics. Then, in college, I discovered *why* I had this bias. It was the appeal of the so-called scientific method, a way of thinking and acting that goes something like this. Let's say I want to make a chemical compound called Y, which no one has ever made. From what I know about chemistry, I *think* I should be able to make Y by mixing equal amounts of A, E, and M, and stirring the mixture for 3 hours while holding the temperature at 90°C. It's just an educated guess, but it has a fancier name: hypothesis. I try it and strike out. I'm a bit smarter. I now know something that *won't* work.

I next make a new guess. I will change one—but only one—of the conditions: raise the temperature to 110°C. That's my second hypothesis. I try it and again strike out. I persist with a third hypothesis, then a fourth, and so on. Each time I learn a tad and eventually find that set of conditions that will yield chemical Y.

What I describe is an orderly thought process that works outside the lab as well as inside. Let's say that instead of wanting to make chemical Y, I want to fix a fluorescent light fixture that no longer works, even with a new bulb. I first learn enough of the basics so I can make some educated guesses. The electricity has to come to the fixture, get past a switch, go in and out of a transformer, fire up a starter, go through the fluorescent tube and back on out through a ground wire. I then set a hypothesis: that the starter is at fault. I try a new one. No luck. Second hypothesis: bad connection on switch. I scrape and reconnect. When that doesn't work, I continue to make changes, one at a time, and see what happens.

As an advocate of this scientific method, I find myself intolerant of those who reject it out of hand. Many of them say they can't be bothered trying to understand how things work. It's somehow beneath them, something best left to their inferiors, those who practice stepwise logic.

But of all those who pride themselves at being above the scientific method, the truly dangerous ones are those who misuse the word *experiment*. In science, an experiment is a well thought-out, controlled exercise aimed at adding knowledge. When I hear some guy say he's experimenting with drugs, I cringe. I'm sure he hasn't learned the basics of drug chemistry. Sure, too, that his experiments won't be well thought out and involve changing just one condition at a time. And is he really trying to learn something?

Enough said. I've never shaken the pro-science bias that began on that 1930s Christmas morning. How do you suppose I'd have turned out if my present had been a *paint* set?

LETTER 59

Tree Frogs and Sharks

On a few nights in Spring, the tree frogs of our neighborhood do a voice recital. I hesitate to call it musical. There's nothing melodic about it, no catchy tune, no toe-tapping rhythm. I wouldn't call it croaking either, at least not the croaking of those big old bullfrogs up north. Our tree frogs, though only half the size of bullfrogs, are much louder, and when they open their collective mouths, the din is steady. Even before one frog stops yakking, others begin. It's as though the woods were full of Democrats and Republicans all talking at once, with no pause to inhale.

Well, not that bad. Frog noise is *good* noise, loud but *good*, like the sound of tall waves coming ashore. Many loud noises are not so soothing: the screams of injured children, speeding sirens, the boom of cannons. Our noisy tree frogs, I am told, are males trying to meet females. What no one tells me is (a) how any female can figure out which male is making which sound, and (b) why one sound has more sex appeal than another.

When I hear those frogs each Spring, I think of the few peaceful jungles I visited during the big war. We seldom went ashore in the war zone except to put survey markers atop hills—and we got shot at while doing so. Mostly we stayed aboard ship near jungles where Japs still lingered. We didn't hanker to slog through mud—in New Guinea, rain was a daily event—or to hike, fully clothed to foil insects, in sauna-steamy air. Also, just getting ashore and back took effort. With no docks in these wretched ports, we just dropped anchor; anyone wishing to go ashore had to lower the wherry and pull oars. Only in a few more "civilized" ports did flat-bottomed boats come ferry sailors on their way to fetch food and mail.

One clammy morning we got two pages of unexpectedly good orders that might better have been cut to one sentence: *Go survey the Hermit Islands harbor.* The orders didn't say why—orders never did—but that was okay. At the time, this small cluster of islands, a hundred miles or so off the coast of New Guinea, was isolated, beautiful, and inhabited only by jungle creatures plus a few natives. We were in for a quiet week on calm, clear water. We could safely clean our guns and drape our bedding over the rails for a proper airing.

I don't recall how many Hermit Islands there were. Six or so, I'd say. I do recall that they formed a circle a few miles in diameter, and that the water between adjacent islands was shallow. Thus, the encircled lagoon that we were to survey was well protected from the turbulence of the sea beyond the perimeter.

Curious natives who came to see what we were up to stayed to help us cut wood and build markers for our surveying. They spoke pidgin-English, as did many folks in that part of the world, so we were able to ask a few questions and understand the answers. "Boy find mango?" we asked. Or, "Boy find banana?" or "Boy catch turtle (for soup)?" and a native might grab the sleeve of my shirt and ask, "Boss give?" We were much too young in those days to fret about politically correct language. In pidgin-English, a black male was "Boy," a white male was "Boss," and a female was "Mary." Anyone who wanted to change all that would have to wander from village to village, inland, and out to sea to teach a new language.

Back and forth we sailed, slowly in straight lines, taking soundings and fixing our positions every 45 seconds. Two of us on the flying bridge used sextants to measure angles between markers on shore. A third yelled "Mark" at 45-second intervals and plotted our exact position. If necessary, he had the helmsman steer to port or starboard. Upon hearing the word "Mark," those with sextants reported their angles, and a man below reported the depth.

We made such progress that by 3 p.m. each day we could anchor and relax. On one afternoon, we saw many shark fins cutting curved paths just fifty feet aft of the stern. Big fins they were, fins of Great Whites, no doubt. Could we possibly catch one? We'd need a mighty big hook. Some stout rope for line, too, and some leader that could stand up against shark teeth. Bait would be no problem. A hunk of beef from the galley should do. But will we be able to hang on to the rope once a shark that big is hooked? and knowing sharks, once one is hooked, will others go after him?

Pourcelli made the hook. He bent a quarter-inch steel bolt stock in a vise, filed a sharp point, and used a hacksaw to cut a barb. For leader, we used flexible steel cable, and tied it to braided linen heaving line as thick as clothes line, and ever so much stronger. We put meat on the hook, tied the hook to a block of wood, let the tide carry the bait aft, and wrapped the line around the drum on a winch so we'd be able to hold on. As an added precaution we loaded pistols and rifles to prevent shark cannibalism. WHAM! An instant hit! The quiet of the Hermit Islands was broken. Gunshots and yelling, flying fin fragments and shark blood in that otherwise blue water. We caught our shark all right. The trouble was, too many of our bullets hit him instead of his predatory chums. He was dead.

Around sundown, I rowed ashore with two of the crew to give away T-shirts and pick up mangos. The jungle creatures, mostly birds and monkeys, I reckon, not frogs, were just tuning up for their all night concerts. It was a comforting sound.

LETTER 60

Studying Hands

My Auntie May was a keen observer of hands. Nearly everyone else's focus in those days was on heads and body shapes. Not Auntie May. After having met someone and gotten beyond earshot, she didn't say, "His eyebrow is one long dash, not two hyphens." Or, "She has wonderful blue eyes, like a September sky." Or, "The poor girl is pear-shaped." Or, "That moustache of his looks to have been put on with a ballpoint pen."

No, what Auntie May used to say was, "Did you notice his (her) hands?" which of course no one else had, and then she'd describe them. She seemed to have had Sherlock Holmes's knack for careful observation. Fingers were fat or bony, gnarled or sleek, long or stubby. Nails were well-tended or not, bitten or not, too brightly painted or not. Some palms were clammy, others calloused. She also read character from hands, though not the way palmists do with dim lights and glass spheres. Auntie May just knew that anyone whose nails were clean couldn't be all bad. Quite often when I was a boy, and in the same room with her, I kept my hands in my pockets.

No one ever explained to me why she was so fascinated by hands. My sister, Mary, thought it was all an adult scheme to make us kids stop chewing our nails and start cleaning them every single time we made mudballs. Except for sewing, at which Auntie May excelled, her own hands weren't remarkable. I never saw her play a piano or cast for bass or shoot marbles.

At middle-age or so, I, too, got interested in hands. My focus wasn't the same as Auntie May's, though. Whereas what she had cared about was the look and feel of hands, I grew curious about hands in action. It began shortly after a couple we knew, Charlie and Gretchen, had their first child, a daughter.

We were, of course, duty bound to view the infant, Oh! and Ah! and proclaim her the prettiest and smartest of all time. We were not obliged to attest to that under oath, and I kept two fingers crossed behind my back. Well, Charlie looked at that babe in the crib and slowly lowered his hand to where the baby could reach up and grab his little finger. Right away she got excited enough to begin kicking and gurgling. "She thinks she's grabbed a Tootsie Roll," I told Charlie, but even he didn't think she was smart enough to know about Tootsie Rolls.

Before long, Charlie couldn't just let that baby lie there. He picked her up the way all fathers pick up their first-borns: as though he were moving a 500-piece assembled jigsaw puzzle bare-handed from one table to another. The baby, seemingly unafraid lest her father drop some of her pieces, was quiet for fully ten minutes, then turned on tears as babies are wont to do. That meant one of three things. She needed to be fed or burped or changed. (And any parent's first two guesses are bound to be wrong). This baby needed to be changed in the worst possible way. Charlie soon found himself holding a stinky diaper with one hand and wishing he could hold his nose with the other.

And that's how I got curious about whether what we do with our hands—even just holding various objects—can shape our mood. The baby felt happy and secure clinging to a finger. Charlie felt happy though apprehensive as he lifted that baby with all its assembled pieces, and as for holding that nasty diaper, well, he felt no joy.

You might enjoy making a few observations on your own. Watch someone hold something and see whether you can figure out his or her mood. Need some examples?

Watch a girl put a worm on a hook. She may feel the way Charlie did with the diaper. Watch a child hold a crayon, and a man trying to thread a needle. See whether you spot a feeling of pride in a boy holding his first fish. Look for determination in a little-leaguer, bat in hand. Sense the reverence in the mind of the priest as he holds the chalice. Ride a plane and find the passenger who has a white-knuckled grip on the arm rest.

From an old Indian named Hawk, I learned about a hand exercise that can bring on a slue of emotions. It's a form of fishing called noodling. To noodle, you find a stream or lake known to be loaded with fish. You go to a spot on the shore where you can lower your hand, palm up, a foot or more into the water as you sit on the bank, and that's all there is to it. You wait patiently for a curious fish to come check out your hand. Should curious fish be too slow to come, strap a worm to your palm with a rubber band.

As you noodle, your mood changes. You're happy, then bored by the wait. You're excited as you watch a fish approach, disappointed when it decides your hand is unappetizing. When at last you lift a wiggling fish from the water, you are once more happy, but now proud as well. You've done it! With neither net nor hook, you've done it!

Perhaps you think noodlers' mood changes come as much from the eyes as the hands. If so, go watch a noodler use his skill in muddy water. He can't see, only feel, what comes to his hand. Might it be a catfish with hypodermic fins? A water moccasin?

You may have heard it said that eyes are windows to the soul. Do you reckon hands are doorknobs?

LETTER 61

When Folks Take Chances

Typically, when I write one of these letters, I have a subject in mind before stringing together two pages of words. If, as sometimes happens, I bog down on a sentence because I can't think of the right word, I reach for a spineless tan book, *THE WORD FINDER*. It was published in 1947. There should have been later editions. My copy may soon crumble.

THE WORD FINDER is neither a dictionary nor a thesaurus. It's the book to use when you have a noun and need an adjective. Let's say you're writing about someone and mention his or her ears. You want a word that will set those ears apart from just any set of ears. You look in *THE WORD FINDER* under "ears" and find maybe a hundred adjectives such as "furry," "cupped," "wiggly," "cauliflower," and "cocked." *THE WORD FINDER* will also provide adverbs to go with your verbs (or adjectives). Under "speak," for example, you'll find "icily," "tensely," "warily," "glibly," and many more.

Today I start this letter, not with an idea, but with a word. I will blindly and gently stab a word in *THE WORD FINDER* with a pencil point, then write whatever comes to mind as I behold that word. Ready?

I can hardly believe it. My word is *chance*. My choice was random, a matter of chance, and my pencil lit on *chance*. That should be a good word to think about and write about. It has a multiple personality. It's a noun (He'll take a chance). It's a verb (You'll have to chance keeping dry). It's an adjective (Theirs was a chance meeting).

A few years ago, I heard a notion worth passing along—namely, that before you can really come to know someone, you must watch how he or she takes chances. That struck me as an inaccurate generalization. After all, I've come to know people quite well who pay little attention to the way they take chances. Even so, I've had fun from time to time spotting abnormal behavior.

And what better place to look for abnormality than in your family's genealogical records on your grandmother's side! I found no extremists, no compulsive gamblers who bet and lost the family farm, and no ancestors who stayed abed rather than face the perils of the outside world. What I found was two males whom I now dub Herb and Jack so as not to embarrass a surviving relative.

Herb hated to take chances. As a boy, he seldom got holes in the knees of his pants, was always on time for school, was never checked into a hospital emergency room, and would not play marbles "for keeps." Out of earshot, his peers called him a sissy. Today he'd be called a nerd or wimp or an even more up-to-date term. The few friends he did make had Herb's cautious temperament.

In adulthood, his social life improved. No longer was he thought of as the lad afraid to compete in rough games. His reluctance to take chances was no longer obvious. Still, it was there, and it served him well. He sought and found stable employment, married an even-tempered woman, lived within his means, had three children, and made only the safest of investments. How would I sum up his life? Long: 92 years. Comfortable, though not wildly exciting. Fairly successful in terms of family harmony and finances.

Jack liked to live on the edge. As a boy, he held lighted firecrackers until the fuse was three-quarters gone. He shinnied a telephone pole to stand on the crossbeam. He swam in the company of water moccasins. Would he have tried to disarm a bomb, given the opportunity? Who knows?

After graduating from high school, more or less honorably, Jack became a self-employed opportunist, a promoter of sorts. He'd dream up a deal (such as buying and selling land), talk someone with money into putting up the cash, then take a share of the profit, if any, just for having had the idea. So Jack still took chances, but now it was someone else's money.

Jack's life was much more exciting than Herb's. He kept hoping that the next deal would make him rich for life. Although that never happened, he seemed happy just dreaming of a luxurious future. His biographer for the genealogical records says he laughed a lot, a baritone laugh, loud, and infectious.

What may be as important as watching others deal with chance is watching ourselves. We still must avoid those foolhardy enough to play "Chicken" or Russian Roulette, but we do well to understand our own comfort levels. We make some choices easily: when to chance crossing a street, whether to chance eating food that could be contaminated. Other choices make us ponder: whether to sell a stock or wait in hope of a higher price, whether to trade in the old car or chance having it break down.

Of this I am sure. As we age, our handling of risk gets steadily more cautious. We take fewer chances as we drive. If we take chances with money, it's small sums—the prices of lottery tickets. We experiment less with the foods we eat. We bundle up lest a virus lurks nearby. We use handrails we never before even noticed. What we don't often do is what Jack did: laugh loudly. Can it be that we worry too much about taking chances and losing?

LETTER 62

The Cobbler and the Hardware Man

There was a time, so long ago I hardly remember, when I enjoyed shopping, at least in certain stores. It was different then. If you will now stroll with me along two blocks of Lockwood Avenue, you'll see how different. We'll drop into a few shops, meet the owners, and look around.

First is Schlufman's Shoe Repair. It is narrow, dimly lit, and it features a linoleum floor, a long counter on our right, and behind it, Mr. Schlufman with his cobbler tools. The air is heavy with vapors of leather, polish, and sweaty feet. To our left are two seats with waist-high side walls and swinging doors in front. That's where kids sat while Mr. Schlufman put heels or half-soles or both on their shoes. Lots of those shoes had been fitted with cardboard inner soles to plug up holes. That was a temporary fix. *Very* temporary after a rain or snow. Each of the kids I knew had two pairs of shoes, one for school and one for Sunday. The school pair wore out fast on account of all the hard use they got.

I never did see a grown-up on one of those walled-in seats. Grown-ups apparently had so many shoes that they could drop off a pair to be cobbled and come back the next day.

Mr. Schlufman understood kids and why they'd naturally fidget, because they had to sit there in stocking feet instead of playing outdoors. He took their minds off their ordeals by getting them to talk about what their friends and family were up to, and he sang them songs whose words and melodies were unknown to them. Mr. Schlufman was a rarity. He was a Jew, and there weren't many Jews in Webster at the time. Most preferred living closer to

St. Louis. Many congregated in University City, the way Germans did in South St. Louis and Italians did on "The Hill."

Before Mr. Schlufman handed a kid his repaired shoes, he polished them on a spinning brush. Then he gave the kid a short lecture on taking better care of shoes. But his advice fell on deaf ears. Mr. Schlufman mended shoes. Kids did not mend their ways.

Let's cross the street now, and move back in time. We enter Gorelock Hardware Store and meet Mr. Mueller, the owner. He has shed his German accent, if he ever had one, but not the German virtue of cleanliness. His store is spotless, his wares stored ever so neatly. One long wall is all shelves, floor to ceiling, yet nothing is beyond Mr. Mueller's reach. He has a ladder on a track, you see, so he can climb up and ride all the way from the front of the store to back, picking items off shelves as he goes.

His definition of hardware is narrow by today's standards. Most of what he sells is metallic: saws and hammers, nails and hinges, bolts, and wire. There are no big boxes marked "some assembly needed." If we buy a wagon here, we pull it out on its own four wheels. We can't buy power tools or appliances or auto parts. Whatever we do buy, we may first touch and try out. Nothing is imprisoned in a plastic cell. We also buy only the quantities we need, not the quantities some packager thinks we *should* buy. We need nails? Mr. Mueller asks us what pennyweight, then walks us to the proper nail keg, where we grab as many as we need and put them on a spring scale. Mr. Mueller pours the nails into a paper sack and takes our money. (No charge for less than a good handful of nails)

As a youngster I often stopped at Gorelock Hardware on my way home from school, if only to get warm. Usually, though, I had a project in need of nails, or sheet lead for ballast, or putty, which Mr. Mueller scooped from a big can and wrapped in heavy paper. Sometimes I was after roller skate wheels to use on my homemade wooden racers. But in Mr. Mueller's inventory was something you'd not expect to find in a hardware store, something every red-blooded boy just had to own: agates. Cat-eye agates and tiger-eye agates, the finest shooter marbles in the world.

And boy, did Mr. Mueller know how to sell them! He kept them in a chamois bag behind the counter. Whenever a boy announced that he was about ready to buy an agate, Mr. Mueller brought a whole new ambiance to his store. On his counter he spread a rectangle of dark green felt and set beside it a library lamp with a dark green glass shade. Proper light is essential in judging agates.

He loosened the drawstring on the chamois bag, peered inside, and brought forth just one agate, which he then placed under the best light. The boy picked it up, set it down, rolled it over to check its whole surface, and tried shooting it against his left palm. Mr. Mueller took other agates from the bag, of course, though he never had more than three agates on the felt at one time. He knew that boys faced with too many choices were hard put to make up their minds.

I didn't realize it at the time. I learned later that buying an agate in Gorelock Hardware Store was like buying an engagement ring at a fine jewelry store. The setting was awesome, the stakes high. Serious business but with a happy outcome. My tiger-eye was the best, a close friend for years. When it disappeared one day, I looked and looked but never found it. I suppose anything that valuable was bound to get stolen.

I'm now out of space for this letter, and we've been to just two shops. Let's walk a little further in the next letter.

LETTER 63

The Dime Store and One-Cent Sales

We turn left as we leave Mr. Mueller's store, and we're still back at an earlier time: about 1930. If we were to walk a quarter block along Lockwood, we'd come to Gore Avenue, hence the name Gorelock Hardware. But let's not go that far. Instead, let's duck into the dimestore. Although its proper name is Woolworth's, it's best known as the 5-and-10 or the dimestore.

It is quite unlike Gorelock Hardware. Instead of being rectangular it is L-shaped with one door on Lockwood and one on Gore. It is untidy and not so clean. What must be the store's whole inventory is heaped onto the belt-high counters that line the aisles. It is a chain store, not one with a local owner like Mr. Mueller. Clerks are neither friendly nor unfriendly, and look as though they lead hardscrabble lives. Which they probably do.

This is a true variety store with something for everyone, and no item priced higher than 10¢. There are writing tablets, tire patches, candy, and socks. For those unable to afford Mr. Schlufman's services, there are heels and half-soles. There are candles, cups and saucers, incense, toys, sheet music, popped popcorn, and small phials of perfume. Just before Christmas each year, this dime store does a brisk business with grade-school-age children. Days later, young mothers bravely pretend to like the way they smell, although some of them wash off their perfume when they leave the house.

Our next stop is another chain store, Rexall Drugs. You find it bare compared to today's drugstores. It lacks so much that had not been invented by 1930: antibiotics, Band-Aids, multiple vitamin pills, inhalers, and aerosols of any kind: for hair spray, shave cream, or deodorant, for example. Missing, too, are products that 1930s people don't think belong in drug stores: cosmetics, toys, recordings, cookies, greeting cards, and bottled soft drinks.

Almost everything in Rexall's is somehow related to health care. If you've been sick enough to have gone to a doctor, you now give your prescription to the white-jacketed druggist. He must *prepare* your medicine, *formulate* it. He cannot merely transfer tablets and liquids from large bottles to small ones. There are too few ready-to-use prescription drugs on the market. He must mix powders thoroughly after weighing each ingredient on an elegant little scale. To make up individual doses (since he has no tableting machine) he fills gelatin capsules or tiny paper packets that can be emptied into glasses of water. When he concocts liquid medicines in graduated glass vessels, he stirs in coloring and flavoring. Even so, his medicines are none too tasty.

The druggist is highly thought of, a cut above the grocer, the cobbler and the barber—more like the banker. That's partly because what he does seems complex and professional, and partly because his goal is to help the ill. His wares are called drugs, a synonym for medicines. Drugs are not illegal substances such as heroin or opium. Those are called dope. People who use dope are not users. They are dope fiends, mankind at the lowest level.

On Rexall's shelves are a few non-prescription drugs. Foul tasting tonics promise new vigor to those who will have a swig of sulphur and iron. (Rumor has it that the worse the taste the better the medicine). If you have an upset stomach and have already tried baking soda, Rexall's two top suggestions are citrate of magnesia (under high pressure in special bottles) and Pepto Bismol. A sore throat? Try a nickel box of Smith Brothers cough drops, which are said to work well even though they are delicious. Stopped up with a cold? Put some tincture of benzoin into your kettle and steam up the sick room. If your problem is a cut or scrape, Rexall will sell you iodine (a real stinger!), gauze, and adhesive tape. For headaches, there's aspirin; for fever, an ice pack; for chills, a hot water bottle.

Just don't come here in search of mood-altering tablets. There
are none. When you're feeling low, Rexall's druggist will steer you
to the non-medical corner: the soda fountain. You may order a
cherry phosphate, a hot fudge sundae, an ice cream soda, or a
malted milk. If one of those doesn't cheer you up, try seconds.

On that happy note, and before you tire of shop hopping,
we'll end this walk. The picture I want to pass along is this. In the
1930s, stores stocked less and charged less. Most of those stores in
Webster were owned by individuals. Rexall's and the dimestore
were exceptions. The attitudes of the individual owners were superb.
All would trust customers who were strapped for cash. Grocers
delivered free of charge. Doctors made house calls. Mr. Zimmer,
our butcher, often called me in off the street to fix me sandwiches
just because I looked hungry—no charge. Mr. Mueller lent me
tools that I'd rarely need—no charge. Walter Weir, owner of the
filling station, drove his truck to our house whenever our cars
wouldn't start—no charge.

Tough times? I suppose. But we were in good company.

LETTER 64

A Blackfoot from Up North

This afternoon I met Jim Eaglefeather, a full-blooded Indian—a Blackfoot, I think he said. He was on his (padded) knees on the sidewalk in front of a store that was closed for renovation. Having just miscut a groove in a panel of yellow pine—a no-count kind of wood to my way of thinking—he turned to his assistant with words about how they might deal with it.

As I stepped cautiously around this curbside carpentry shop, I smiled and shook my head ever so slightly. The pine panel, hideously scarred, was a goner: kindling. My smile and headshake must have led Jim Eaglefeather to conclude that I knew something about woodworking. He at once began to explain what had gone wrong. He needn't have. The curve in that ugly groove told me he hadn't held his router firmly against the fence. Charring of the wood was obviously due to his having used a dull router bit.

With the sun low in the sky, there was nothing left for Jim and his assistant to do but pack up. Tomorrow, Jim would make or buy a new panel and borrow or buy a sharp bit. Meanwhile, they were talkative, and in no hurry. Which was fine by me. Seldom do I meet a full-blooded Indian. There are few of them close by.

Would I have known he was an American Indian if he hadn't told me his name? I'm not sure. He had the jet black hair and reddish bronze skin, but then so do many Mexicans in our midst. His hair, being done in a queue, was like the rat tails that I see on boys and men of all colors. He wore a lot of jewelry for a man, and it was of a kind that I'd expect an Indian to favor: wrist bands, beads, and hair ornaments (no earrings) crafted of turquoise and silver. But folks other than Indians also find such jewelry most appealing.

After we had yakked awhile about which species of woods and which tools were our favorites, I asked Jim how he came to settle here. I recalled (I know not how) that the Blackfoot Indians were members of the Algonquin Nation up near the Canadian border, and maybe even beyond it. Indeed, that is exactly where Jim had spent his early years, in the woods of northern Minnesota, at a time when many Indians thereabouts moved—or *were* moved—from forests to towns. Their vast homelands were seized and turned into national parks.

"Were you anywhere near Quetico Provincial Park?" I asked, and then added, "Years ago I took three of my sons there. We went in by canoe, portaged from lake to lake, and camped out. Every boy should do that, see what the world was like before man messed it up. In Quetico there are no buildings, no roads or billboards or telephone poles. The only sounds are from animals and thunder. We drank lake water from our cupped hands."

Jim was all too familiar with Quetico. He had lived on the edge of it, gotten his food there by fishing, hunting, and gathering. He had run trap lines there to get furs to trade. It was a primitive life, he conceded, but not half bad. He was freer than he would be later on. The rules were few and simply stated: Don't lie or steal, for instance. Penalties, too, were easy to understand if also quite severe. Once, when Jim was quite young, he was taken by his parents to witness the punishment of a Blackfoot who had been caught stealing. His penalty was to run the gauntlet—that is, to run between two long rows of Indians who pounded him with large clubs and hurled stones at him. He survived the run, bloodied, and with broken bones, and was allowed to go on living with the tribe; but from that day forward, no one was to speak to him.

As Jim Eaglefeather's life gradually changed to the "paleface" way, he became a guide for white vacationers, then went to white schools. He married and started a small contractor business. After his wife came down with a paralyzing disease, he brought her to Houston for expert care. Today, he still has the contractor business plus a home-based, silver-and-turquoise jewelry business. If all goes well, he will soon teach students at a local college how to make Indian jewelry.

The Eaglefeathers live in an especially tough part of Houston where gangs no longer kill only their rivals. Sometimes their victims are ordinary folks who happen either to irk them or just be in the way. Life is not as it had been in Minnesota. There are more laws, more lawbreakers, no gauntlets.

Quite by chance, Jim found a way to keep gang members at bay. One crisp, clear morning as he stood in his front yard, he remembered the Blackfoot custom of thanking various spirits for providing a very fine day. So Jim got himself a sack of tobacco, returned to the front yard, withdrew a pinch of tobacco, and tossed it to the north while chanting loudly his thanks to the Spirit of the North. The language of his chant was neither English nor Spanish. Once the Spirit of the North had been thanked, Jim went on to the other five spirits: South, East, West, Sky-Above, and Earth. Each got kind words plus a bit of tobacco.

Well, some of the gang members watched this and spread the word: This man's a witch. He can put a curse on you, make you drop dead just by wishing it. Gang members who kill without qualm won't go anywhere near Jim Eaglefeather and even try to get out of his sight lest a beam from his evil eye vaporize them.

Perhaps you wonder why I write to you about this Indian whom I may never again see. So do I.

LETTER 65

Having Fun With Language

Fun sometimes visits you at odd times and for odd reasons. Sometimes it's even free. You've no need to buy anything, not even tickets to be entertained by musicians or athletes. Sometimes fun comes to you with no effort on your part.

Have you ever had fun with the English language? I hope so. I certainly have, though not in the early *learning* stages. I found little joy in memorizing rules of grammar and diagraming sentences, and I doubt that I laughed even once while building my basic vocabulary. Spelling contests, boys versus girls, were okay, except that the girls usually won, and everyone knew why. Girls had their noses tucked into spelling books while boys wrestled and made mudballs.

Thanks to the iron-fisted nuns who pounded all those language principles into my head, I left grade school with a fair knowledge of English. That was important. In those days, a person's grammar, like his or her manners, was a sure sign of social class. If a boy said, "She don't have no car," or if he chewed with his mouth open, he was looked down upon by *cultured* folks. He wasn't hated or even disliked, simply pitied and avoided.

In high school, my grasp of English tightened. There were weekly compositions to write and classical works to read and analyze. There were courses in Latin and Greek, from which I learned the roots of English words. "Where's the fun in that?" you may ask. Patience! The fun was yet to come.

By the time I joined the Navy, I had, in my vocabulary, the perfect word to describe what naval know-it-alls had done to the

English language. They had *transmogrified* it: changed it in ways that led to a ridiculous end-product. Naval memos and orders were drab as a November sky. They were short on adjectives, riddled with acronyms, and humorless. The words *I* and *we* were not used. Instead of writing, "*I have decided . . . ,*" authors wrote, "*It has been decided . . . ,*" with no clue of who the decider was. But a language as bad as the Navy's has one redeeming quality. It is a great tool for practical jokers.

Ensign Kurt Curtis and I, both stateside on temporary duty, watched all incoming mail for so-called permanent orders. Mine would let me regain civilian status. The war had ended, and I had put in enough time to merit prompt release. Kurt had not. He was a late starter, a green Californian shivering in Washington D.C., destined to be in uniform for months to come. His prayers were for orders that would carry him west, all expenses paid (for he had little money), where he could now and then see his girlfriend. He was most unhappy with the East and Easterners, and with winter in a world colored gray and tan. He was a patsy for a practical joke. Our Commanding Officer and I agreed on that, and on the gist of the bogus orders we'd draft.

Kurt's jaw sagged as he read what was in that envelope. Who ever heard of a ship called HBT 714? And based in New York City? Still, the orders were official. Of that Kurt had no doubt. The format was right. His name, rank, and number were correct, and there were seven copies of a single page of Navy jargon. An English translation would have read: *Get your things together. Take a train to NYC. Find the HBT 714 and give the captain a copy of these orders. Be there within 72 hours.*

So Kurt would have to head east, not west. All that remained was for some of us experienced officers to tell him about the HBT class of vessels. "Every day in New York the city's garbage is loaded onto big flat-bottomed boats nicknamed 'honey barges.' These are pushed a few miles out to sea and dumped. The HBT 714 is what does the pushing. It's a *H*oney *B*arge *T*ug. You might want to check it out in *JANE'S SHIP DIRECTORY.*"

Seeing Kurt find little joy in this explanation, we charged ahead. "There's a good side to your assignment, you know. It's *safe* duty, and you're in port every night. You also don't have the top brass looking over your shoulder—or anyone else if you don't bathe often. The downside of HBT duty are the escorts you'll have whenever you put to sea. There'll be thousands of gulls overhead the whole time you're outward bound, and because they recycle garbage, you may want to wear a raincoat and rain hat. In the summer there will be black clouds in between the garbage and the gulls. Those are flies. Some are there just to eat, others to arrange hatching places for their maggots, and still others just to pester you. Long sleeves, gloves, and mosquito netting over your head should protect you. Remember that your HBT will be *pushing* barges, not pulling them at the end of a long cable. You'll be in close. You're apt to pick up odors you don't like. Try using a gas mask."

We didn't prolong Kurt's agony. Our goal had been to see whether we could truly convince him that his orders were genuine. Once his expression and demeanor had made that clear to us, we set him straight. Two days later he got his real orders: shore duty in San Diego. I think he meant it when he said, "You guys sure had me depressed for a while, but that has only made these official orders all the better."

LETTER 66

What Your Great-Grandmother Was Like

As I pitched old papers yesterday, I came across this eulogy I wrote right after my mother (your great-grandmother) died. No doubt it needs editing. It was a spontaneous bit of writing done at a time when my thoughts were not of grammar. I include it in these letters to let you know something about one of your very best ancestors. The name "Gommie" was given to my mother by one of her grandsons who couldn't pronounce "Grandma" or much else.

*   *   *

When God created Gommie, He meant to give us a current example of what a Christian life should be. He overdid. For most of us, trying to describe the full range of Gommie's Christian characteristics is too great a challenge. Evidently, God intended for us to focus on only a few of her strong points. Four come immediately to mind.

First is what might be termed a mixture of hope and faith: a deep conviction that if she were to hope hard enough, everything would somehow turn out all right.

You see, Gommie was destined to live more than ninety years through a series of crises. As a very young girl, she was called upon to help teach her brother, who had been rendered deaf before age two, how to read lips, how to speak, and indeed how to live a full, normal life. That took twenty years of part-time effort. Gommie knew it would turn out well, and it did. Before she was thirty-five, she was widowed with five children, the youngest being nineteen months old. For most folks, this would have been panic time. For Gommie, it was the start of a new round of trials. She watched one child receive last rites, temporarily blinded by meningitis . . . another go rigid with tetanus.

She sent all three sons to sea in World War II, never doubting they would return, but she prayed all the same, just for added insurance, as though God might get too busy with other matters and need a reminder. She buried her mother and father, her only brother, her only sister, and hardest of all, two of her five children— two who were quite special to her. It took courage. It took hope. It took Gommie. Who else among us would be able to say, at age ninety, and only an hour or so after hearing that her 55-year-old son had died, "Haven't I been fortunate to have had such a happy life all these years?"

Gommie's second strong point: unselfishness. In a world replete with materialists and acquisitive people, Gommie was a maverick. Although she deeply appreciated the gifts people gave her, and she took immense comfort in owning the house that was home for 58 years, she never really longed for more of the material things of life. Intangibles, yes: companionship . . . conversation . . . the camaraderie which is part of large-family life (Gommie was very pro large families) . . . and the chance to see not only her children's children (all 22 of them) but their children as well. Gommie didn't want a "better" home, a new car, a modern TV set, or even new clothes. It is better, she thought, to do without so her children could have much more. She paid for five college educations, gave her children the best of food and clothing, and helped them get started buying their own homes. She ran a summer home, which, from June to September, was open to family and friends, and, not infrequently, near-strangers. How much all this was made possible because of Gommie's self-sacrifice, none of us knows. To hear her tell it, there really was no sacrifice. She wanted nothing she didn't already have.

Gommie's third virtue was a pervasive appreciation of beauty. With very few exceptions, she saw beauty in all she beheld. If she didn't see it on the surface, she found it inside. Her sometimes nondescript dogs had attractive personalities. In the giant oak tree in her side yard, she saw what Joyce Kilmer had seen. A menacing storm on Lake Michigan was beautiful, not fearsome. Beneath the homeliest human face there lurked some wonderful personality trait. Gommie discovered beauty in Shakespeare and Bach, in the creatures on her bird feeder, in the 24 to 36 people who each year gathered around her Christmas dinner table.

To most of us, Gommie's fourth virtue, her sense of humor, was the most obvious. There are far too few in our midst who can laugh when one of their children, on roller skates, tries unsuccessfully to deliver a piece of lemon meringue pie to the dining room table. Few, too, who could laugh as they drove barefoot from the beach in a Model A Ford two-door with five children, an English setter, three innertubes, and upwards of a dozen recently captured snapping turtles loose on the floorboard. We shall miss that sense of humor. Gommie inherited the seed of it from her father, then brought it to bloom on her own. It turned out to be a perennial. It never went dormant—not even on the last afternoon of her life when she suggested that the hospital chef drop around to her kitchen for a cooking lesson.

We have much to be grateful for. Gommie's passing was painless for her and for all three living children who were by her side. She had always hoped never to have to leave her home, and as with so many other hopes she had, everything turned out all right. Except for her last few days she *stayed* in the home she loved.

During her lifetime, Gommie relied heavily on Saint Anthony to help her find lost keys, mislaid records, wandering dogs, and strayed children. She never doubted his ability, and he never disappointed her. Let us hope that Saint Anthony can now help us find what we have just lost: this magnificent influence on so many of us.

LETTER 67

How Folks Copy Nature

Did I mention this in one of these letters? Man finds something marvelous in Nature, pokes around at it, discovers a bit about it, and brags about how smart he is for having investigated so expertly. (Incidentally, I use the word *Man* to mean all sorts of human beings—male, female, eunuch, hermaphrodite). If he likes what he sees, he may make copies of it, though not terribly good copies, not nearly so exquisite as the originals. The false teeth he makes don't stay put. His artificial joints wear out. His plastic flowers last longer than garden-fresh ones but lack their delicate beauty. His fake ducks attract live ones, but they don't lay eggs or sprout feathers or waddle or grow tasty meat.

As he basks in self-glory, Man gives too little credit to the Maker of all that natural beauty around him. I find that strange in an amusing sort of way. I can't get upset about it or go preaching religion to him. Instead, I like to look at—and smile at—some of his copies.

Take his houses, for instance. In building a house, he copies parts of the human body as near as I can tell. The skeleton is I-bars and lumber, mostly 2 x 4s. Metal hinges let doors pivot the way the human elbow does. Whereas the body has a layer of fat to keep heat from moving in or out too quickly, the house has bats or blobs of insulation.

People wear hats or open their umbrellas to keep from being drenched by rain and scorched by sun. Houses wear roofs for the same reasons. A houses's eyelids, its drapes, open and close to let in light or keep it out. Bodies burn food for warmth; houses burn fuel. Bodies have intestines and renal systems, in part to get rid of waste; houses have plumbing, including toilets and garbage disposals and intestinal pipes. When a house gets constipated, the laxative is Drano, the enema a snake.

As Man tried to put copies of the human nervous system into houses, he didn't get very far. He used lots of wire, all right, and quite a few switches, but his copy was mighty crude compared to the human wiring diagram. Instead of even trying for a copy of the human brain, he settled for a few tiny brains no better than a pinch of chicken brain. One of those was the thermostat. It compares temperatures in a room, oven, refrigerator, or washing machine to preset temperatures, and decides whether to throw switches. The house's security system is perhaps a slightly better brain. It has to check more than just temperature before deciding whether to flip a switch.

A house, like a person, has built-in resistance to small critters. It isn't an invincible resistance, though. People *do* succumb to viruses, houses to termites. Bigger 'critters' can wound and even kill. A falling tree collapses a house or flattens a man.

Houses, like bodies, are covered with skin, some of which can blister in torrid sunlight. The skin gets dirty and needs washing. It develops rashes, usually caused by fungi. It benefits from cosmetics: paints applied to siding and trim. It shows its age, although more by creaking than by wrinkling.

When Man beheld stalks of bamboo, he found them so remarkably flexible that he used them as fishing poles. Those tapered bundles of long fibers bent but would not break when tugged at by the feistiest of fish. So Man said "Ah!" and set out to bundle some other fibers (e.g. glass and graphite). In some ways, the copies were better than the originals, though lots more expensive.

And how did Man figure out how to make fibers? Was it by watching spiders and silkworms? Through a tiny hole, each of them pushes a thick liquid that keeps its cylindrical shape after it oozes through the hole and "gels." The greater the volume of liquid pushed through the hole or pulled through from the far side, the longer the fiber. A spider attaches the start of its fiber to, say, a ceiling, then uses its falling body weight to pull the liquid through the tiny hole. Man attaches the start of his fiber to a wind-up spool, and the hole he uses is made in metal, not spider tissue, but the principle is the same: liquid→hole→"gel"→pull.

The camera is Man's copy of the eye. Each has a lens: a double-convex lens. Each has an iris (diaphragm) that opens wide in dark rooms and all but closes on a sunny beach. Each can focus on objects nearby or far away. Each can be fitted with corrective lenses. Each can wear sunglasses (filters). There are differences, of course. The eye needs no film or tape, and it develops and files its pictures, immediately, and at no cost. Still, its pictures can't be shown to others.

Isn't it nice to know that if Man's progress depends on his making copies, Nature still has so many originals to offer him? Some he has yet to discover; others are just way too complex for him.

LETTER 68

The Flat Cat

I'm in a jocose mood. It's a carryover from last night. Right before I fell asleep, I laughed quietly and convulsively. Once before when this happened, your grandmother woke up, fussed about my having shaken the bed, and ordered me to stop reading Thurber tales late at night. What shook the bed last night wasn't Thurber. It was my memory of an article in a St. Louis newspaper.

The article was about a man, his six-year-old daughter, a middle-aged woman, and a flattened cat. I don't recall any of their names, or even whether the cat *had* a name, so I'll give the people aliases. Finding suitable names should not be a problem. Your grandmother has collected strange names of real people, and I've filed them away alphabetically. Here are ten good ones:

> Earl Barneycastle, Shaelynn Desiree Dawn Beasley, Ussery
> Orlanda Byrd, Seven Caloudas, Exzayveon Campbell, Misty
> Dawn Chapman, Madison Cloberdants, Orgo Craig, Elmer
> Eigenschenk, Heaven Noel Flores.

The man that I now name Orgo Craig, has taken his daughter, Misty, to a mall on a Saturday. He has no idea what they are shopping for, nor does she. As they leave their parked car and walk toward the shops, they come upon a flattened cat. Orgo's notion of what to do is quite simple: walk around it or step over it. After all, it no longer needs human help.

Now this cat has not been lying there long. There's a lot of scarlet mixed with grays and browns. Crows have not yet spotted it, or if they have, they're afraid to dine in a busy parking lot.

Misty is saddened by the sight. She can't just walk away or around or over. The poor cat must not be left lying there like that. It deserves a proper burial.

I should point out that Misty, like most young girls, knows what it takes to have her way when her parents disagree with her. To get the better of her mother, Misty must pout and weep, and sometimes scream or stamp. Even then, her mother may stand firm. But to get her father to give in, all Misty needs to do is give him *that special look*. She need not make a sound. He'll understand; he'll melt. It's a basic tenet of daughter-versus-father philosophy.

So Orgo knows he must do whatever it takes to inter this heap of offal, this gory splat that once was a cat. The question is: how to go about it? Maybe he can somehow wrap the mess in newspaper. Easier said than done. Even if he can find some newspaper in a trash barrel, he is not about to touch this tangle of fur and intestines, or even kick it onto the newspaper. He is squeamish. He also wonders about the diseases that might lie there on the asphalt. There's no telling where that cat has been. He knows that cats like to party and that their parties often sound mighty wild. The risk of social disease is high.

Orgo returns to the car hoping to find rags. What he finds is much better: a Nieman Marcus shopping bag and a cheap, short-handled windshield scraper. Luckily, he is able to scoop the cat into the bag without being seen by friends or strangers. He trots the bag back to the car and sets it on the trunk lid. He can decide later how to tie it to the bumper for the trip home. One thing sure, this was an outdoors cat. It does not belong indoors, not even in the trunk.

As Orgo and Misty set out once more for the shops, another character arrives. Let's call her Heaven Noel Flores. Having parked her car well away from Orgo's, she walks close enough to it to see the Nieman Marcus bag on the trunk lid. My lucky day, she thinks. How could anyone be so careless as to buy something in a classy store and then just leave it like that?

Ms. Flores's eyes sweep the parking lot in search of witnesses. None in sight, or so she thinks as she lifts the bag by its handles. She walks toward the shops, not hurriedly, and not stopping to see what is inside the just-stolen bag. Her immediate goal is to lose herself in the crowd. There will be plenty of time later to check on this bagged treasure.

What she does not realize is that Orgo had seen her seize the bag. Although he has high hopes of seeing her discover that her loot is not really Nieman Marcus merchandise, there is Misty to consider. She needs to be shielded from what has happened. Until this can all be straightened out, the funeral will have to wait. Orgo takes Misty to a small shop and tells her to amuse herself there until he gets back from some of his own "shopping."

He finds and follows Ms. Flores who goes, not to a shop, but to a restaurant where she orders lunch before taking a peak inside the bag. That's when she faints at the sight of all those entrails mixed with bits of fur, and what seem to be small paws.

The restaurant manager calls for an ambulance, and Ms. Flores is about to be carted away, still not fully conscious, when a waiter comes running. "Here," he says. "This belongs to her." And he hands the bag to the paramedic.

LETTER 69

Skate Keys and Rumble Seats

To a few friends, age 70+, I said, "If you were to ask one of your grandchildren what a *skate key* was, you'd probably get a shrug and a blank look. The same thing might happen if you were to ask about *party lines* or *rumble seats*. What are some other terms so clear to us but not to our grandchildren?" I wanted to use one or more such terms as the subject of one of these letters. With luck, I'd give you another glimpse of life as it once was.

You younger folks need no *skate key* when you blade or skate. You slip your feet into special "shoes" with wheels attached, tie laces or press Velcro, and take off. You're helmeted and padded, injury-proof. You make better speed than we did, and your glide is much quieter. You even have better places to hone your skills: bike paths, ramps, paved play areas, indoor rinks.

We had to attach our roller skates to our regular shoes, and that's why we carried *skate keys*. They weren't really keys at all. They were small, key-shaped wrenches. Except for a leather ankle strap, our skates were all steel. We adjusted each skate to the right length and tightened a nut to lock that length in place. We then strapped on the skate and used the skate key to tighten a clamp that held the skate and shoe together up front.

If you wonder why we had to adjust the skate's *length*, it was a matter of money. We didn't throw away our skates just because our feet grew. Also, we eventually passed skates along to siblings with smaller feet. In some homes, skates were family property; kids took turns.

Our real problem wasn't putting on skates. It was finding a proper place to skate. Parents thought kids should use sidewalks, not streets. But sidewalks were all wrong. They were concrete slabs five feet long, laid end to end, and separated by gaps wide enough to snag our small skate wheels. If only people had learned to pave driveways and paths with asphalt!

Under the sidewalks-only rule, we nearly quit skating. Although we had broken no bones, we were bruised and cut and scraped. We also dreaded having to get stitched up by a doctor who either had no pain killer or who saw no need to waste it on kids' cuts.

But suddenly all the neighborhood parents relented. Maybe they felt sorry for us. Or maybe they wanted us to stop dumping all those ripped and bloody clothes in the hampers. Whatever the reason, we kids had won a rare victory over our parents. If we could find a patch of street where cars almost never went, we could skate there. Our choice was the dead-end of Sherwood Drive. We went there week-day afternoons until our interest in skating faded, and we played a weird sort of hockey: broomsticks, tin cans for pucks, the storm sewer opening for a goal.

The games were hard on skate wheels. From the worn-out ones, we salvaged the ball bearings for later use in slingshots and marble games. I should remember how much Mr. Mueller charged us for new wheels—5¢? 10¢?—but I don't. I bought quite a few in my time, and not just to put on skates. I used them on a scooter that I made, and on many model race cars.

Y'all have no cause to envy us our skating days. On your in-line wheels, you go miles in an hour. We spent hours in a space the size of a living room floor. What you *should* envy us are the *rumble seats* we had.

Picture this car, if you will. It's a coupe. Its covered section has just enough room for the driver and one passenger. Out back, folded up under what looks to be a trunk lid, is a seat wide enough for two more passengers. That's the *rumble seat*. To get into it, once you've opened the lid, you step up two rubber pads on the rear fender. When you're back there, you're out in the weather. There's no cover.

What was so great about *rumble seats*? Well it has to do with a popular social practice: dating. If a boy in high school or college had $1.00-$1.25 to spend and could get a car or a ride, he called a girl and asked her for a date for Friday or Saturday night. If she said no, he called another girl. But always, it was the boy who had to make the call, pay for the movie and for the sundaes or whatever after the movie, and furnish the transportation. If the boy couldn't get a car for the night of the date, he double-dated—that is, he and his girl tagged along with another couple.

Now if the other couple just happened to have a car with a rumble seat, so much the better. Riding along back there with the wind in his face a boy—a *normal boy*—just felt obligated to keep his girl warm by snuggling, and a girl—a *normal girl*—thought he was most considerate, even when the wind wasn't all that chilly.

LETTER 70

The Tin Lizzie Worth Fifteen Cartwheels

I've decided to explain more of those old terms.

We had nicknames for money. A quarter was *two bits*, a half-dollar coin *four bits*. We called the paper dollar a *buck* and the silver dollar a *cartwheel*. The five-dollar bill was a *fin*, the ten a *sawbuck*, the twenty a *double sawbuck*, the hundred a *C-note*. Of course this was all talk. We almost never held a bill as large as a *fin*, and we never did hold a three-dollar-bill, for there was no such thing, but we mentioned it in our insults: "He's as odd as a three-dollar bill." Barber shops had a jingle, "Shave and a haircut, *two bits*," but that was before my first whisker poked through. I had to pay *two bits* just for a haircut.

In our house were several objects whose names must be foreign to you. My *chiffonnier* was later called a dresser, and then a chest of drawers. I still have it, still use it. It was custom made in the 1930s: solid walnut, no plywood. In the top drawer I once kept *garters* and gold *collar buttons*. The garters, when I wore them, kept my socks from dropping to my ankles. A few of my shirts had stiffly starched detachable collars. To attach them, I used the collar buttons.

Some of our sayings are all but forgotten now. *Don't get your dander up* meant don't get mad. When something mechanical broke down, it was *on the Fritz*. Anyone really old was *long in the tooth*. To get someone to go away we ordered him to *scram* or *beat it*.

Perhaps you know what a *privy* is, but I'll bet you never used one or smelled one. You *do* know how to *gee* and *haw*, though not by those terms. *Gee* means turn right; *haw* means turn left. Mules learn those words early in life. Have you an *icebox* in your kitchen? Of course not. Where would you find an *iceman* to bring you blocks of ice every few days?

Throughout my boyhood, we were never on a *party line*. Mother considered it a poor way to skimp. Here's how party lines worked. The phone company offered low rates to those willing to share a phone line with strangers. If subscriber X agreed, the phone company set up a party line to be used by, say, X, Y, and Z. Any one of them could make a phone call provided none of the others was using the line. It was, of course, irritating for Y to pick up his phone and hear X or Z talking to friends or creditors. Cost saving was supposed to make up for the irritation.

Even in grade school, we kids could see the opportunity for party-line mischief. All we had to do (from Jimmy Corbin's house) was listen in on party-line conversations and offer comments. When an adult female voice complained of being unable to find elegant dresses that fit, we suggested she try a tent and awning company.

It's too bad you weren't around to see the *tin lizzie*, known also as the Model T Ford. It came in several body styles but only one color: black. Until 1928, when Ford's Model A appeared, the tin lizzie was *the* family car in the U.S. Folks judged it (charitably) to be reliable, affordable, and easy to drive. Whatever electricity it needed came, not from a battery, but from a magneto. Start the tin lizzie with a crank, and the magneto supplied enough power to run the engine and brighten the headlights. The driver had three foot pedals to push (forward, reverse, and brake) and a hand lever to speed up or slow down. If the brake was worn out—and it often was—the driver pushed the reverse pedal. That did only a *fair* job of stopping the car.

Five of us took off in Claud Camuzzi's *tin lizzie* for state high school tournaments. Claud and Ken were golfers; Dave, Jack, and I played tennis. We had our doubts, before we started, whether that car would hold up for 125 hilly miles. It was a good enough tin lizzie, a *phaeton* with only two small rips in its canvas top, and Claud had paid top money ($15) for it only two months earlier. Still, a trip that long would be quite a test.

On the down side of the third hill, that car got to going *lickety-split*, and Dave, the cautious one in our midst, said he thought Claud should go slower. Claud told him that that might not be possible. The brakes were shot, and stomping on the reverse pedal didn't seem to do much good on really steep hills. So on we drove. With each new hill came a new thrill. That tin lizzie strained and shuddered to climb hills, then plummeted like an elevator with a snapped cable. We hadn't been on the road two hours when things got sportier: driving rain, dreadful visibility, slick roads, bald tires. Even $15 tin lizzies didn't come with new tires.

By the end of the trip we were soaked, hungry, and chilled, but mostly relieved to be on a flat street. As Claud drove along the main street at a legal speed, a traffic light half a block ahead turned red. Claud floored the reverse pedal. Too late! We broad-sided a crossing car, a lawyer's car. The police and the lawyer made Claud try to prove that his car had brakes. He drove it slowly and brought it to a stop, but he held his foot on the pedal a mite too long, and the car began to back up. In the end, the lawyer opted not to sue or have Claud jailed. Five wretched kids plus a junker of a car—a lost cause. There was an old-fashioned saying for what that lawyer must have thought: *You can't squeeze blood out of a turnip.*

LETTER 71

What It's Like To Grow Old

Yesterday while walking south on Lakeshore Drive, I met a tail-wagging Golden Retriever tethered to a woman in her thirties. He might have been smiling. I couldn't tell because his mouth was busy holding a teddy bear by its hind feet, a large teddy bear, half again the size of the dog's head. The woman at the far end of the leash didn't wait for me to ask. She evidently had met any number of curious strangers. "He won't go for a walk without his teddy bear," she explained.

It's nice to meet a happy dog with a personality. Most dogs today are too penned up to be happy. Seldom do they get to go bum around with other dogs, but are instead stuck with people.

I turned around after a half-mile, and sure enough, on my way home, I again met that Golden. This time he *was* smiling. His human companion held the teddy bear. "As soon as we turn around he drops his teddy bear, and won't budge until I pick it up," she told me. I should have asked what happened when the two of them walked around several blocks rather than doing an about-face. Would the dog sense the half-way mark and drop his toy? I wish more people were like this Golden: happy, harmless, and pleasantly eccentric. He is a middle-aged dog. Will he be like this when he gets old? I hope so.

Why do I imagine his aging? It's because these days thoughts of aging—especially my own—invade my head the way bees go into a half-empty coke can.

If you think that growing old is all bad, and you probably do, you're about 75% right. The arithmetic of aging bears you out.

Wrinkles and aches are added. Cartilage and long-time friends are subtracted. Attention is divided. Worries, descendants, and skin blotches multiply. Height contracts; gas expands. The body sags and grays. Some of its parts wear out. Others fall out or are taken out, and one by one those sources of pleasure dry up: the stomach has trouble with spicy foods, reflexes refuse to hurry, stamina is just a word, the brain wants to nap.

Ah! but there's also a bit of happiness in aging. Folks think about us oldsters the way I think about that Golden Retriever. They don't mind our being eccentric. Or if they do mind, they don't say so. We can be odd when we're babies and again when we're old, and not be criticized for it. Babies are said to be cute, old people to be quaint. Only during those in-between years must we conform. If at that time we butter our bread with our fingers we're regarded as neither cute nor quaint, but downright *strange*, unfit for places in polite society.

Folks are also nice to us oldsters in other ways. They judge us to be falling apart faster than we really are. If we let them believe that, all sorts of wonderful things happen. We get driven around. The numbers on our tax forms get set right. Our snow gets shoveled, our groceries delivered, our carpets vacuumed, and all the while, these caring folks feel warm inside for having helped the frail and forgetful in their midst.

There's just one catch. Sometimes an oldster doesn't want to be helped. He or she wants *not* to be helped because to accept help is to admit weakness of mind or muscle or both.

When you're old and male, you get lots more smiles from young females than you did while middle-aged. Now if only they were *romantic* smiles!

The worst part about getting old is that it's a fear-filled time of life. Oldsters fear harder and oftener and about more dangers than ever before. They're afraid of being alone, of being duped, of getting sick, of getting into accidents, of going broke, of having families forsake them, of being put into "homes," of getting lost, of becoming burdens. Real fears or imaginary? Makes no difference. Nature provides at least *some* relief from all this fear. The old have had many years to accumulate happy memories which they can now recall.

Lest the world feel a tad sad about its old folks, there's a blessing worth noting. Oldsters are very nearly free of responsibility. No one expects anything of them. Well, almost no one. Tax people will still expect seniors' checks, and grandchildren will expect birthday presents. But few younger folks will press seniors to *act* or to *hurry*.

I've concluded that a person's age determines how he or she reacts to change. Young folks accept it—unless it upsets their lives *too* drastically—and figure it's for the better. They move from one job to another, one city to another, one spouse to another. They don't even seethe, as we old folks do, when an automated phone system orders them to dial googol numbers or forces them to listen to mortuary music as they wait for the sound of a human voice. Old folks have had their fill of change. They're ready for a steady-as-you-go life. They prefer familiar foods, well-worn shoes, and self-sculpted chair seats. Even so, old folks like to brag about all the changes they've witnessed: telephones, penicillin, computers and TV, heart transplants, and tailored DNA.

On this afternoon's walk I shall learn that eccentric Golden's name. Yesterday we just smiled at each other in passing. It's time we were introduced.

LETTER 72

Our Ailing English Language

English is on the endangered language list. It will be slow to die, for its enemies are a patient, if also determined, lot. Like arsenic poisoners, they take their time. Known by some as the *Anything Goes Mob*, they flaunt the rules of grammar openly and often.

Granted, that set of rules (or laws) is complex enough to invite flaunting. Who can memorize all those laws with all those many "exceptions": I-before-E *except* after C; when to use *which* rather than *that*; when to repeat a word immediately within a sentence (It's all right to say *too, too* cold or *very, very* hot, but not *the the* coffee)?

And then there are those many words with multiple meanings:

> The *present* is as good a time as any to *present* a *present*.
> The *invalid* signed an *invalid* form.
> As a trash collector, you can't *refuse refuse*.
> Do the *Polish polish* their silver?
> His garden will *produce produce* if the rabbits don't eat it.
> How could she *desert* her family in the *desert*?
> He's mighty *wound* up over that tiny *wound* on his hand.
> The people in the third *row* stirred up quite a *row*.
> I *object* to his putting that *object* in his front yard.
> Catch a black *bass*, sing a *bass* note, beat a *bass* drum.
> Get a *close* friend to *close* your garage door.
> The farmer must *sow* wheat, then feed his *sow*.
> The king will *subject* every *subject* in his realm to taxes.
> An April *shower* may ruin an outdoor bridal *shower*.

We've had these complexities of the language right along. What's new are attitudes toward the language. The *Anything Goes Mob*, evidently a very large group, would have us all break the laws of language. This, of course, upsets us law abiders. We regard the person who speaks proper English as educated, cultured, civilized. Proper English, like clean fingernails, is a sign of how high a person has risen above the chimpanzee level.

There are reasons aplenty for the growth of the *Anything Goes Mob*. Certain groups would like to see their own languages gain ground on English. Some want Spanish to become a strong second language in the U.S. Others want an Afro-American lingo better recognized by schools. The French, it would seem, hope to keep English from becoming the universal language.

But what really sparked the growth of the *Anything Goes Mob* was the feminist movement. Before that took hold, we could speak the word "mankind" meaning human beings of all sorts: large and small, young and old, male and female, every color; and when someone spoke or wrote the word "man" (without referring to a particular male), the meaning was clear: no particular gender. To have said, "Man is a creature of habit," or "Man has his faults," meant females as well as males.

Feminists objected. They insisted we all be neutered. A Chairman had to became a Chairperson. No longer could we call the police station and ask to speak to a police*man*. The feminists were kind enough to spare us a few male-sounding words. The Navy could still train a midship*man* or a sea*man*. *Man*hole covers didn't become peoplehole covers. Our garbage*man* didn't change his title. The "*Men*" signs on rest room doors didn't come down.

These concessions were quite welcome. Still, the English language was about to be gravely injured. Why? Because there were no pronouns to go with all those neutered or asexual or hermaphroditic nouns. For example, what pronouns fit the blanks in this sentence: "If someone has an idea in _____ head, let _____ now raise _____ hand." The subject of the sentence is singular (someONE). So is the verb (HAS). See the problem? This someone can't have an idea in *their* head. Each person, even a neutered person, has his or her or own head—a single head—and lends it to no one.

In pre-feminist days the sentence would have read "If someone has an idea in *his* head, let *him* now raise *his* hand." And in my grade school, more girls than boys raised hands. Today, to keep both the feminists and us law-abiding linguists happy, we must write awkwardly: "If someone has an idea in *his* or *her* head, let *him* or *her* now raise *his* or *her* hand."

There is fine word for what has happened to the language: transmogrified. (I've used that word in earlier letters). It means changed in a way that has led to a ridiculous result. Perhaps someone will develop some new words, new pronouns (her-r-him, his-r-hers, heeshee).

A lot depends upon what we want the language to do. In New Guinea years ago I managed to "converse" with natives using pidgin English and gestures. We didn't pass one another much information or learn much about one another. You might say we just got by, using a language with few rules. But today, in the U.S.A., I expect lots more from the language. I want it to tell me about the person who speaks it or writes it.

LETTER 73

My Happiest Day

Here's a challenge for you. Answer the question: What was the happiest day of your life? If you're like most folks, you've had so many happy days you're hard put to name the happiest. Once you're married you're apt to be scared into saying, "My wedding day." Any other reply could get you a semi-friendly swat.

But what of all those other great days? The day you got your first bike or first car or first kiss? That special birthday: age sixteen and able to drive, or age twenty-one when you became (legally) a grown-up? Maybe the day you graduated was your happiest. Or was it the day you were given a prestigious trophy? Could it have been a special Christmas, or the day you got a substantial promotion, or the day you got engaged?

For me, the No. 1 day on the *Happy List* was none of the above, and guess what! I can't remember the exact date or even what day of the week it was. I know it was late July, 1945. The build-up for it began nearly two months earlier. That's when our captain, John, handed me two sheets of paper.

Come back with me to that steamy day in May, 1945. We are at anchor in Leyte Gulf. Things are quiet here now, not like they were less than a year ago when the world's all-time biggest naval battle raged. Now you can get 10-to-1 odds from American pilots that the war will be over by September. The Japs are short of fuel and planes and experienced pilots. About all they can do is dispatch young pilots with only enough fuel for one-way trips. They are the suicide pilots, the kamikazes.

The first paper John hands me is a copy of orders to W. W. Fiebig. He is to stop doing whatever he is doing, go find the USS YMS 393, and report to John as my replacement. The other paper orders me to head home once W. W. Fiebig shows up. I am to make my own travel arrangements and take thirty days' leave starting the day I set foot in the continental U.S.A.

Well, I know what to do first. I must find W. W. Fiebig as soon as he gets within a hundred miles of our ship. I can't just sit and wait. For all I know he may not be eager to climb aboard a wooden-hulled ship and get shot at and bombed. Why, he may even be just plain slow in the head about finding his way. I hope he isn't looking for our ship in Europe. I must get friends ashore to let me know if he arrives by ship or plane, or if he picks up mail or checks into Officers' Quarters. I must also ask a ship's carpenter to be ready to make me a sea chest.

Just in case you don't know about sea chests, I'll tell you. Sailors, when they come aboard, do not carry suitcases. There's no room to store empty suitcases. Enlisted men pack their belongings in duffle bags. Officers use wooden sea chests, which are knocked apart to save storage space.

I have a decision to make. When W. W. Fiebig *does* show up, should I take the fastest form of transportation (military planes) or the slowest. I'm really anxious to get home. I haven't seen your grandmother for about 22 months. When I left, Ken (father of some of you, uncle to the others) was 10 days old. Now he's walking and talking. I'm also ready to leave the war zone, however quiet it may now be. I long to be one of those who make good on this year's slogan: *BACK ALIVE IN '45.* The argument against hurrying home is the chance of being shipped back out after 30 days. The Navy does like to put experienced sailors back on fighting ships.

W. W. Fiebig is here! It took him a while—late May to early July—but I'm glad to see him. It's time to pack my sea chest and shave this beard. I've opted for a *fairly* slow trip back, a troop transport bound for San Francisco. What I turned down was a *really* slow freighter headed for New Orleans via the Panama Canal. Too bad I'm not allowed to tell your grandmother what ship I'll be on or when it docks. I just tell her where we'll meet in San Francisco, and approximately when.

The troop transport is pretty comfortable. It's big enough not to roll much and slow enough not to pitch much. The galley is staffed with Javanese (not Japanese!) cooks, so I eat tasty curry entrees. But these same Javanese also know how to fix my kind of breakfast: two fried eggs atop a stack of hotcakes encircled with strips of bacon. The sky is clear of enemy planes and scary clouds. I don't have to stand midnight-to-4AM watches. It's a pleasant trip. Or it would be except for the sight of my fellow passengers. So many warriors going home without the arms and feet and eyes they had brought, so many hideous scars.

We sail along, the breezes a lot crisper than those near the equator. What will it be like to wear a sweater again? Ah! Land ho! The Golden Gate Bridge is dead ahead. I must get topside as we pass beneath it. I must see its underside and treasure the moment. I must be alone lest someone see these tears trickling down my cheek. Grown men don't weep, and naval officers? Never.

We are anchored and may not go ashore tonight, so I sleep fitfully. I half-expect some sort of welcoming as I come ashore in the morning, maybe a small band or a few people with banners, if not for me, at least for all the wounded. I am met instead by a customs officer who goes through the stuff in my sea chest, finds nothing of interest to him, and sends me on my way. Twenty minutes later, your grandmother and I are reunited—the happiest day of my life.

LETTER 74

The Number One Invention

When I play singles these days, my opponents are all younger than I. My peers either play doubles wearing elastic bands on their elbows and knees, or they play golf so as never to run. George, who is just four years my junior, is an exception. He hates doubles, says doubles is something you order in a bar, and as for golf, he claims he'd as soon ride a hearse as a golf cart. George exaggerates.

One day last week, after we had played two sets and sat court side in the shade, George started up one of our bragging-about-grandkids bouts. He should know better. He has only four grandchildren. Surely at least one of my fifteen can top whatever one of his four does. Arithmetic is on my side.

"Timmy asked me a question I couldn't answer: 'Grandpa, what's the best invention since you were born?'" George said. "He may have thought I'd say it was the automobile, but I'm not *that* old! I told him I'd have to think about it. What do you think was the best invention of the last 70-odd years?"

I couldn't answer him right off either, probably because there have been so very many inventions in my lifetime. Someone once told me that Edison had over a thousand patents when he died. Of course, lots of his were before my time, but thousands of other inventors followed him. Instead of giving George my quick nomination for *best* invention, I got us started down memory lane. We tried to recall as *many* inventions, major and minor, as we could.

Being court side, I was without paper and pencil. Too bad. I'm bound to miss a few of the items we covered, but here are the ones that stuck in my head. For the home, practically every appliance was invented after I was born: the electric washing machine, toaster, clothes dryer, refrigerator, microwave oven, mixer, blender, vacuum cleaner. Although the radio had been invented earlier, few homes had radios for quite a while because of a lack of broadcasting stations.

Entertainment? What you see today—and some that has come and gone—was invented during George's and my lives. TV→Color TV→VCRs→video games. As for sound, the inventions included transistor radios, stereo systems, tape recorders, and CDs. For frivolous fun there were frisbees, hula hoops, silly putty, and skateboards. Movies were invented and gradually improved: silent films→talkies→color→3D and IMAX.

If discoveries are to be counted along with inventions, the list grows. DNA. By-pass surgery. Organ transplants. Penicillin.

The Big War got inventors moving fast. They had to and did come up with synthetic rubber after the Japs grabbed most of the world's rubber trees. They put nylon into parachutes and invented 2,4-D to kill Jap food crops. They figured out how to unleash atomic energy, and built superior bomb-sights. They came up with radar and, later, with guided missiles.

George and I pared our best invention list to three:

DNA—We chose this because its future seems awesome. As scientists now modify DNA samples, they stand to improve and lengthen human lives. Bad germs can be "fixed" so they don't have offspring. Crops can be made resistant to insects and fungi. Livestock can be cloned to be uniformly "superior." What is scary is that scientists may "improve" people in wrong ways.

PLASTICS—Nature gave us some pretty good raw materials with which to make things: wood, metals, stone; and Man has added one very good class: plastics. They're in or around or over just about everything we have. The fibers of our carpets and (part of) our clothes are plastic. So too, the paint on our houses and the varnish on our furniture. The films of our shower curtains, our grocery sacks, the gears of our alarm clocks, our sports equipment, our tires and steering wheels all contain plastic. Often we use plastics to improve natural materials: plastic glues in plywood, plastic composites in fishing rods, tennis racquets, and golf clubs.

COMPUTER—This is my choice for the best of the bunch. It has been the heart of the technical revolution. It started out simply enough. It was a high speed adding machine for accountants. But those close to the great machine spotted its greater powers. It was a quick learner, and once it was taught properly, it solved complex problems reliably at lightning speed. It could deal with words as well as numbers, learn from experience (playing chess against human opponents, for example), handle telephone networks, draw pictures and graphs, store and retrieve information, and throw switches in timely fashion.

But best of all, it could get human beings to consider whole new ways to tackle their problems. Engineers could test designs and materials by simulation rather than actual trial. Doctors could get rapid analyses of complex data. A useful Internet system could be created. Satellites could be launched. Space travel was possible.

Nor were we ordinary folks left out. We had a whole new way to go about writing, for example. Now we could revise over and over, as often as we pleased, without using erasers or scissors or staples or glue, and if we didn't like to type, we could dictate to the computer and watch our words appear on the screen.

LETTER 75

Memorable Meals in Faraway Places

Some folks say I am lucky to have seen so much of the world. I suppose that's so. East as far as Budapest. West to Seoul, Korea. North to Alaska. South to some uninhabited spot in Australia. The most fun I ever had traveling was my trip to Europe with the Boy Scouts. I've seen mountains and glaciers, museums and cathedrals, castles and hovels, deserts and jungles, royalty, and Mussolini. I've ridden ocean liners and New Guinea dugouts, helicopters and jumbo jets, tin lizzies and Jaguars.

Lots of our retiree friends like to travel for any of several reasons. They see it as an educational experience or a way to escape their humdrum lives at home. Some seem bent on spending money that might otherwise go to the IRS, and some, I'm sure, see travel mainly as a way to make new friends.

Sad to say, travel no longer tempts me. I got to where I hated living out of suitcases, eating strange food at strange hours, standing in queues, and rushing to catch busses and planes. Certain hardships aren't all that bad, and can be looked back upon as funny. Like showering in Europe. In many European cities, the hotel rooms are tiny compared to those in the U.S. When you shower, you must stand still. If you turn or take even a short step, you're apt to hit a handle or curtain or be out of the shower completely. If you drop the thumb-sized bar of soap that the hotel issues you, you're not quite sure about bending to pick it up.

Before I retired, in those days when I had nothing better to do with my time than work for money, I traveled abroad now and then. Of the places I went, Japan was my favorite. Strange, isn't it?

I used to shoot at these people, and they used to shoot back or try dropping a bomb on me. But that was years ago. I called them Japs then or worse. Now we smile at one another, bow to one another, and do business.

Going to Japan was like visiting another world. Whereas Europe was like an old (shriveled?) U. S., Japan was something else. The people were different—better in some ways, worse in others. In Tokyo, I could leave cash or a watch or a camera atop my hotel dresser and be certain it would not be stolen. Workaholics were everywhere: from board rooms to factory floors and secretaries' desks. Roads were repaired at night, not during busy daylight hours. Every car looked freshly washed, and there must have been a law against driving any car with a dent or rust spot. I counted all such cars I could spot in a week: 2!

Women's Lib hadn't gotten very far when I was there. A woman was still apt to walk behind her man rather than alongside him, but now she was free to step on his shadow. In offices, women held inferior positions and knew better than to get ahead of a man when an elevator door opened. In the evenings wives stayed home; husbands, if they chose to, found female "friends."

The southern island of Japan is Kyushu. It is the place where the gods are said to have watched the rising sun and created Japan. It is also where I ate two never-to-be-forgotten meals. Unlike Tokyo, Kyushu has stayed old-fashioned. The natives wear kimonos and sandals, not suits and shoes. In rural Kyushu, the plumbing is primitive, the traffic is light, and English is all but unspoken.

We drove along Kyushu's eastern coast, my business companions and I, heading for a chemical plant further north. For lunch, we visited a seaside restaurant where fish swam in indoor canals and patrons walked footbridges to get to their tables. We sat, Japanese style, on floor cushions around a low table. We saw no menus, simply took what was served.

It was a huge platter piled high with chipped ice, on top of which were all sorts of raw seafood: shrimp, squid, fish, octopus, clam, turtle, lobster; and buried in the mound of chipped ice was a fish about the size of those in the restaurant canals. He was evidently too cold to wiggle free, but there he lay, working his jaw as though he were chewing gum. As the meal progressed and the ice melted, the truth was laid bare. The gasping fish had undergone surgery. Someone had cut slices from him without killing him, and put those slices atop the ice. That fish watched us eat him! Now I like my fish fresh, but that's a bit too fresh, don't you agree?

At another memorable meal, I was served a Japanese delicacy: a bowl teeming with live minnows. To make sure they were really active, the waitress added several drops of vinegar. My host explained that these very special creatures, whose name meant "dancing fish" in English, were not to be chewed, but swallowed whole. I was to feel them wiggle on their way to my stomach, and it would be quite rude for me to refuse. Ugh!

LETTER 76

Idioms That Have Kicked the Bucket

Idiom. You almost never hear that word. It's a word used by teachers of English, and promptly forgotten by students. Although most of us can't define it, we utter idioms in everyday conversations. Perhaps we say, "Her boss *sacked* her," or "He *kicked the bucket.*" Our messages have nothing to do with sacks or buckets or kicking; they are about firing and dying. An idiom, then, is an expression whose meaning is not clear from the meaning of the word or words that make it up.

Idioms, like people, may live long or die young. Which is why I thought to write this letter about idioms that (I think) went to idiom heaven before you got to know them. They were part of the language of my youth.

A boy I knew named Clarence got *fleeced.* I think he was the only Clarence I ever knew back then. Very few parents hung a sissy name like that on sons; they might get nicknamed Clara. Well, Clarence saw this ad for a bug killer. Guaranteed to kill every kind of bug—ticks, flies, roaches, ants, bedbugs, you name it. Just follow the instructions. 100% effective or your money back. Despite Clarence's sissy name, he was a regular boy when it came to murdering bugs, so he answered the ad and enclosed a dollar. The price was high, to be sure, but for 100% kill, it might be worth it. The popular bug spray those days was *FLIT,* which was nowhere near 100% effective.

Within the week, Clarence's package arrived: two blocks of wood, one marked A, the other B, plus instructions. Place the bug on top of Block B, the instructions said, then place Block A directly over the bug and press down hard. Clarence had been *fleeced*. I'm not sure he even tried to get a fly to sit quietly atop Block B long enough to be squashed by Block A. You might say Clarence had been *bamboozled*, but that isn't an idiom.

Do grade school kids still play hide 'n seek? I think so. I hope so. It's a good game. We used to play it until one day we realized it had a flaw. No one liked being IT—the kid who put his forehead against a tree (home base), closed his eyes, and counted to 100 (not too fast) while everyone else hid. He then went seeking. Once he found a playmate and outran him to the home base tree, that playmate became IT. The title meant that of all the players, he was the worst at hiding or running or both. IT was not an honorable title.

So we made a few changes in the game. Rather, we invented a new game called *Ditch 'Em*, which of course had nothing to do with ditches and was therefore an idiom. To *ditch* someone meant getting away from him or her and hiding very successfully. Daring criminals *ditched* cops in those days. Young girls *ditched* boys they didn't like, and vice versa.

In *Ditch 'Em (a boys-only game)*, the boy with the enviable title of IT was the only one to hide. All others had to seek him out. Whoever found him and beat him back to home base took over the IT crown. For the game to work, we had to allow a lot of time for hiding (15 minutes) and a large playing field (3 city blocks). We had to tie up our dogs during the game because even smart dogs don't know enough to keep hiding places secret. We imposed no limits on where, within 3 blocks, IT could hide. He could stay outdoors or go indoors—even into a friendly neighbor's attic.

I once hid for three hours under the floor of Al Frampton's gazebo. But Jimmy set the record. He climbed a huge maple tree with foliage was so thick you couldn't see him from the ground. He sat up there until all the rest of us went home to supper. Then he climbed down and that night called each of us to ask, "Give up?"

*   *   *

Our high school physics teacher, Mr. Perk, gave us strict orders before he let us handle those little gauges called galvanometers. "There are three buttons, one red, and two black. You may press either of the two black ones. You may press the red one and a black one at the same time. Do *NOT* press two black ones at the same time. Do *NOT* press all three at once."

Well, I just knew what John, my lab partner, would do. He'd press all three just to see what would happen, and press them he did. There was hardly a sound—just a puff of blue smoke as the arrow on the gauge curled too far too fast, and broke into three pieces. Mr. Perk, spotting the blue cloud, marched to our lab bench. Without speaking, he took a card from his coat pocket, wrote "John Carroll $10," and walked away. We could tell he had *blown a gasket,* though he didn't shout.

And John? Well, he was *in a pickle* and knew it. If his parents found out—and they would if the school insisted that someone *cough up* $10—John would be *a dead duck.* What was he to do? Ten dollars was a heap of money. His *back was to the wall.*

*   *   *

Am I *all wet* (wrong) to think that you grandchildren don't hear these old idioms? Do you *talk turkey* (speak frankly)? Do stores ever *soak* (overcharge) you? Did you ever dread taking a test and find it was *duck soup* (easy)? Have you *taken a shine to* (started to like) someone?

LETTER 77

Collar Buttons and Debut Parties

On many an evening, I sink into my leather chair, prop up my feet, and half-watch TV as I either whittle or use my laptop computer. On the nights before your grandmother hosts her quilt coven, I have to tidy up around my chair. It doesn't take long. I stuff most of my toys—woodcarving apron, knives, file folders, pens—into paper sacks and trot them upstairs. You'd think it would be snap to restore the disorder around my chair after the quilters leave. Not so. Something gets lost every time, and I'm all but certain that the quilters are guiltless. When they come to our house, it's to talk and eat, not to pilfer.

Last Thursday it was my stapler. Disappeared. Not in any paper sack. Nowhere. During parts of the next two days, I searched in all the logical places plus a few not too logical: under beds, in my sock drawer, on pantry shelves; and all the while, it was right where (I claim) your grandmother moved it, beneath an empty candy box in the breakfast room.

The payoff for all that searching was much better than just finding the stapler. I came across two gold collar buttons, three studs, and a pair of cufflinks. I hadn't seen them in decades. They and I are antiques now.

During my high school and college years, the country's economy was rotten. First was the Great Depression, badly named because times were far from great. We came out of that for awhile as President Roosevelt created various make-work and give-away programs. By 1937, those programs proved to be but a temporary fix, and we began the Roosevelt Depression. Despite the widespread suffering and poverty of those depression years, some of those few folks who still had money spent it freely. Rich fathers of young girls threw lavish debut parties, one per girl, and that's why those collar buttons, studs, and cufflinks came into my life, and my stiff shirts.

For a boy to be invited to a debut party, he simply had to be on an "approved" list and come dressed in a tuxedo or tails. How boys got onto the "approved" list was a secret that no one ever shared with me. Money evidently was not a requirement. My theory then was and now is that each boy on that list went to any of four proper schools and had taken at least one debutante out on a date. Somehow my name got on the list, and I went to debut parties, cufflinks and all, with never a thought about how the money spent on those parties might better have gone to the poor. Teenagers in those days (as now) lived in teenager-only worlds whose borders were less than an hour's drive away.

Only the settings changed from one party to the next. All else was constant. At each party, there were girls in long dresses, fine food aplenty, boys in tuxes or tails, diligent chaperons, no alcohol, and a band whose song book included *Stardust* and *Night and Day*. Everyone, it seemed, knew everyone else. We kids had trouble memorizing Latin words and poetry lines, but we could put a hundred names with a hundred faces. We ate and danced under the stars in warm weather, and in a hotel ballroom or a country club in winter. There was a lot of cutting-in on the dance floor; seldom was a couple "stuck" with each other for more than ten minutes, even couples that wouldn't mind being "stuck." The dancing was a rather gentle contact sport, far less athletic than the jitterbugging that was so popular in open-to-the-public dance halls.

Ah! those were happy times. Not until decades later did I realize that during the debut era, I sank to a hypocritical low. The real me (or should that be I?) drove a Model A Ford with no more than a quarter's worth of gas in the tank. I had more fun with friends who were *not* on the "approved" list than with those on it, and I got by on a slim budget. The fake me (or I) knew that debutantes don't ride in Model A's or make a practice of dating low-income boys. So I drove the family car on dates, avoided money talk, and donned my tux.

The question now is what to do with these bits of hardware for my long-gone dress shirts. My name has fallen off the "approved" list. If I were to be invited to a debut party, it would be as a stern chaperon. Do they even have chaperons now? Do fathers still throw debut parties for their daughters? In the 1930s, when a father threw such a party, his message was: "This is my charming daughter. She comes from good stock and a good school. She's beautiful and healthy and polished. Before long, she will make some suitable boy a fine wife. So, you boys on the 'approved' list, keep her in mind." Today such a message would surely rile feminists.

Has the debut party now become a group event: one party for a slue of debutantes rather than one party per girl? In some cities I believe it has.

But the really important change has been in dress shirts. They're one-piece now. No more detachable collars to launder separately, starch heavily, and fasten front and back to the torso of the shirt with collar buttons. So what shall I do with my rediscovered obsolete gold collar buttons? I should get rid of them, I suppose, and I would, except that they take up so little space.

LETTER 78

Greenbelt Musings

When I'm in Texas and can't get up a tennis game, I sometimes walk a stretch of the Greenbelt. That's a path we have that meanders over fifty miles. It's for walkers and bikers, not those who ride horses or motorcycles, and it goes through woods and alongside lakes and under streets. On these walks I seldom see anything unusual unless you count that Rhodesian Ridgeback named Zeus, or the Greyhound named Matlock, who is fast enough to catch squirrels.

I don't really cotton to walking, even though, I'm told, it's fine exercise. I prefer something livelier. Walking, even on the Greenbelt, is too much like swimming laps: good for the body but none too entertaining. I get around this by having random thoughts.

Last week, a snake crossed the Greenbelt in front of me. He was in a hurry, not wanting to be stepped on. He evidently had no idea that I have never stomped on a snake, and I never will. It was so brief an encounter that I wouldn't mention it, except that it got me thinking that snakes are a lot like cats.

Now I know what you're about to say. That cats are nothing like snakes . . . that snakes have fewer legs, no fur and no fleas, don't spit up hair balls, and don't usually get spayed.

But forget the differences. Ponder what cats and snakes have in common. Both hiss. Both like to sneak around when they're not sleeping their lives away—shapeless lumps in warm spots. Both are smooth to the touch if you don't mind touching them. Both like to attack creatures much smaller than themselves. Neither will do anything its owner wants done, like fetching a newspaper, or staying in a corner, or shaking hands, or guarding a house. Some folks say cats are too aloof, not too stupid, to do such things, but those folks don't explain how they're so sure of that. Other folks say that although snakes can't learn to shake hands, any snake that climbs a tree is smart enough to get back down on its own.

What other dissimilar pairs have something in common? How about grammar and body odor? When we hear someone say, "Me and her went to a party," or "She don't like cabbage," we make a snap judgment of that someone. Whiffing someone's B.O. has the same effect on us.

Before I came up with more pairs to compare, I was distracted by a biker with an odd cargo. Sticking out of his backpack was a head, a small furry head, the head of a miniature poodle. The wee critter was quite content to be stuffed into a denim pocket and taken for a ride facing backward.

I walked on. My next random thought was of a headline that had amused me: *BELCHER TO SPEAK AT WOMEN'S CLUB*. A devilish typesetter could have had fun with that. He or she could change it to *SPEAKER TO BELCH AT WOMEN'S CLUB* and no doubt get a larger, more curious bunch of luncheon diners.

Beside the stretch of Greenbelt that I walked that day, there are few flowers. It's mostly trees with ground cover of vines and ferns and weeds, the sort of ground cover that Nature makes by rejecting human help. So when I did spot flowers, I really noticed them. Some were smiling. Not big broad smiles you understand, more like *Mona Lisa* smiles. Those flowers were probably pleased by a mild shower we had had earlier. Whether their smiles would be bigger after a real downpour I don't know. I doubt it, but then I've never gotten too friendly with flowers. I'm not one to talk to flowers. The only times that I tried it I got no response—not a sound or a frown or a smile—and we went our separate ways.

I once wrote about a water lily that spoke ever so softly and helped a skunk stop smelling so bad. The skunk, you see, was unhappy because whenever he tried to befriend rabbits and other non-skunk animals, his body odor was too much for them. (I wrote that story long before I thought about grammar being like B.O.).

This has turned into such a peculiar letter I may shred it. My intent was okay. I wanted to explain that just plain walking, even on our fine Greenbelt, can be deadly dull. Nothing much happens, and the scenery doesn't change much along any particular stretch. So to liven up these walks, I must make the most of small sights: a dog peeking out of a backpack, a smiling flower, a scared snake; and I must welcome random thoughts, however trivial, however zany.

And once I'm back from a walk, I phone someone who would rather hit a tennis ball than pound the Greenbelt pavement.

LETTER 79

Writing As a Pastime

New technology will humbug you. It will flaunt its benefits even as it sets out to carve out a chunk of your humanity. I know. It has done that to me more than once.

The first time was in grade school, and the technology was a little machine with a crank, a pencil sharpener. This great invention, I was told, would brighten the lives of everyone in the class. Indeed, it was faster than I was with my knife, and it left the bare wood smoother—as if that should matter—but it couldn't make points like mine. Mine were sharp as a wasp's stinger. What's more, I *liked* sharpening pencils with a knife. All the boys in the class did; we had an on-going competition, although I don't recall that we ever crowned a sharpening champ.

The girls, as usual, were against us. They neither carried knives nor knew how to use them, so they cranked the sharpener, wrote or drew with mediocre pencil points, and smiled at the teacher. Those girls often flashed fake smiles, hoping to be taken for angels. Eventually, we boys had to accept that little machine and give up that *human* skill in using knives. We even gave up a bit of masculinity as well.

Technology got me again when I was seventeen and had all four driving skills: steering, braking, working the accelerator, and shifting. The toughest of these, and the one I did best, was handle the stick shift. That, more than the other three, made me feel confident, in control. I could start a car in third gear on an icy road and use second gear coming down a steep hill. I knew just when to let out the clutch to start a coasting car with a weak battery. I could double-clutch to keep gears from grinding, and along came the *automatic* shift.

That didn't utterly destroy my stick-shifting skill, but whenever I drove a "regular" car like your grandmother's, I had to let a gizmo under the hood make all shifting decisions.

My reason for telling you about pencil sharpeners and automatic shifts is simple enough. I think you should develop skills even though technology will surely make them passé. Example: writing. I've had fun with it (although not when I *had* to write in high school), and some of you might also enjoy it.

Today, technology is out to get writers. There's a push on for speed and brevity. Use phones and pictures and e-mail and recorded messages to communicate, we're told. Forget the personal touch, forget such details as spelling, don't build a vocabulary, make what you say sound robotic. I disagree.

When I began writing this stack of letters, it was to be a present to you, something to amuse you when you wondered about your ancestors. It may have done more for me than it will for you. As I wrote each letter, I got to relive a few moments or hours from long ago. The pictures were vivid. I saw very clearly the faces of relatives who died before your time, even chatted and laughed with them in old cars and at beach suppers. I got scared all over again, and sad, and puzzled. I revisited folks I admired, others that I pitied, and some who were just good company.

If you believe me that writing can be fun, here's an exercise to get you started: five steps to a good paragraph. With an open dictionary in your lap and your eyes closed, do a finger stab. (My finger hit the word *gully*).

STEP 1—Quickly jot down what the word calls to mind. (Gully means a rut or a ditch. It rhymes with sully. Lop off the 'y', and it's gull. Turn it inside out, drop an 'l' and add a 'y', and it's ugly). Now choose one of those thoughts as the subject of your paragraph. (I chose *gull*, as in *seagull*).

STEP 2—Write a periodic sentence that isn't just subject-verb-object. Try a question: Are those gull eggs in my front yard? Or an exclamation: What a mess! Or a complex sentence: The guy who dug that gully was either drunk or daft.

STEP 3—Write the rest of the paragraph using a mixture of sentence structures. Maybe one long, three short, and one medium. A good mix makes for good reading. Be not afraid to have a few "ands," "buts," and "yets" in the paragraph.

STEP 4—Somewhere in the paragraph, put a *slightly* unusual word. Nothing too elegant. Maybe just scarlet instead of red, or apricot instead of orange. Furry ears, rickety legs, tapered fingers, sausage-like arms.

STEP 5—If possible, use a figure of speech in the paragraph. I like similes, metaphors and analogies—for example: drab as ditch water; the day broke its early morning promise; his grasp of reality is limp; jaundiced street lights.

Here's my *gully* paragraph written with those rules in mind:

Gully. That's what it was. The pier was paved with those gray and white birds and their gray and white droppings. For a hundred feet above the pier, the air was filled with feathers, fowl, fertilizer, and the raucous, garbled conversation of birds in search of food. Some would fail; more would succeed—at the expense of inexperienced fish. I watched the pier from a safe distance, wearing protective clothing, and I thought of New York in the morning. The teeming masses, all out in search of their sustenance . . . their droppings . . . the garbled din . . . the confusion rising more like a hundred stories than a hundred feet. The only thing missing was the feathers.

LETTER 80

Sorting Stuff

Are you the sort who sorts? You must be. America is a nation of sorters. I was slow to learn that, probably not until my high school years, even though the evidence was in plain sight. I knew that someone in the Post Office sorted mail, of course, and that bridge players sorted their cards. Teachers had made me sort words alphabetically. Mother had explained her box of recipe cards grouped under such titles as "deserts" and "salads." I even knew that some scientist (Mendeleev?) had found a neat way to sort all the chemical elements into the Periodic Table. Still, I just hadn't seen all this sorting as a human compulsion.

We all sort. Some of us do dull sorting (laundry). Some sort for a living (accountants who tuck figures under proper headings). Some sort for the fun of it (stamp collectors), and some find ways to get out of sorting. A friend of the family always wears a safety pin in one sock. Why? So that when he takes off his socks he can pin them together before they go to the washing machine. Neither he nor his mother has to sort to match clean pairs.

Some folks are content when all that their sorting does is convert a mess into something "neat." Such folks are not infants. Infants don't care whether their clothes are sorted and put in drawers or piled in a pyramid. Nor are such folks teenagers who use messes as a way to defy neat-freak parents.

The happiest sorters, I think, must be those who come across an item that simply doesn't fit into any known category. In the world of biologists are sorters called taxonomists. They look at various critters and bugs and plants, then assign them to proper classes. Years ago, even before my time, one of these taxonomists must have had a blue-banner day. He heard about or came across a platypus.

The platypus was not quite right for any of the tags biologists had set up for creeping, crawling, slithering, flying, swimming things. He had muskrat-like fur, a heel spur connected to a poison gland, and the flat bill of a duck. His mate laid eggs, two at a time, then proceeded to suckle her young, not with the well developed glands of respectable mammals, but with modified sweat glands. Neither she nor her husband had wings; both shared the jerboa's fondness of night life; both had retractable foot webbing.

We ordinary folks won't discover anything so spectacular as we sort. Still, we have reason to be happy. We can turn some of the grubbier sorting over to the computer. It's great at sorting words alphabetically, numbers by size, and people according to whether they are tennis players, out-of-town friends, plumbers, or whatever, and we can still hope for a heart-warming discovery. Somewhere in that box of photos waiting to be sorted may be one, not of a platypus, but of an all-but-forgotten childhood chum.

Hopes like that are nice to have. They hang around. I can put off sorting pictures for as long as I please and still hope to find a keeper or two. Knowing that, I procrastinate. I am in no hurry to complete all my sortings, and run out of discoveries.

One secret to a happy life is to wake up each morning with a backlog of tasks, a backlog too long to complete in a day. You awake knowing you'll keep busy, not bored. Some of those tasks are bound to involve sorting, for there are always papers, clothes, and bits of hardware to be sorted. The contents of overloaded drawers need to be sorted and rearranged.

As I maintain my huge backlog of sorting chores, I live with my share of mess. Which is okay. Mine are manageable messes, like one I saw in an old W. C. Fields movie. Fields had a large roll-top desk in his office. Instead of putting papers into files, he shoved them into the desk day after day until only the roll-top could keep the papers from falling on the floor, and then Fields went on vacation. His boss, needing a contract that he had given to Fields, went to find it in the roll-top desk, released a torrent of paper, and gave up. Fields, when his vacation ended and he was asked for the contract, pulled up the roll-top, thrust his arm elbow deep into the heap of papers, and, without even looking at what he had grabbed, handed his boss the contract.

For most of her life, my Auntie May was a sorter whose things were always properly grouped and properly placed. She could always find that spool of lavender thread or those receipts for last April's food. Late in life, she began an almost frenzied house cleaning. Pictures, old letters, mementos of all sorts got dumped by the armful. Not looked at, and dumped. Not fondled one last time, and dumped. Just dumped. For Auntie May, all hope of discovery was gone. It was sad to see.

But she gave me an idea. One day I may have to move to a smaller home. Friends who have done that now have precious little stuff waiting to be sorted, and therefore not much hope for discovery. I think I will save my messes, find them a storage space with temperature control and visitation rights and a comfortable chair. Somewhere in those messes are a bolo I brought back from the Pacific, and a check stub for some crazy purchase I made in the 1950s, and the chisel Pop used when he taught me how make darts out of shingles, and—what else? That's the mystery. That's the hope. That's why I must always have messes yet to be sorted.

LETTER 81

Parent-Child Conversations

Subject: Kids talking to parents, and vice versa. How has that changed in three generations? and what hasn't changed?

The main changes have been in where and when the talking is done. Most of our discussions during the 1920s and 1930s went on each night starting at 6 PM. That's when we had supper. We sat around that oak table, each of us in his or her own position. Friends, when they heard that Mother's menu was *right*, got themselves invited. We always had enough chairs, enough table leaves, enough food. Our talk was all spontaneous, nothing very deep. We laughed out loud a lot, usually about something crazy someone had said or done, and we argued a lot. My sisters recited my evil doings of the day. Mother coached us on table manners: elbows off the table, no slouching, no talking with a full mouth, no leaving the table without asking to be excused.

Aside from those dinner sessions and the dish-drying chores that followed, our talks with one another were hit-or-miss. We kids were too busy with school, play, and homework to have time to sit around and talk with adults. Mother, too, had more than enough to do, and then there was that unwritten law saying that adults leave kids alone unless the kids are hurt, hungry, or misbehaving. Adults didn't drive kids to games or officiate. I'm fairly sure that Mother never saw me play tennis.

By the time your generation reached school age, the dining room table was no longer for family gatherings. Mothers cooked less as prepackaged suppers came forth from freezers and fast-food places. Nor were there dish-drying conversations; automatic dishwashers took care of that. Adults had repealed the law about staying out of kids' games, so they, like their kids, ate on the run in order to meet game schedules.

Now instead of getting het up over which generation, yours or mine, had the better deal, consider what did *not* change. At the top of my list is the way parents and kids talked to one another about *SEX*.

I first learned about sex from a boy my age. I thought he just wanted to see whether I'd believe so wild a story. I didn't. Not then, not until I had heard it from several other boys. I asked each of them how he was so sure, but I never got an answer. None of them had heard it from parents or teachers.

There's a very good explanation of why parents were not—and are not—the first to tell kids about sex. Kids want to hear about anatomy and action; parents want to talk about the aftermath, and even when parents do speak of the action, it's in vague terms: egg-laying birds and pollen-carrying bees.

I know why they don't use spiders as examples. Spiders' sex practices are too much like people's.

In the spider world, the male is typically the aggressor. The female, who much prefers food to sex, grows stout enough to outweigh the male by a bunch. She also has poor eyesight. This is something the male must keep in mind. If he doesn't distract her, he may be mistaken for something she'd like to eat. So he thinks up various strategies that will let him have sex but not be eaten. He isn't always smart enough, though. Black widow spiders are self-made widows.

So here's the scene. A hefty, hungry female spins a web and hangs on to a strand, which is her way to detect a trapped bug. The male approaches the web. He has sex in mind. He knows he can't just run at the female and hope to have his way. If he's one of the simpler species of spider, he strums a strand in a certain way. She gets his message, "I'm available. Are you?" and either saunters out for a tryst or tells him to bug off. The whole thing is a little like a señor's serenading a señorita, strumming a guitar rather than a web strand. Granted, the señorita is much prettier than any fat spider, and is not so quick to run to a trysting spot.

The male of another species can't count on serenading to make the lady spider swoon. He sneaks up on her and tickles her with both forelegs (like human touching) to get her mind off eating. In still another species, the male pretends he's a man bringing chocolates to a lady. He gift-wraps an insect, tosses it into the web, and goes after her as she eats.

A devious spider dances frantically around the female. With her poor eyesight and all that twirling, she gets too dizzy to resist. And then there are the criminal species. The crab spider wrestles his girl, bites her legs while he ties her down with a silken thread, and forces himself on her. But the real pervert is Drassodes. He finds and imprisons a very young female, raises her to early maturity, then ravishes her before she's strong enough to reject him.

Makes you wonder, doesn't it? Do spiders teach *their* offspring about sex by explaining what people do?

LETTER 82

Dirt

You may have wondered, though probably not, when I would write you a letter about dirt. The time is now. The dirt I have in mind is mud, grime, ashes, soot, and dust. I'll have nothing to say about political dirt or pig-sty dirt—just *clean* dirt.

In the 1920s, long before developers bought great chunks of land and built scads of houses at a time, the Gautiers bought the vacant lot on the north side of our yard. Which was okay by us neighborhood kids. A new house would mean scarps of lumber and metal. Besides, giving up that lot wouldn't be very tough. It was too heavily wooded for baseball or football or soccer. Not that the Gautiers cared, or even thought about, how we kids felt. They just hired an architect to design them a house and a contractor to build it the old-fashioned way.

First Step: Remove tons of dirt, enough to make a basement-size hole . . . no bulldozers or back-hoes or jackhammers—just muscular men with shovels, pick-axes, and wheelbarrows, plus a team of horses. The basement, you see, was a very important part of every home. It was cool in summer (no air conditioning in the 1920s), warm in winter, and safe during tornados. It was where you put up the ping-pong table and the dart board. It was where dirty clothes came down the clothes chute. It was where the furnace oil tank and the furnace and the hot water heater and the deep laundry tubs were. It was where the work bench and tools were, and the cabinet full of home-canned foods. It was where Christmas presents were hidden, and in some homes, where photo darkrooms were walled off. Folks partied in basements, rode their exercise bikes, and on torrid nights slept.

So, the perimeter of the Gautier basement-to-be was marked with stakes and string. Men began to dig, with shovels where the ground was soft and pick-axes where it wasn't. Others carried away the dirt in wheelbarrows. One man drove a team of horses, pulling first a plow and then a flat steel scoop. Little by little the hole deepened, and one side sloped so that horses and men could get into and out of the hole.

As the dirt was removed, it was piled into two long mounds along east and west sides of the hole. That gave us a proper battle ground for a mudball fight. Johnny Longmire and I were the western army. The Lewis brothers fought from behind the east wall. Although lots of ammo flew back and forth, there were very few direct hits. The walls were far enough apart, you see, that we had to lob our mudballs like mortar shells. Thus, we had plenty of time to spot and duck incoming enemy shells. It wouldn't have mattered much if we had gotten hit. We were pretty much covered with mud anyway from lying on those mounds and making all those mudballs.

Weeks later, we had our own project. In the Lewis's back yard, we built a tunnel by digging a ditch, then covering it with boards, and adding a top layer of dirt. It was narrow for the first ten feet with a round "room" at the far end. The plan was that at least three of us boys could hide out in that room whenever we had to escape bullies or parents or wild animals; and three of us did hide out there once, just for practice. The next day it rained. As much as we liked playing with mud, we saw no joy in sitting underground in a flooded, dark little room. Better to face the bully or parent or wild beast.

As kids, we were on very good terms with dirt, and not just around building sites. When our arms or the backs of our hands were dirty and sweaty, we could roll up tiny cylinders that looked like black bread sticks. When we waded golf course creeks in search of crawdads, we rather enjoyed feeling cool mud ooze between our toes. We learned that in good dirt we could grow melons, and in great dirt we could house fishing worms.

So what happened? For years we were fond of dirt, and, I think, it liked us. Certainly it sought our company. We boys were dirty more often than clean. But there came a time—I don't know the exact date—when we turned against dirt. We spoke badly about it, scrubbed it from our clothes and hair, vacuumed it into dark bags, swept it from our homes. When we saw it beneath our fingernails, we no longer thought of mudballs.

A big mistake, for dirt has not let our change of heart go unnoticed. If we could hate dirt, it could hate us. Behold the evidence. Dirt avoids us by hiding in corners and behind picture frames or inside coil springs. It irritates us by getting in our eyes and noses, and by clinging to the walls of our bathtubs. It has us pay for our hatred by helping termites attack us, and fungi go after our paint; and if its hatred gets really intense, it takes away whole homes with mud slides.

In the 1930s, dirt got very upset with folks in the Plains for chopping down too many trees. Those trees had kept dirt from being blown away. Well, that dirt got even all right. It made sure the farmers who had done the chopping would have mighty poor crops, and it got after some dirt-hating city folks by invading their homes and lungs.

I'm fairly sure that dirt still likes kids, and that it doesn't hate *all* adults. It's fond of those who feed it well, make beds for it, see that it isn't thirsty, and visit it often. It rewards them with flowers and food, and on those who shape it nicely, it bestows sculptures. Now although I'm neither a gardener nor a sculptor, I don't hate dirt. It was very nice to me in my mudball days, and, like it or not, we will all *be* dirt one day.

LETTER 83

A Fine Friendship Cut Short

Most of us made our strongest friendships during our teens. That's because doing so was simple. There were none of the obstacles that adults faced. If a boy wanted to get together with a friend, he just did it. No need to get permission from his wife or make excuses to a boss. Teens formed no-strings-attached friendships. Just being together was enough. No one kept track of whose turn it was to entertain. That would come later. So, too, would business friendships in which a favor received meant a favor owed.

In 1934, I met Ken Becker. Mother had rented one of the Wren cottages up on the hill in Saugatuck, and the Beckers had rented another. Ken was a few months older than I, trimmer, and probably smarter. He came from Chicago, he told me, had no brothers or sisters, wondered what kids our age did for fun in Saugatuck, and asked whether he and I might play tennis. I had never played. He said he'd teach me. He had had lessons. Wow! No boy I knew back in St. Louis had ever had a tennis lesson. Music lessons, maybe, and swimming lessons, and for a few sissies, dancing lessons, but not tennis lessons.

It was a matter of luck, our meeting that summer and hitting it off. Except for age, we had nothing in common. I fished a lot, he not at all. Neither of us had a friend that the other one knew. He lived in an urban high-rise, I in a suburban house with vacant wooded lots nearby. Religion was more important to me than to him. He could spend money much more freely than I could.

Tennis was all we needed. I learned, slowly. We played every morning that the courts were dry. I didn't win a set all summer.

Ken had every shot, knew always where on the court to be, and could play for hours, alert through the final point.

The following summer, we took up where we had left off. His parents had bought a cottage on the lakeshore, but every morning, he met me at the public tennis court in town. Although I had improved enough over the winter to play on my high school team, I was no match for Ken. Not once did I win a set. He was just too good. Championship potential.

His being on the lakeshore brought something new to our friendship. He had been drawn into the lakeshore crowd, kids with active social lives: nightly beach parties, hay rides, scavenger hunts, cottage gatherings; and as Ken's friend, I was welcomed by these fun-loving kids. I now had a whole set of new friends, including your grandmother.

For another summer (or was it two?) we played tennis every morning, and at last I won two sets. We played small Michigan tournaments as a doubles team and as singles opponents, and we did rather well. Then in October, our friendship ended. Ken died of a blood clot after an emergency operation. It was hard to lose that good a friend, very hard.

For Ken's parents, it was, of course, devastating. To lose a son, an only child, a son so young, a son with such promise. His death was, I am sure, the ruination of their lives.

Ken's father, rich from real estate deals, had bought everything his family could want: a whole-floor apartment, a maid and a chauffeur, a LaSalle sedan for his wife, a 16-cylinder Cadillac for himself, and a robin's egg blue Oldsmobile convertible for Ken. With Ken's death, his parents' goal, their ambition for him, was gone. His father took to drink, some of his deals turned sour, his bank balance shrank. The Beckers had to sell the big apartment, give up the fancy cars, let go the maid and chauffeur, even sell the little cottage in Michigan.

As I watched, I reached an extraordinary conclusion. If I had to choose between having just one child or none at all, I would opt for none. I couldn't risk going through what the Beckers did. Nor could your grandmother. Which explains in part why we had six children, and aren't you glad we did?

Is bigger better? I think so. In a big family, there's always more happening, more tales brought home, more crises to hold parents' interest, more young friends in the house, more kinds of music to hear, and more variety of food to eat. Kids learn how to share, how to handle kidding and teasing, how to be happy even when they don't get everything on their wish lists. They can't be overly selfish or greedy and still get along with their siblings.

Which brings me to a puzzlement. Why was it that I, destined to become so pro big-family, chose an only child to be my best friend? Who knows? I'm just glad I did. Because of him I found two life-long joys: your grandmother and tennis—plus a name for our first son.

By rights, Ken should have been spoiled, never having had to want for anything or compete with a sibling, but I don't think he was. His parents made rules and enforced them. He never got into even half-serious trouble, never drank, never brought home a bad report card, always dated the right sorts of girls. I wish he had lived longer than eighteen years.

LETTER 84

Taking Trips Long Ago

Come back with me to the late 1920s and early 1930s. See what traveling was like. It was almost never so bad as that trip to the State Tennis Tournament in Claud's tin lizzie. That was a memorable enough ride, yet not typical.

First we'll travel just a couple of miles, and we'll go by car. If the weather were nicer, we'd ride bikes. It's February in Webster Groves, though. There's snow on the ground and lots more of it waiting to fall from those putty-colored clouds. The wind could rip a kite if any kid were stupid enough to fly one. We need to wear sheepskin helmets and boots today, heavy jackets, and mittens.

I wish we were going in Scorchy Orchard's family car. It's a Franklin, the only make of car with an air-cooled engine. Once Scorchy's dad starts up that Franklin and lets it run a very few minutes, the front floorboards heat the feet first, then the whole car. Franklins aren't very popular. Folks tell scary tales about them: charred shoe soles and blistered feet. Could that be how Scorchy got his nickname?

We go in the Clark family's Model A Ford (much newer than the well-worn one I bought years later). Its starter barely gets the engine parts to budge. That's because the oil is thick as tar. Low viscosity oil for winter has yet to be invented. There's no heater in this Model A. If there were, it would be the size of a small toaster and would warm the inside of the car about as quickly. There are no snow tires, of course, and no defroster. As moisture from our breath freezes on the windows we rub it away with our mittens. On a few hills, the City has spread ashes, not salt. There aren't many cars out on a day such as this, and those that are just crawl along. We're on the back seat, teeth chattering, blanket (called a *lap robe*) tucked around us, glad that we're riding only two miles or so.

Now let's take a longer trip—Webster Groves to Saugatuck, 420 miles, still in Mother's Model A, but in June. The roads, except for a stretch by Michigan City, are two-lane. When we get stuck behind a slow mover, we stay there for miles waiting for a safe time to pass. We dare not pass on a hill or curve, only when we're sure there isn't an oncoming car. The Model A with one adult, five kids, one or more dogs, and very little horsepower is slow to pick up speed. Most of the highways are macadam (gravel embedded in tar). A few are loose gravel; fewer still are concrete; asphalt is unknown. Because our car has no trunk, almost everything we'll need during the summer has been shipped by train to Fennville. Frank Wicks will fetch it for us in his beat-up flat-bed truck.

We go north averaging maybe 35 mph. We kids squirm and hit one another, and sing, and ask how much longer the trip will take. A game holds our attention briefly. One child watches the right side of the road, another the left. Spotting a cow is worth 5 points, a horse 10. Passing a cemetery wipes out a player's score. We stop often to fill stomachs, empty bladders, stretch muscles, and calm nerves. We try not to stay overnight on the way. If we do, it could be at a *tourist home*. (Back then some people with homes along the highway put *Tourist Home* signs in front yards and rented rooms to travelers).

For our next trip, we go by night train from St. Louis to Chicago. This is not a whole-family sort of trip—too pricey. We go to the Delmar station near the University City Loop at 8 or 9 PM. There on a railroad siding sits a Pullman Car, a car designed to let folks lie down and get a moderately good night's sleep. A conductor takes our tickets. A porter takes our bags, shows us our bunks, asks us what time we'd like to be wakened, and wishes us good night. There are upper and lower bunks, each surrounded by curtains, and each with a low "ceiling." To sit upright inside those curtains is impossible. To undress and dress takes a limber body and a sense of humor. The two bathrooms are on opposite ends of the car. For passengers who are willing to pay double the regular fare, there's a drawing room whose name puzzles me, for there are neither sketch pads nor pencils in sight. It's simply a roomy compartment where two people can ride and dress standing up.

At about 11:30 PM, a train from Union Station pauses long enough to back into our siding, and, with a bit of a jolt, grab hold of our Pullman car for the trip north. We are pulled by a coal-fired steam locomotive. The driver who sits in the cab (the engineer in striped overall and cap) is the idol of young males. He's right up there with the fireman and the policeman on boys' want-to-be lists. He's in full charge of that huge black machine. Gates close for him without his even asking. No one dares get in his way. He visits distant places, climbs mountains, rings a bell bigger than those in schoolyards, speeds through tunnels, blows an ear-splitting horn.

We sleep fairly well. In the morning, the porter wakens us in time to wash, shave, dress, and eat breakfast in the dining car. We share a small table with strangers. The tablecloths are stacked four deep; the top one comes off after each group of diners leaves. The food, though well below gourmet-grade, is tasty and ample.

Our train pulls into the station right on time. We are downtown in Chicago. We can walk to our hotel. We don't even have to wait for our luggage or go looking for it. The porter hands it to us as we step down from our Pullman car.

LETTER 85

Homemade Stuff

On my way to Texas via St. Louis at summer's end, I got two bottles of grape juice, a gift from Linda White. She's married now with two teenage sons and a hard-to-spell last name, but I still think of her as the White girl. That's what she was when I first knew her as the toddler next door. Today she's taller than I am, a lot stronger, and not wrinkly.

Linda has found the good life on a Wisconsin farm without whole-house heating. She raises edibles and critters. She clears land and kills chickens. She churns butter, hunts deer with a bow, cans vegetables and fruit, and sells surplus produce.

Although she's an "organic" farmer, she must, of course, use such *in*organic chemicals as water and minerals of iron and phosphorous. Her inner voice probably says, "I use all sorts of chemicals turned out by lowly life forms, but nothing man-made. I use dirt rife with living and dead fungi, insects, mold, and bacteria. I use droppings from birds, farm animals, and worms."

Linda's grape juice, drunk first thing in the morning, was a fine start to the day. Besides pleasing my taste buds, the juice stirred up thoughts of things homemade. Mother used to put up grape juice every year using fruit she bought by the lug. Our sugar and flour used to come in cotton bags, and no one I knew pitched those bags without using them. Poor folks even cut them up, dyed them, and stitched them together into clothes. Ours became book bags, all-purpose bags, dust rags or, during grape season, the bags that were filled with crushed grapes and hung from a hook on the underside of the kitchen table. Juice dripped slowly and quietly into a large glazed crock. Well, some of it did. Lots of it got intercepted by thirsty kids before it got to the pool in the crock. Whether that juice was tastier than Linda's, I can't be sure. Too long a time between tastes.

During 1930s, Mother delighted (I think) in canning things in the summer. In a steamy kitchen in our little Michigan house, she filled Mason jars with peaches, pears, applesauce, apricots, strawberry preserves, orange marmalade, sour (pie) cherries, and sweet cherries. One crop Mother would not can was beans. She liked beans. We kids did, too (as much as normal kids liked any vegetable), but Mother had heard that home-canned beans were sometimes laced with enough botulism bacteria to kill people. This was one more health worry of the times. We couldn't go near a parrot lest we get parrot fever. We didn't touch a wild rabbit because it might have tularemia. If we stepped on rusty nails or got burned by a firecracker, we had to have those old-fashioned tetanus shots that made some of us deathly ill. Raw milk, even from a pet cow, was not to be tasted or we might get undulant fever.

City and suburban folks don't do much canning these days, as best I can tell. Most of what is saved for the off-season goes into freezers, not put hot into hot Mason jars.

Are homemade products better than store-bought ones, or do we simply *think* they're better? I don't have a single answer. When I make wood furniture, I take my time and try hard, knowing that computerized factory tools are bound to outdo me on precision and consistency. When your grandmother bakes bread, I *think* its quality is tops. The loaves are not of uniform size or density, and slices don't brown so quickly in today's toasters. Still, I'd rate that bread above any from commercial bakeries.

Personal touch is what sets homemade things on top. Also, they're often one of a kind. Occasionally, as on Valentine Day in my fifth grade, the personal touch was not quite right. Each of us had been told to bring 30+ valentines, one for each classmate, and drop them into a large box wrapped in red crepe paper. We could buy them at the dime store if we could afford to do so, or we could make them. We were not to put comic valentines in the box, lest we hurt some kid's feelings.

Whenever we made a valentine, it was not for that box. It was for someone special: a mother, a grandmother, a generous aunt. To make such a valentine (from a dime store kit) required careful cutting and pasting of paper hearts, arrows, lace, and printed words. Wonder of wonders! In that Valentine Day box was a handmade masterpiece addressed to me. It was from Nancy.

Impossible! We boys in the class had an understanding about girls. We talked *about* them but not *to* them. We teased one another about "liking" one of them, usually without evidence. We classified them: lookers, brains, athletes, stuck-ups. Nancy was a looker. She was, in every boy's book, the top looker. She was also a stuck-up. Maybe her looks were what made her stuck up, or maybe her parents taught her to steer clear of boys, all of whom are born evil and get worse as they age. So we boys sneaked looks at Nancy as she pretended we weren't even in the room.

So why would she not only have sent me a valentine but actually *made* me one? Well, I took a ribbing about that all right. Privately, I was not displeased that the whole class thought Nancy and I "liked" each other. One classmate, though, knew better. Oscar Brockmeyer had cut and pasted and forged the name of that raven-haired beauty.

For a homemade item to be better than a store-bought one, its maker has to have happy thoughts, the kind your grandmother has when she quilts and cans and bakes. Oscar's thoughts were not like that, although I'm sure he had fun as he watched me get that mushy valentine.

LETTER 86

Shrinking

It's like a mosquito buzzing my ear in the dark. Only it isn't a mosquito, and it buzzes my ear in bright daylight. It's a word I keep hearing: *downsize*. It goes at my eyes, too. Newspapers quote company presidents who say they're about to *downsize*. Which I suppose is nicer than saying they're about to fire a few hundred people. By now I'm used to fad words and fad phrases. Remember the "like" craze when you'd hear someone say, "I'm *like* having a party but first I have to *like* buy food"? Remember when folks threw a *ya know* into every other sentence?

Rather than stew over that wretched word, *downsize*, I tried using it in a different context. Many of our friends have *downsized* their living quarters, moved into condos. Old folks tend to do that. They usually say they're glad after they've done it, but insist on defending their decision: no yard to mow, easier to lock up and leave, etc., and they shrug off the loss of space and the freedom to own, say, a big dog or a big garden.

The specter won't go away. Even your grandmother and I, who figure we've drunk from the Fountain of Youth, know that some day we may have to *downsize*. Either that or be struck by lightning, and we're not sure which to prefer. We can't—or won't—imagine living in space too small to house our toys, our treasured trash, and us. We kid about doing a test run, living one day a week in two walk-in closets and an adjoining bathroom. We haven't done it yet. The closets are already too full.

What we have done is go on an occasional neatness kick. We tackle part of a closet or a garage, pitch a little, and rearrange the rest, often by packing it in stackable boxes. The goal is to create empty space. If we were to make enough empty space, we'd convince ourselves we could live in *downsized* quarters. We move very slowly toward that goal. I know why. When we decide whether to pitch something, we have too many sound reasons not to:

Items so small we wouldn't save space by pitching them (keys that fit only long-gone locks) . . . items unused for years but simply must keep (wedding dress) . . . items very seldom used but the need for them might arise (pipe wrenches) . . . items that may become quite valuable (old plates, Indian head pennies) . . . items that are irreplaceable even though no one would want to replace them (snapshots) . . . items we're afraid to pitch (tax records) . . . items our descendants may want—but probably won't (old-fashioned furniture) . . . items we can't bear to part with because they were gifts from relatives or estates (crystal bowls) . . . items that took one of us many hours to make (quilts) . . . and items we just can't make up our minds about.

Although we haven't freed up enough space to house a pair of gerbils, I've come up with a good idea. For years I've crammed stuff into boxes, scribbled a cryptic list of box contents, and forgotten where I put things. I'd then paw through boxes and look at lists to find, say, a can of walnut wood putty. After looking at the cryptic lists on a dozen boxes, I found the word putty on three, and I had to search those boxes to find the walnut putty.

On one of my neatness kicks, I decided to have the computer do my box searching for me. I start with an empty box and write its 3-letter name (e.g. APT, BOG, CAM) in large letters on all its sides. As I pack items into the box, I give my laptop computer a *detailed* description of each item (one-ounce can of walnut wood putty). I store the descriptions of all items for all boxes in a word-processing file called STORED. Later, when I've forgotten where I put things and what I might have called them, I tell the computer to search for walnut—because I don't recall whether the can is filled with wood putty or wood dough—and the computer stops at each mention of walnut. When I see the one I want I know it is in Box CAM which is on a shelf in the garage.

During one of these box-packing ventures I unearthed my old slide rule. I haven't held it for years, decades. In its day, it was top-of-the-line, a K & E log-log decitrig duplex. Ah! but you don't even know what slide rules were, let alone what kinds there were. Sometimes known as slip-sticks, they were gadgets we used for all manner of mathematics except addition and subtraction. We could multiply and divide, raise numbers to any power, and find logarithms and functions of angles. Hand-held calculators were yet to be invented.

A good slide rule, like mine, came in an orange leather case with a belt loop. I could wear it or carry it. Either way, it was a mark of distinction. Only the science majors and engineers had them. The "intellectually inferior" folks in liberal arts, fine arts, social studies, and business could neither define "logarithm" nor use one. So I flaunted my slide rule like a peacock in front of a peahen. But I also used it. It went with me into some tough exams. It taught me some fine math techniques. It was my friend, and now I can't just cast it aside. I'll never use it except to see whether I still can, but no matter. It has a home for life.

Which brings me to yet another reason not to *downsize*. As long as we live amid all this stuff and are slow to sort it and box it, we can look forward to heart-warming *discoveries*. Last month I found and ran my fingers over that slide rule. What will I find to pack this month? I delight in the anticipation.

LETTER 87

Chairs: Easy and Not So Easy

What better place than where I am to write this letter? Today's topic is sitting, and that's what I'm doing. I'm in (or on?) my blue leather chair with a laptop computer where it should be: on my lap. Perhaps because this chair rates an A+ for comfort, I've been musing about various chairs in my life, and about what else I have sat upon, such as benches and stools.

I'm not a compulsive sitter, more a manic-depressive. After a good meal or tiring exercise, I'm happy to sink into this leather chair. I seldom sit in bleachers or movie theaters, but that once made for happy sitting. What depresses me is *having* to sit. Society expects it of me, demands it.

Christ Cland was my first barber. Throughout my boyhood, I never knew anyone else with that first name, although he pronounced it like the first part of "crystal," folks thought it odd that anyone should be called Christ. My first visit to his barber shop was, I have been told, chaotic. He put a board across the arms of his barber chair, lifted me onto it, and kept ordering me to hold still while tear-soaked hair got into my eyes and mouth, and down inside my shirt. He might as well have told an eel to sit still. Young boys are built to squirm, not sit.

Nor did my grade-school teachers understand that boys are born with squirm genes. To sit for hours spelling words, reading aloud, and reciting times-tables is not like chasing a soccer ball or climbing a tree. During school hours, I wasn't always at my little wooden desk. For misbehaving, I got to stand in the cloakroom, and if I *really* misbehaved I got to sit on one of five very uncomfortable chairs lined up outside the principal's office. There were always other boys there to talk to—the principal spent most of her day scolding—but never any girls. Schools are different now. Ritalin, counselors, no discipline. Still, the male squirm gene lives on.

Later in life, I sat on command in so many ways. I sat while commuting. I sat in meetings and boring concerts. I sat beside an IRS agent's desk and at funeral services. I sat outside and in the offices of doctors and dentists.

It may have been in a dentist's chair that I discovered my very poor pain tolerance. In the 1920s, my dentist believed in courage, not anaesthesia. He had me sit with my white-knuckled grip on the chair arms as he probed and drilled and filled. I was not to wince or whimper or make a sudden move when his drill found a great nerve. Nor was I to faint. He never told me not to collapse and die in his chair, though more than once I thought I might do just that.

So consider yourself lucky to have been born after such fine dental developments as local anaesthetics and water-cooled drills. You won't have fun in a dentist's chair, but neither will you think you might die there.

The way folks took care of certain chairs long ago seems almost comical today. These were called easy chairs, usually kept in living rooms, seldom sat upon, and then only by sitters in clean clothes because the fabric coverings were not washable, and there were no sprays to protect against stains. Parents put slipcovers on these chairs, shielded them from direct sunlight, draped sheets over them to keep off dust, and trained their children never to put feet on furniture. There were even small lacy pieces of cloth with a name so long it was never on spelling tests: antimacassars. One piece kept hair oil off the chair back; a piece on each chair arm guarded against grimy hands.

Don't be too quick to conclude that those chairs were worse than yours. Those were more than just places to sit. They had eye appeal. Some were showcases for owners' skills—needlepoint, for instance—and they shaped behavior. Let's say you went to a girl's house intent on taking her to a movie. If she wasn't ready when you rang the doorbell, her mother or father showed you to the living room and an easy chair. If she were on time, that would make them all look too eager. You knew this was coming. You were about to be grilled. You sat much straighter than you usually did and kept your head with the hair glop well away from all fabric. You were glad you did a proper job of brushing all those dog hairs off your pants. You knew that being alone with a girl's parents could induce sweaty palms, so you kept tight control of your hands.

Two of the wooden chairs I've made are a bit like those oldies: as much to look at as to sit on, and with surfaces too delicate for today's rough treatment. I like seeing them, running my hands over them, remembering the days spent making them. I hope they find a caring home.

Think of the many places a person sits—or imagines sitting—during a lifetime. The high chair with polka dots of strained peas and beets . . . the throne used only by royalty and movie stars . . . the dreaded electric chair . . . the bean-bag chair designed for the under-50 crowd . . . the park bench used in turn by lovers, no-hopers, brown-baggers, and pigeons . . . the seats of sport cars, tractors, planes, and bicycles . . . the witness chair in a criminal court . . . the board room chair beside a huge rosewood table . . . the wooden folding chair used at school plays and graduations . . . the wheelchair for the unfortunate.

While on watch as officer-of-the-deck during the big war, I sometimes sat on the captain's chair on the bridge. Think of it as a bar stool with a swivel and a back rest, and bolted to the wheelhouse deck (as though anyone would use it in a heavy sea). I did a lot of daydreaming in that chair when there were no Japs nearby. Once—maybe more than once—I imagined myself very young again, sitting on the arm of Pop's rocking chair as he "read" me *Huckleberry Finn*. The arm of that chair was a lot more comfortable than the captain's chair.

LETTER 88

Huge Mistakes

Last month, I began to ask friends this question, "What was the biggest mistake Americans ever made?" In five weeks, I've gotten lots of different answers and no clean winner. There were some duplications, of course—slavery, and dropping the A-bomb, for instance—but no single mistake was named by even a quarter of the folks I polled. That's not too surprising. Americans have made huge mistakes aplenty.

Several of the answers from that poll fall under the heading: *Making Life Simpler at Too Great Cost.* Aerosols that messed up the ozone layer . . . disposable diapers adding to waste disposal problems . . . frozen meals that made whole-family suppers infrequent . . . punching telephone keys as ordered by recordings . . . cell phones that can cause car crashes . . . security systems that do what they should but sometimes scream when spooked by imaginary burglars.

Another broad heading I found was: *Setting Aside Moral Laws.* Folks living together without getting married . . . politicians lying under oath . . . abortionists killing unborn babies in numbers that exceed Hitler's . . . so-called mercy killings.

And a few mistakes fell under my heading: *Working on the Wrong Problem.* Concentrating more on the *size* of the population than on its *quality* . . . building roads and rapid transit systems instead of communication systems to let folks travel less . . . letting troublemakers such as Hitler and Sadam live long enough to carry out the killing of thousands . . . letting courts focus on *how* things are done rather than on *what gets done.*

Although my friends didn't agree on a single biggest mistake, Jack gave me one worth writing about: *Hurrying.* I'm not sure who first made that mistake or when, but it has turned into a biggie. It's a pervasive mistake, too.

Somehow, Americans got obsessed with the notion of saving time, which is a fine notion if the time saved is put to good use. Too often it is not. We drive too fast hoping to save minutes or hours only to waste weeks in a hospital or years in a wheelchair or an eternity elsewhere.

We hurry through meals. Whereas we once sat and chewed and talked and laughed, we now gulp and wolf and run. We even hurry in the preparation of meals, and why not? If the eaters can't take time to savor, why should the cook bother? Why create a pie with just the right kind of apples, just the best flaky crust, just the right balance of sugar and cinnamon? Why not simply buy a factory-made pie and let it go at that? And as for the rest of the supper, well, there are plenty of factory-made packets and bags waiting to be melted in the microwave. Better still, why not go out for supper or order-in? Why not think of the gleaming kitchen as a room to show off to strangers on house tours.

The first three letters of *hurry* came from the word *hurt.* Which makes sense. Hurriers hurt themselves and others in many ways, many places. Physically and psychologically.

A hurrier swerves in front of me on the freeway. If he swerves too fast he smashes my car. If not, he scares me momentarily, then angers me. If I holler at him, he gets red-faced and maybe scares me all over again. I've read of road rage. It's a lose-lose situation.

On the job the boss says, "We don't want it right; we want it Wednesday," or words to that effect. What he means is that I must not take time to do my very best. I must hurry. He may also suggest that I hurry to catch a plane or go to a meeting or read a report or get back from lunch.

A doctor's office is a hurrier showcase. A doctor waits for no man. Or woman. Patients wait, first in—where else—the waiting room, then in holding cells. The doctor over-books so there's always a patient ready to be "checked." For each visit, the doctor will charge, say $50+, and, with luck, will spend no more than five minutes before hurrying to the patient in the next holding cell. At $600+ an hour, he can't take time for plain-English explanations of ailments or medications. One can only wonder how much time he takes to study patients' files and test results. Does his hurrying scare me? A little. Does it anger me to be made to wait and then to be hurried out the door? Yep.

Now and then, I either pity the trapped hurrier or get that serves-him-right feeling. There's a three-car accident in the road ahead of him, and he's boxed in on all sides. He slams the dashboard with his fist. He mutters something, profanity maybe, judging from his flushed face. He uses his cell phone and fidgets. The fury never leaves his face.

Before ending this letter, I must mention the non-hurriers in our midst. Back in the 1930s, parents told their children, "Don't be in a hurry to grow up. Take your time. Enjoy your youth. Get an education so you can get a good job. Don't rush into marriage." But we knew better. We grew up fast and married young. Today's children don't do that. They take more time to get educated and come away smarter, and their approach to marriage is painfully *un*hurried. I think they figure they should analyze prospective mates and not rely on *feelings* the way we did. Will they have better marriages? Let's hope.

LETTER 89

Sleeping

For one-third of their lives, folks sleep. It's time well spent, usually very relaxing. I'm disappointed in myself for waiting until Letter 89 to write about sleep, which in many ways hasn't changed a lot from my generation to yours. How could it? When we're sound asleep, we can't bother to think of ways to change what we've been doing, and when we're awake we can't remember what being asleep was like.

The young still sleep more soundly than old folks, and those of all ages occasionally sleep fitfully for any of many reasons. Thunder claps. A tummy rumbles. An animal, maybe a wolf, howls. A fever parches the mouth. A ghost or a burglar or Santa Claus makes mysterious sounds. A cold draft brings on a shiver. Voices from another room can be heard but not understood. A worry that should have gone to bed in the head is up and about. A sick relative may need help at any moment. A leg cramps. Someone snores. A nightmare gets the heart racing, the body trembling, the brain short-circuited.

Why, when we are wakened by a nightmare, can we not realize how preposterous it is? In one of only two nightmares I ever had, Uncle Walter and I are fishing. We are in a flat-bottom boat moving downstream quite rapidly; Uncle Walter is in the bow keeping an eye out for rocks and fallen trees. He is, you may recall, totally deaf. I am in the stern hoping to land a fish. All of a sudden, something huge takes my bait, most likely a monster blue catfish, and yanks me clean out of the boat. I yell to Uncle Walter, who can't hear me and who keeps scooting downstream. The monster catfish, angry about the hook in his mouth, comes to the surface, eyes me, and streaks toward me. I can swim but nowhere near fast enough. I'm a goner. Or will be unless I wake up. Which I do. But it all seemed so real.

War zones, I found, are punk places for sleeping. In one twenty-four hour period we had Jap planes overhead thirty-six times. Bombs, shells, noise aplenty, and I didn't dare sleep through all the excitement.

Shortly before leaving the U.S. to do battle, I had some memorable sleep during a long train ride. I had boarded the train in Los Angeles, a string of antique rail cars pulled by a coal-burning, soot-spewing locomotive that may or may not have been overhauled after leaving the dump site. Times were tough. What steel there was went for military use. Liquid fuel, too—gasoline and diesel fuel—were in short supply. But I was on a happy mission. Our first-born was fresh-born off in Neenah, Wisconsin. I'd see him at the end of the train ride. A bit of sleep discomfort was a small price to pay. I hoped the train wouldn't die en route.

To board a train, even a moribund coal-burner, you had first to buy a ticket, then to get to the station gate ahead of time. Way, way, ahead of time, maybe five hours. There were no reserved seats. The number of tickets sold might be triple the number of seats on the train. For the two-night, three-day trip I was about to take, there would be many standees, and guess who couldn't get off duty early enough to be close to the front of the mob when the gate opened and the foot race for seats began?

By day, I half-stood and half-sat on the narrow armrests of seats. I couldn't sleep that way at night and couldn't lie down in the aisle for fear of being stepped on. I spread newspaper on the steel platform between cars and lay down in full officer's uniform, no blanket, a black blizzard of soot, sulfur-scented air, a bed that lurched and throbbed. When I got to Neenah, son Ken didn't even notice that I was filthier than I had been during my mudball years. He was less than a week old.

Sleeping equipment has changed since I was a youth. We didn't have innerspring mattresses or electric blankets or queen-size beds.

We slept with open windows, winter and summer. We slept on real linen sheets and pillowcases, not plain old cotton or polyester blend. The insides of our pillows were soft down feathers, not molded plastic foam. In cold weather, we piled on the wool blankets three or four deep, a heavy layer. Some of those blankets were the kind Mother hated and we boys liked. They were khaki colored and available at any Army Surplus Store for two dollars apiece. We had two, but only two, down comforters, not enough for five kids and our mother. You may never have seen a down comforter. Ours had a maroon, satin skin, were about three inches thick, provided splendid light-weight warmth, and kept sliding off the bed because the satin was so smooth.

Although the linens on which we slept had a better feel than today's sheets, they needed more personal attention. Washing them without a real washing machine was work. They then had to be wrung out and carried to a clothesline, preferably one outdoors where the wind could whip them and the sun brighten them. They were then taken down, loaded into wicker baskets, and brought to the breakfast room for ironing. Why the breakfast room? Because that's where Mother kept the mangle. Small pieces of laundry could be pressed on an ironing board, but a dozen sheets from six beds are better put through the mangle. It was an awesome machine that squeezed sheets between a cloth-covered cylinder and a red hot chunk of metal. Fingers beware!

I'm sure we kids didn't appreciate the work it took to ensure that we were comfy in bed. We just lay there, sticky in the summer, weighted down in winter, happy most nights.

LETTER 90

Conversations With Plants

I don't speak to plants. Some folks do, but not I. They're balmy, not I. Plants can't hear. Even corn with ears can't hear. Peel back those green lips on an "ear" of corn and what do you see? Rows of yellow teeth, that's what. Now it's true that some plants can chew and swallow—the Venus fly trap for one—and lots of plants drink rainwater. But I'm sure that plants can't hear, and even if they could, how could they understand all the world's languages?

When someone tells me she (it's almost always a girl) talks to plants, I give her this Oh, sure! look, ask her what she tells her plants and how she knows the plants understand.

I once wrote about a water lily that not only could hear but could speak in a whisper. What's more, that water lily could understand all sorts of animal and insect languages, so whenever a hummingbird or bee whiffed her perfume and came calling, she and her visitor had a right fine chat.

She had an easy-to-remember name: Lily; and when she was approached one day by a young skunk named Rather, who lived in the woods nearby, she listened to his sad tale. He didn't like the way he smelled, which was dreadful, because no animal other than another skunk wanted to be anywhere near him. He longed to frolic with rabbits. He even wished that some boy or girl would pet him, maybe even adopt him.

Lily told him, in simple skunk language, that she'd see what she could do to rid him of his nasty odor. She'd need the help of certain friends, and it would take time, but she felt certain that Rather's problem could be solved. She spoke to a wasp who agreed

to drill a perfectly round hole in the sac where Rather's stinky stuff
was stored. The hole had to be round so it could be properly plugged
later on. A jagged hole would be hard to plug.

Once the stinky stuff was drained, Rather would have to rinse
out the sac and wash every inch of his fur. This, Lily felt, meant
swimming underwater, and Rather was not what you'd call a
swimmer, not even on top of the water, so Lily would have to ask a
friendly bass to give Rather swimming lessons.

Getting cleaned inside and out wasn't all that Rather needed.
He had to have his sac filled with nice-smelling liquid, and plug
up that round hole. Lily talked a bee into gathering nectar, squirting
it into the sac, and plugging that round hole with beeswax. In the
end, Rather got most of his wish. He was now able to frolic with
rabbits. Other woodland creatures no longer shunned him. He
still had a bit of a problem with people, though. When they looked
at his black fur and white stripe and bushy tail, they just
automatically screamed or ran away or both. This didn't really
bother Rather, who was happy with animals who didn't judge him
on how he looked.

Despite my having written about a lily that could listen and
whisper, I'm not sure it's possible; hence my refusal to talk to
plants. But my reasoning is more complex than that. I've *tried*
talking to plants, and gotten no response. I've cursed weeds loudly
enough to be heard, even said I'd yank them from their homes in
my garden and send them off with the trash man, threatened to
put deadly poison in their drinking water. They paid no attention.
They kept growing and having children.

The first telephone in the house of my youth had a mouthpiece
shaped like a daffodil, although being black, it wasn't very pretty.
When I spoke into that mouthpiece, my voice traveled through
wires in ways I didn't understand, and, being so naive, I wondered
whether my voice might move through one of those yellow
mouthpieces in the garden. Maybe some friend put the idea in my
head. I don't remember. Nor do I remember whether I got the
knees of my knickers muddy when I knelt beside that patch of
daffodils. What I do remember is complimenting those flowers on

their color and shape, and urging them to start smelling like roses if they wanted to be popular. They never did. They didn't hear me. I'm sure of it.

If plants could hear, what would I say to them? Now and again I wonder about that. To carry on a one-way conversation with a plant, I'd have to choose a proper topic for each species. I know what I'd tell a Brussels sprout, but it probably wouldn't drop dead on my say-so.

I'd avoid talking to plants with such mean-sounding names as snapdragons, impatients, poison ivy, and deadly nightshade, any one of which might take offense at my comments.

I'd compliment the crocus for having the courage to poke through snow while all others stay holed up. I'd urge the sweet potato to turn into a yam, and the violet to hold its head high, not half-buried by a blanket of green. I'd gently order grass to grow no taller than two inches.

Geranium? "Put forth a few more red blossoms; they attract hummingbirds." Pansy? "You're fabulous at coming up with color combinations. Now if you could just stop wilting when the summer sun hits you."

When people my age talk to plants or cats or empty space, they're apt to get in trouble. Normal folks whisper such words as "senile." So, as I said at the start of this letter, I don't talk to plants—only to TV sets and computers and tools that don't behave.

LETTER 91

Hopes For Grandchildren

I had no choice. The dean of the college I attended said, unsmilingly, "You *have* to take several philosophy courses to graduate." I hated those courses. They seemed so fuzzy, so impractical, so jejune, rather like courses in psychology or history. I much preferred courses in science and math in which the answers to questions weren't so wishy-washy.

Whatever joy there might be in learning, I felt, must be in cooking up chemicals, peering into a microscope, cutting up dead things, and getting electricity to go where I wanted it to go.

What I was too young to understand was that a course may be quite dull and still develop some part of the brain. Math teaches us to think logically. Foreign language courses pave the memory paths of our brains as we store lists of unfamiliar words. Philosophy works on the "mulling over" parts of old brains. Young brains don't take to mulling; hence, there are very few young philosophers. Still, for some of us, there comes an age when just sitting and thinking about life—just mulling—with no hope of coming up with *really right* answers, is rather pleasant. Not practical, just pleasant.

My latest mulling exercise was about the hopes I have for each of you grandchildren. I'll now tell you what I came up with and try not to be preachy, for should my hopes be at odds with your ambitions, it will be you, not I, who chooses.

Hope #1: *That you find the right person, marry him or her, stay married, and raise children.*

This will take some doing. The world seems to reject the whole notion. Lots of folks say—and maybe believe—that there's no need to find the right mate the first time around because mates can be traded in for newer models . . . and no need to marry rather than enter into a "commitment" (meaning no binding commitment) . . . and no need to have children, surely not many children, for they would take time and money that parents would rather not give up.

As I write these letters, the folks who think like that are still in the minority, and why do I hope you don't join them? Mostly because I've had a happy life so far with a fine wife, a durable marriage, and a half-dozen kids. Also, I've known too many sad-faced people who opted for mini-commitment lives.

Hope #2: *That you find work that you like and that lets you grow.*

If you're super-picky, this too will take some doing. The trick is to figure out the position you really want, the *ideal* job, then ask yourself, "In what ways might a job fall short of my ideal and still be acceptable?" Does it have to be in a certain city? Must it be based on some narrowly defined skill that I already have? Must it be a low-risk job? Would I take a bit less money to get more exciting work? Does my employer have to be a company (or a government, or myself)?"

While working 30-odd years, I found myself better suited to variety (chemist, economist, applied mathematician, etc.) than to specialization. I could not have made a life-long career of, say, accounting. Some folks can. More power to them! I also learned that in each job there were great features and wretched features. The *ideal* job? I never found it. It's a myth.

Hope #3 *That you have one or more real adventures.*

What will it be? Choose a good one, not fighting a war. One of my better ones was going to a Boy Scout World Jamboree in Hungary. At age 14, I visited nine countries, prowled castles, torture chambers, museums, and cathedrals, and met scouts from far away—some of whom came by camel.

Hope #4 *That you gather just the right amount of money.*

Since one of my earlier letters was about attitudes toward money, I've little to add. Too little money will make a whole family miserable. Too much money will invite predators, spoil children, and push others into the sin of envy.

Hope #5 *That you find the right place to live.*

May it be a place where you have fine neighbors, where neither the climate nor the crowding fray your nerves, and where there is opportunity to play and learn and hear happy sounds.

Hope #6 *That you build a proper set of consuming interests*

In a *proper* set are at least five interests. Each should be the sort that you can turn to on short notice and become completely absorbed in for an hour or two. I sit down to write, for instance, and block out whatever worries lurk in a crease in my brain. When I make a piece of furniture, my mind is on the tools and the wood, not worries. Playing tennis affects me the same way, and the *proper* set should let you exercise both your head and body each day.

*   *   *

It seems I have more hopes for you than I can handle in this letter. May you have great health, a clear conscience, and a sense of humor. I hope you laugh often, and loudly enough to be heard.

LETTER 92

I've Got Dibs

When did I stop using that powerful word? Long ago. Long before I was old enough to vote. Come to think of it, I haven't heard the word spoken since I can't remember when. I never did know what part of speech it is, noun or verb or pronoun, and it may even be a code word for one or more whole sentences. The word? *Dibs*! It was quite popular with kids in large families. Maybe it just disappeared when families shrank.

Picture this. Mother was about to drive us kids to church, one in the front seat of our old two-door Ford, and four in the back. Which was not a good place to be, for it was rather like a cage. Kids, like animals, poked one another, pinched, shoved, pulled hair, and squealed. Mother said she bought two-door cars instead of four-doors because she didn't want to litter the streets with her children's bodies. Although none of us had ever known a kid who flew out a car door, Mother took no chances.

To get that favored front seat, I had simply to be the first to say, "Dibs on the front seat." *Dibs* meant it's mine; nothing can change that; not even Mother can override that first *Dibs*.

The usefulness of *Dibs* went way beyond car seats. It was used to stake out claims of all sorts: at home, at school, in vacant lots, anywhere. The meaning of *Dibs* was known to all kids, even those in undersized families, and to most adults. If I said, "Dibs on the bow," before any of my friends did, I got to shoot the first arrow. If at home I was first to say, "Dibs on listening to *Chandu the Magician*," no one could turn the radio dial to hear *The Shadow Knows*.

Mother's cooking set off many *Dibs*. Long before some of her dishes reached the table, one of my siblings or I would shout, "Dibs on licking the pan." Any supper that featured roast chicken or turkey brought forth shouts of "Dibs on a drumstick," as losers had to settle for thighs. We did eat well, despite the Depression, always enough to satisfy the appetites of a family of five kids, Mother, a maid, sometimes a friend or two, and always one or more dogs. We felt sorry for members of small families who occasionally made meals of leftovers. Except for a few hated vegetables, we had no leftovers. A rib roast on the table was there to be eaten. Ditto for a leg of lamb or a pork loin.

It was Mother's desserts that triggered most *Dibs* frenzies. Before any of us could holler a dessert *Dibs*, he or she had to have finished the mandatory part of the meal. When a top-rated dessert was soon to be served, we fell silent and ate in earnest. I recall having wolfed suppers so I could be first to exclaim, "Dibs on an end-piece," of a square cake with chocolate icing. Whenever Mother cut an extra large piece of pie (coconut cream, cherry, blueberry, apple, pumpkin, banana cream, apricot) or an extra large slice of cake (sponge, angel food, marble, devil's food, heavenly hash), the cries of "Dibs" were deafening.

One summer, after I was grown and married and working, I endured the St. Louis heat while your grandmother and great-grandmother (my mother) stayed cool in Michigan. Also stranded in St. Louis were my two brothers nicknamed Q.U. and Fat, and my sister Alice. We pooled our money and cooking skills (?) and ate basic, no-frills suppers at Mother's house: canned things, cold things, things that didn't involve messy pans. Then someone suggested making a layer cake with chocolate icing. The first person home from work would make it the following night. After that, we'd take turns making a cake or pie each night.

We had all we needed for the layer cake: Mother's recipe, flour, sugar, milk, eggs, pan, butter, chocolate, and baking powder to make the cake rise. As the first one home from work, I began the creation of an astonishing cake. Although I followed directions carefully, the cake hardly rose. Each layer, instead of being an inch or so thick, was somewhere between one-quarter and one-third of an inch. Oh, well. I put generous coats of icing between the layers and on top, hoping for the illusion of a properly made cake. It looked like a chocolate-covered square of plywood.

Fat came home from work. "It's supposed to be much higher than that," he said. "We'd better start over and add two layers to what you have." So we did. Same result. Two more skinny layers and a cake well below normal height.

"What happened?" Q.U. asked when he came home. "Did you drop it, or sit on it, or forget to light the oven?" He tried his hand at following the recipe. That took us to six layers, and our cake was actually losing height because my two layers were compressed by all the weight above them. Alice's reaction was scornful: typical boys—can't read directions, can't measure, can't set the oven temperature. I think she was surprised when her two layers were dead ringers for the six made earlier.

We had been slow to learn that cakes rise only when the baking powder has oomph. Ours did not. So what should we do with this eight-layer leaden confection? We had too much money invested in it to throw it out. "I know," Q.U. said. "We'll invite Charles (a friend of Q.U.'s) to supper. He has the appetite of an elephant, and he's way too polite not to eat at least a quarter of this cake." And Q.U. was right.

But no one, not even Charles, said "Dibs" on any part of that cake.

LETTER 93

My Knickers Years

You don't recall my telling you that in grade school I wore knickers. They came down to an inch or so below my knees. They were made of various types of cloth, patterned and plain, and ideally dyed to the color of dirt. Except for the blue-serge Sunday knickers that couldn't be worn while having fun of any sort, all my knickers had beat-up knees by the time they were two weeks old. We boys did a lot of falling and sliding and climbing and getting down on the ground as we wrestled and shot marbles. Our flesh-and-bone knees took quite a pounding too. Each of mine got sewed up in doctors' offices.

No one told us why boys had to wait until high school to wear long pants. It was one of those unwritten laws we dared not break. I reckon it was because young boys' long pants would get caught in bicycle sprockets. Or because long pants on fast-growing boys would be up to wading level in no time.

Girls wore uniforms—plaid skirts and blouses with squarish flaps at the backs of their necks—and we knew why. The principal thought that if the girls weren't uniformed, they'd try to compete for best-dressed title. If boys thought at all about their own clothing, they gave it a Pass or Fail grade on masculinity. Style was merely a word.

We boys naturally wondered what those squarish flaps on the girls' blouses were good for. Not much, we concluded, until the day Oscar figured how to have fun with Nancy's (she sat in front of him). He snuck a small matchbox full of inch-worms into school, and when Sister Helen was writing on the board with her back to the class, Oscar planted those inch-worms one at a time onto the bottom of Nancy's flap. Well, they moved pretty slowly, and only five or six of them headed north. This gave Oscar enough time, when Sister Helen turned around, to raise his hand for a bathroom break. When Nancy jumped up and started slapping the back of her neck, Oscar was nowhere to be seen—or blamed.

Knickers had one design flaw that bothered adults more than it did us boys. The socks we wore needed garters, and were long enough to cover our calves and go up under the bottoms of the knickers. The garters, rings of elastic tape sewed by mothers, seldom did what they should have done. A single jump or a short sprint, and our socks went down. Parents saw this and said, "Pull up your socks." Which we did, because to disobey a parent was sinful. But when parents weren't around to issue orders, we let our socks fall with abandon.

Our schooling involved a fair bit of church time, and those wooden kneelers, harder than anything outdoors, were unkind to knickers as well as to young knees.

The Catholic Mass back then was very different from today's. It was said in Latin, which was not our native language, so we followed what was going on by using a small book, a missal. Its left-hand pages were Latin and its right-hand pages English. Whereas today's Mass is somewhat social, with folks holding hands and shaking hands, Mass in the 1920s and 1930s was far from an audience participation event. I went to Mass for a one-on-one visit with God using the priest as my intermediary. I was expected to be on my best behavior, and I usually was; and I was expected to be neat and clean, which I often was not.

In church, the girls always had to wear a hat or cap or a square of lace. The boys were forbidden to wear anything on their heads, not even feathers. We sang very little, spoke not at all, and tried to think a lot about how we were going to stop being so bad. We had it on good authority that going to hell was a lot worse than being sent to the cloak room.

To be good in those days included giving up things. Sacrifice was a virtue. During Lent, we gave up candy. Every Friday of the year, we ate no meat. Every Sunday we went to Mass, even when it meant giving up a chance to go fishing. To go to Communion at Mass meant fasting: nothing to eat or drink from midnight until after Mass. Between midnight and 10 AM, any boy worth his salt could get mighty hungry. Any girl, too, I suppose, but I wouldn't know about that.

On the school days that we went to Mass and Communion, I was doubly blessed. I got a dime to spend at a bakery just two blocks from church. With that dime, I could buy half a crumb coffee cake. What could be better on a really empty stomach than half a crumb coffee cake! A whole one maybe.

The decision wasn't always easy, though. That bakery also sold delicious cinnamon rolls, two for a nickel. With four inside me, I could last until noon lunch. Those cinnamon rolls stood taller than the ones I get today, and they were firmer. To make one the baker sprinkled generous amounts of cinnamon, sugar, and raisins on flattened dough, rolled it up tightly, let it rise, baked it, and topped it with white frosting.

Some folks just bite into a cinnamon roll, and some take a fork to it. My way is best. I unroll it, pick out and eat each raisin as I find it, then tear off a de-raisined chunk to chew as I continue to uncover the next raisins.

When I went on to high school, I was proud to wear long pants, a symbol of my becoming a man. Was I right to savor the end of my knickers years? Wasn't it fun enough uncurling cinnamon rolls and watching inch-worms race to the finish line?

LETTER 94

How the Young View the Old

While traveling on business, I found Asian countries far more interesting than European ones. Europe was too much like an old, compressed U.S.A. Once in an elevator in Rome, a British tourist asked me how I liked Italy. I said, "Just fine. It's nice being where everything is older than I am. I'd like it even better if certain things weren't so small. This morning I dropped the soap in the shower in my hotel room and couldn't lean over to pick it up. I had to get out to do that, then get back in." He smiled. "You Yanks have to understand," he said "over here everything is so old it's shriveled up."

We Yanks do ignore that smallness when we make Europe-vs-U.S.A. comparisons. We envy the French their high-speed railroad, and forget that to go even from one end of France to the other is hardly like crossing the U.S.A. I've had friends tell me that Italian gasoline prices were double ours, then fail to mention that Italians rode motorbikes and tiny cars, and didn't drive very far because they had less highway than, say, the single state of California.

Although Asia is even older than Europe, and some of it even more compressed, I was fascinated by how *different* it was: the customs, the clothes, the food, the social behavior. Strange that I could like Japan, whose people tried to kill me with bombs and bullets. (At one business meeting, I got to know a Japanese executive named Watanabe. He and I had survived a particular battle in World War II, and may very well have shot at each other. I'm glad his aim was bad). All that was long ago. Instead of making war, we were now making deals, buying and selling, forming partnerships.

Of the Japanese customs I found out about, one that I like has to do with the way they regard old folks. Put simply, they think the older the wiser, the more deserving of respect. At my age, that sounds good.

Each year on his father's birthday, the oldest son must come sweep out his father's house. The son may be an executive or a laborer; he may have to travel far or miss some important event. No matter, he must show up. Of course, he doesn't really have to push a broom. He simply goes to show respect and make sure his father is taken care of.

Which brings me at long last to the theme of this letter: how young folks in the U.S.A. regard us old fogies and biddies. Do you respect us? Think we're quirky? Pity us? Envy us? Figure we're not in touch with the time, living in the past?

Perhaps you have no feelings for oldsters in general, just individuals. If you do form opinions about my generation, give us credit for things we did *not* take. Here's a list I read in a local newspaper. It's anonymous so I can't give credit, much as I'd like to. We did *not* take:

- the melody out of music
- the pride out of appearance
- the romance out of love
- the commitment out of marriage
- the togetherness out of family
- the learning out of education
- the service out of patriotism
- the civility out of behavior
- the refinement out of language
- the responsibility out of parenthood

So you see, we're not only old, we're old-fashioned, nostalgic. We wish later generations hadn't done all that taking.

Tom Brokaw, a TV newscaster, has written a book titled *The Greatest Generation*—your grandparents' generation. He's overly kind to us, doesn't mention some of the dumb things we did, some of the mean things and selfish things and cowardly things. His message, as I read it, is that we were the greatest because we, more than any other generation, had to face the worst crises in history, and we didn't crack or cower or rebel.

Most of the book is about two of those crises, the Great Depression and World War II. Be glad that your generation will never face crises such as those. Today, folks wring their hands when unemployment inches up over 5% or 6%. In the 1930s, it got up over 24%. There was no unemployment insurance, just one wage earner per household, and larger families to feed. Today, when someone goes to war, he or she feels it's a big sacrifice to be away from family for a six-month tour of duty. In World War II, the norm was closer to two years, and there was no way for a soldier or sailor to hear his young children or get word of what they had been up to a week or two earlier.

People were destitute in the 1930s; but except for a few bank robbers and gangsters, they shivered, ate little, and lived in deplorable shacks rather than steal; and during World War II, with rationing at home and bloodshed abroad, folks just pitched in and made do.

Decide what you will about our generation. Just don't feel the need to visit me on my birthday, broom in hand, ready to sweep away my precious clutter. Better that you tote a tennis racquet.

LETTER 95

Zany Laws and Lawmakers

There's something missing in my make-up. Will Rogers, back in the '20s and '30s, could look at what politicians were up to, laugh, and get others to laugh with him. Cartoonists and comedians can do that today. I have to be told the political joke or shown the cartoon. I can't just spot the humor in the way government operates.

We have on the books many laws that are silly, out-of-date, and never enforced. Why don't we just toss them out? Examples: If you tie your elephant to a parking meter in Florida, you must put coins in the meter. In Alabama, you must not drive while blindfolded. In Texas, you must not shoot a buffalo from the second story of a hotel. In St. Louis, it's against the law to drink beer from a bucket while sitting on a curbstone. Detroit forbids you to let your pig run free unless it has a nose ring. (You can find these and other zany laws at Internet sites).

Certain words ought not be spoken during happy, peaceful gatherings. Fire! Government! Bomb! Hold-up! Politicians! Folks react in myriad ways when they hear such words. Heartbeats race or skip. Fingers tremble, faces twitch, tummies tighten. And what do folks think about when they hear, say, "Government"? Many and varied thoughts: red tape, scandal, appalling waste, groups of faceless officials who would rather talk than think. My own thoughts are about all the inconsistencies in government.

We have a tax code tens of thousands of pages long. Its language spans the whole scale from atrocious to gibberish. All of us must obey this code, even those Florida voters who couldn't tell where the pointy ends of arrows pointed. So Washington spends millions to simplify the voting process but not the tax code.

There are laws that require truth in advertising and labelling, and there are slogans about no one's being above the law. Politicians run huge ad campaigns to get elected to jobs that pay less than the campaigns cost. Does anyone believe the advertising is truthful? How come no one expects a politician to live up to what was only a campaign promise?

Terrorists struck. The government, presumably feeling guilty for having let terrorists aboard a plane and therefore put people in harm's way, paid victims' families big money. Something like $1.8 million per family on average. Illegal immigrants' families qualified. But only for the September 11, 2001 attack. No such payments to Oklahoma City families. Nor has there been big money for families of soldiers killed fighting terrorists.

The government trusts DNA evidence. There's nothing quite like it to get someone out of or into jail for a serious crime. One person's DNA is like no one else's (except an identical twin's), and it certainly is not like any non-human creature's. So how does the government regard an embryo's DNA? It's human; it's not like the mother's or the father's; and it comes from living tissue. So whose DNA is it?

A company with an asset that gets used up or worn out over time, may deduct a certain sum each year on tax returns. It applies to buildings, machinery, mines, oil wells, even (at one time) to milk cows. What it does not apply to is people. A worker may have a useful life of 30-35 years on the job, at which time he or she, like a worn-out machine, is retired. How come the government won't give him or her an annual tax deduction?

For generations, the government has been the senior partner in the tobacco business, taking in far more than tobacco companies have. At times it even took over 50% in taxes on the companies' profits. The government's Public Health Service, as its name suggests, was paid to safeguard our health. The government's National Institute of Health had the largest research budget of any institution on earth. So the senior partner, well equipped to find out about the dangers of smoking and protect citizens, didn't do so. Better to let the junior partners, the tobacco companies, take full blame.

About the only time politics and I meet face to face is when I vote. I really shouldn't be allowed to vote, for I seldom know anything important about the candidates, and I'm easily confused by weird wording. Example: Should the school board not amend Article X, which forbids students from refusing to pay for food they have refused to eat? Vote Yes or No.

Now and again friends have asked me, "If you don't like the way government operates, why don't you run for office?" A fair question, I suppose. Not a bright one, but fair. I have a slue of good excuses. I'm too stingy to spend big bucks on an ad campaign. I'm not a lawyer, and that's what most of the politicians with clout are. I'd have to spend too much time with unlikable people. I'm in favor of shrinking government, and no politician wants to hear that. I'm too old now. There was a time when the folks in power were, as a group, like the people they represented. No longer. The percentage of old people in Congress is smaller than in the general population.

So I now apologize to you. In my last letter, I bragged about how great my generation has been, but I didn't admit that we are about to hand you a government that we made more complex and less efficient. See what you can do to make up for our mishandling.

LETTER 96

Those Capital Sins of Youth

There must have been times during my youth when I was bored. Driven indoors by rain, there was little fun to be had other than teasing my sisters, and that was short-lived, for once they began to weep or scream or both, I was in trouble. So what to do? There were no good kids' programs on the radio. I wasn't the sort of boy who sat and read a book in the middle of the day—or hung out with boys who did. I hadn't yet got my chemistry set. There were no TVs. Nor were there public indoor places I could visit: gyms, swimming pools, skating rinks, daytime movie theaters. Board games, even Parcheesi and Checkers, brought only an hour or so of joy.

I was young enough to regard girls as less attractive than a good baseball glove or almost any dog. The only exception I can think of was the black Chow that lived in the stucco house by the corner of Simmons and Gray. What a rotten dog! He hated everyone, and vice versa. We had to get our bikes going fast before we got to his house, then pull up our legs as high as we could and coast. That dog never barked, just came lickety split out of nowhere with his tail curled up like a scorpion's stinger. He was hungry for young boys' drumsticks, but he wouldn't jump high to get them.

We never bothered to learn that Chow's name. Instead, we shouted names we made up and wished him the very worst. Still, we never really acted to get even with him. We considered walking a big fighting dog down by that stucco house, maybe Barthel's *Bam*, to whup that Chow, until someone told us a Chow's fur is too thick for a normal dog (even a big normal dog) to bite through and draw blood.

We were going to sic the dogcatcher on him, but none of us had the nerve to pick up the phone. Anyone who did that was sure to have a troubled conscience, maybe for his whole life. To help a dogcatcher was to help the devil himself. Dogcatchers were the most hateful creatures on earth. Never mind that they were not right in the head. They were pond scum. They were the meanest of all human beings, if indeed they were human, and they were covered in the book of juvenile law. Right after "Never Snitch on a Friend" was "Never Help a Dogcatcher."

Back to my boredom. Even on a rainy day, with nothing to do and nowhere to go, I dared not be *obviously* bored. If there was one thing Mother hated more than hearing a child speak of being bored, it was seeing a child acting bored. I used to wonder why Mother felt that way; my best guess was the seven deadly sins.

Mother was sure that folks ought to think about the deadly sins the way we boys thought of dogcatchers. She couldn't teach us about all seven while we were very young, of course. Covetousness was hard to pronounce, harder to spell, impossible to define. Lust was something we'd have to learn about later.

We knew about anger all right, though not how to avoid it when we didn't get our way. Pride was a fuzzy concept. To be proud of getting a good grade in arithmetic or of hitting a home run was not a sin. To think of oneself as an all-around great guy or girl was indeed sinful. Stuck-up folks were doomed unless they turned humble later on. Envy was another fuzzy term. Envying another boy his sleeker bike or fatter allowance was OK unless you let the feeling fester too long.

Gluttony was what made Henry VIII so fat. Young boys couldn't be gluttons; they needed to eat heartily to grow and to be as active as hooked bass.

The seventh big-time sin, sloth, was one that Mother felt no one, young or old, should commit. What's more, she held that sloth was something more than sitting like a sleepy toad. A person could be guilty of sloth merely by having a lazy attitude, and to say "There's nothing to do" or "I'm bored" was proof positive of sinfulness.

So if ever I was bored, I never let on, never uttered those evil words. Sinning in secret like that troubled my conscience, as you might imagine, so little by little I found ways *not* to be bored. At first, I forced myself to do something physical so Mother could see I was busy. That wasn't too good a solution on rainy days because finding pleasant physical activities was tough.

In time, I convinced Mother that by keeping *mentally* busy, my soul would not be spotted by the sin of sloth. Later still, I found that mental activity was indeed a splendid way to fend off boredom. Which explains why I like imponderables and daydreams.

I seldom feel bored unless too ill to think clearly. When all else fails, I focus on an imponderable. Try to ponder this. A kangaroo mother keeps her baby, her joey, in her pouch for many months. The joey is neither diapered nor, for a while at least, potty trained. The mother, as I understand it, doesn't bathe regularly. So what's it like inside that pouch, the joey's boyhood home. Think about that!

Mother taught me some good lessons about life. I have better memories than any joey in all Australia.

LETTER 97

Catching Up With Long-Gone Sounds

If your memory is good, and if you've read all my earlier letters, you know I'm against hurrying. It makes us mess up whatever we're doing. It makes us cut ourselves, break our bones, stretch the elastic in our hearts, even kill some of us. Still, there's one kind of hurrying I can't hate. Suppose I could go *really* fast, much faster than the speed of sound.

I hear tell that when someone makes a noise, the sound goes on and on. This is very hard to imagine. As I sit here in the family room I could sneeze at any moment. If I do, how will the sound get out the door or window, not be heard by neighbors, and wander off? Up the chimney if I were to forget to close the damper?

Still, I once lost a bet to Ken Becker because I had doubts about how far sound traveled. He lived in a twenty-four-floor apartment building in Chicago overlooking Lake Michigan. He said if we were to go up on roof we could hear what people way down on the beach were saying, and he was right.

When Mr. Perk, my high school physics teacher, explained sound, there were no jet planes, only propellor-driven planes. No one could move faster than the speed of sound. No one could possibly catch up to sounds made in the past, and we still can't because the interesting sounds of yesteryear have too big a head start. UNLESS they're moving in a circle, going round and round, in the Earth's atmosphere. Mr. Perk said that sound waves can move only in some medium, like air or water, not in a vacuum, so those sounds from the past can't very well wander off into the vacuum of outer space.

Which is just as well. Can you imagine how puzzled a Martian would be if he heard that belching contest we fifth-grade boys had?

Although boys still have belching contests, there are many sounds no longer made. Listening to a steam locomotive used to conjure up all sorts of images. The chug-chug was really the gasp-gasp of a locomotive struggling to pull the weight of a whole train up and over a hill. Was the train headed for a place we had only read about or heard about? Did the steam whistle scream to let some motorist know that the train could neither swerve nor stop for a car on the tracks? Was the engineer's family worried about him? How many hoboes were hiding down low, down near those wheels that can cut a man in half?

No longer do I hear the sound of a typewriter. Not that I miss its having been replaced by the quiet of the keyboard. Sirens, though still around, don't take the long path from low note to high that they used to, and some sirens are long gone. My bicycle siren for instance. It was hinge-mounted over my front wheel. To set it in motion, I pulled a string. The siren dipped down; its drive shaft landed on the tire; it spun; it sang out. The faster I rode, the higher the musical note.

I still hear bells: different bells in different places for different reasons. My teachers used to shake hand-held brass bells, a sad sound that meant recess was over. When a doorbell rang, the noise came from a pair of real bells side by side being struck by a nervous little hammer. Chimes and taped tunes would come later. In the house of my youth, the ring of the doorbell carried the message: The person at the door is not a friend; it's a tradesman or a stranger. Friends, you see, knew that the door was unlocked and that there was no need to make us stop what we were doing just to open the door for them.

Telephone bells, like doorbells, had rapid-pulse hammers. So did alarm clocks. You'd have thought we'd have had trouble telling which bell was ringing. Not at all. We must have had keen ears. We knew right away whether to go the front door, back door, or phone. If the alarm clock rang, we tried to ignore it.

Certain sounds can still be reheard but only with fair effort. The honk of a Klaxon horn on a very old car. A dog baying at the moon. Linen sheets on a clothesline snapping in a chilly wind. The sigh of a tortoise as it shuts its front door.

There are many sounds I want not to rehear. The howl of a typhoon. Sobbing, wherever I heard it. Maniacal ravings. Those sounds I used to hear at night when I was quite young. One came from my closet, a rustling sound from a creature as hard to see as a pigeon in dense fog, a non-human ogre, not at all friendly.

The sounds I'd most like to rehear if they're still out there, and if I can travel fast enough to catch them, are my mother's voice. I'd even listen gladly to any of many scoldings I once got. Like the ones that began with, "Stop teasing Alice (or any of my other siblings)." Every now and then, Mother had to suppress a smile during a scolding because I had been rather clever about the way I had teased. When a company came out with a plug-in switch that would make Christmas tree lights blink on and off, I figured it would work on Alice's reading lamp. It did, and Alice, not being electrically savvy, changed bulbs, shook the lamp, and muttered.

Mother was less amused when I put all those white rats in Alice's underwear drawer. I should have known those rats would stray and mate, she said. Even so, I'd gladly take that scolding all over again. If only I could travel *really* fast.

LETTER 98

Paid-for Discipline

For peppier lives, folks should exercise their brains and the rest of their bodies each day. The slogan about that is *Use it or lose it.* Ideally, folks find ways to exercise brain and brawn simultaneously. That's what I do when I play competitive tennis. I think strategy and tactics as I twist and lunge and swat. Sometimes cruel weather drives me indoors. My body then goes to the athletic club where my brain takes a rest until it comes home to a computer problem or some other puzzler.

It's not a good place to think, the athletic club. The machines are humorless, the fellow members sweaty and grim-faced. While there, I climb dozens of flights of stairs without rising above ground level. On a gerbil machine, I walk miles down a path to nowhere. I ride a bicycle up and down hills that are visible only as dots on little screen, a screen that keeps saying, "Pump faster." I row a boat as heavy as a scow across an imaginary lake, yet the only water I see is my own perspiration. As others pump iron, I opt for light weights, and tell folks I pump aluminum. I go to the athletic club for a work-out, and that's what it is: work—unexciting work.

To fend off boredom, some members pipe music into their ears. Others watch silent TV screens where inferior actors pretend to live hopelessly complicated lives. Still others try to read as they jog in place, and their eyeballs bounce off socket walls.

The club members are a fair sampling of the folks hereabouts. I see young kids, fogies, and crones, fats and skinnies. Some, as muscular as Tarzan, hardly need more body building. Others are so frail, I admire their optimism but doubt that work-outs will help them. Clothing ranges from chic to shabby, from slinky to baggy. In the parking lot are Jaguars and pick-ups with scabs of rust.

Today when I visited the club, the girl at the front desk urged me to spend an hour with a *Chair Aerobics* class. I balked, but the girl was young and pretty and persuasive. "Try it. It's more active than it sounds. You might like it well enough to enroll in the next class," she said. "If not, all you'll lose is an hour." So I did. I sat on a bridge-table chair, stretched an elastic belt, swung a broom handle, breathed deeply, and got up and down repeatedly. The class was as much a social gathering as a physical workshop: taped music, laughter, chatting, announcement of a group luncheon.

I didn't enroll. The course fee was tiny, and the folks were having more fun than those on gerbil machines, but I felt I'd get better exercise on my own. On the drive home, my brain awoke. I had what was (for me) profound notion: We pay a lot to have others discipline us rather than discipline ourselves.

Actually, I had had that notion in a limited way long ago. When I came home from the Big War and started to work for $240 a month, there was more to buy than money to pay for it. There was no getting out of signing a mortgage to buy our first house, but what about a car? And furniture? We had my old bedroom furniture, a crib for soon-to-arrive Josie Jr., a cot for Ken, and a second-hand dining room table with chairs. The pre-war car was too costly to keep; it was time to use streetcars and bicycles.

The solution, we were told, was to borrow money. Everyone did it, we learned. With some Depression-type thinking, we decided it was better to save the price of, say, a car, buy it, and start saving for the next one. To borrow would simply mean being *forced* to save not only the price of the car but interest as well. What's more, thanks to the need to make those forced payments, we'd be unable to save for the next car or the one after that. By using self-discipline, we could save ourselves about 10% a year on the purchase price of all the cars we'd ever buy.

So we had a bare living room for quite a while, and did without a car. Today, with money easier to come by, folks think nothing of paying others to impose discipline, and not merely to buy cars and such. Kids take tennis lessons. They don't simply learn by playing the game, watching how good players do it, practicing against a wall, and reading the advice of professionals. They (or their parents) pay someone to say, "Do this. Don't do that. Watch me."

Many of those kids will be better players than I was, and that's good. But learning the hard way wasn't bad. When I finally taught myself to hit an overhead smash with both feet off the ground I was one happy fellow.

Drinkers and smokers pay to hear the order: Stop That! Would-be pianists and bridge players seldom teach themselves. They sign up for lessons and to have someone say, "Do this. Don't do that. Practice. Come back Tuesday."

Make no mistake, though. Quite often it's worthwhile to forget the self-discipline and pay someone to take over. A small girl won't teach herself ballet. A young couple can't wait for a house until they've saved the purchase price, and those folks in that chair aerobics class would be home in recliner chairs if they hadn't paid a teacher to order them about.

I fret less about the cost of imposed discipline (unless it's as much as credit card rates) than about the principle. I hate to admit I'm too weak to discipline myself.

LETTER 99

The Importance of Timing

Yesterday at the hardware store, I overheard a burlap-haired woman in overalls say, "He was in the right place at the right time." She probably envied someone his success and dismissed it as good luck. Indeed, good timing often *is* a matter of luck. Which may explain why, during a lifetime, each of us gets a mixture of good, bad, and so-so timing. Most of mine has been good.

That is not to say that I ever stood before a supermarket counter, cash in hand, at just the right moment to buy a winning lottery ticket. I was born at a right time, though, *after* my sister Alice was, and as everyone knows, it's best not to be first. When parents get their first-born, they don't know what to do. The advice heaped on them by relatives, friends, experts, fools, and books boggles their minds. They experiment willy-nilly. They try to make that tiny person responsible at way too young an age. When the second-born arrives, the parents are self-confident, easy going. Crises are rarer, and the first-born is supposed to help care for the second.

The timing of my birth (May 22, 1919) was right in other ways. In the childhood years ahead, I would live where kids and dogs roamed freely, where families didn't fracture, where grown-ups didn't mess with kids' games, where durable friendships were quickly made. I would have good trees to climb, good food aplenty. I would see the earliest of a slue of inventions: the refrigerator and the radio.

In 1928, my timing went from good to dreadful. That's when I lost my father. Although I'm sure it was much tougher on Mother than on me, I was mighty sad and mighty scared. At age nine, I found it easy to imagine the worst, e.g. being ousted from our home and adopted by a wizened couple dressed in black and carrying black leather whips.

Now you'd think my timing might have stayed bad as the Great Depression began in the 1930s. That surely was a bad time for lots of folks. About a quarter of the nation's homes had no wage-earners, no savings to speak of, too little income to make house payments. Health insurance and unemployment insurance were concepts, not realities.

But for the Great Depression, I was lucky to be in the right place at the right time. When jobs were nearly impossible to find, I was too young to seek one (except for summer jobs, which at ten cents an hour would not support a family). Mother had opted to have our father's life insurance paid to her in the form of monthly checks throughout her lifetime, so our family had a steady income. Prices of nearly everything were low. We could live relatively well, better than most. No need to move out of our house or to be handed over to adoptive parents with black leather whips. Mother put all five of us kids through grade school, high school, and college. She was even able to buy a summer home in Michigan.

In 1933, my good timing took me to a Boy Scout World Jamboree in Godolla, Hungary. Twenty of us from the St. Louis area were invited. We spent two months visiting nine European countries. There is, I think, no age better than fourteen for a boy to have such an experience.

In the mid-1930s, I was again in the right place at the right time. It was then, in Michigan, that I met Ken Becker who (a) got me started playing tennis; (b) became the closest friend I ever had; and (c) got me into the "Lakeshore Bunch," the teenage group in which I discovered your grandmother.

My timing in the 1940s was a mixed bag. I was the right age to be a warrior, which was not so good. I managed to be in places where bombs were not landing and shells were not striking, which was good. I was also the right age to marry and to start raising a family, which was excellent.

It was in the 1940s that I learned this very important lesson: *Learn to recognize when you are in a right place at a right time.* It was as though a tiny voice had whispered, "Make the most of the moment. Don't let it get away from you. Make a decision. Act."

Maybe it was sheer good luck that put your grandmother and me together in Michigan, but suppose I hadn't recognized it. Suppose I hadn't acted. Well, I might have wound up with a shrew, or a floozie, or a harpy for a wife, and a passel of grandchildren less talented, and handsome than y'all.

And *how* did I recognize "right" times? I wish I knew. For many years I've asked myself, "Is the timing right to buy a house (or a car or shares of stock), to accept a job offer, to retire?" Somehow, my judgments about timing seem to have been pretty good without my ever knowing how I made them. The mysterious process strikes me as 80% intuition, 10% brainpower, and 10% luck.

If only there were some way to *arrange* to be in right places at right times. Too often that is beyond the reach of us human beings. We're blessed or we're not, lucky or not.

LETTER 100

To Plant a Tree

Some day you will notice, after you have worked long and hard on a project, that you have a day of despair. Let's say your project is a garden. You dig and weed and mulch. You turn clay soil into luscious loam. You buy bulbs and seeds and potted plants. You rim your plot with stones and spray poisons on pests that visit your garden. Most of the time you are rightly proud for having brought forth those few square yards of brightly-colored beauty. They look *so neat* and smell *so good*.

Then one day, for no apparent reason, your pride is injured. Dreadful questions crowd your mind. Does anyone really admire this garden? When people compliment you on it are they just being polite? If you were to be bedridden for a month or more, who, if anyone, would tend the garden? Should you have done something else with all the time you spent gardening?

Having a despair day (or longer) must be normal. It's common enough, and not just among gardeners. A lot of what we create doesn't "look neat and smell good" for very long, but that's nothing to get teary-eyed about. Better to enjoy the short-lived beauty. This collection of letters is at the milestone number (100). Like a garden, it has a short life-expectancy. But also like a garden, it has been fun for me to till the past and watch fond memories blossom.

Someone—I've no idea who—once came up with a three-phrase suggestion about how to prolong one's impact on the world: *to plant a tree, to write a book, to have a son.* That sage must have been a pre-feminist male or he'd have said "son or daughter." No doubt he figured sons would preserve family names. Although I can pat a tree, a book, and four sons, and say, "I had something to do with their being here," I wasn't acting on the sage's phrases. I hadn't read them soon enough for that.

I have a new tree, not my first, in the side yard. It's a very young oak, just seven inches high, but very smart. It knows it should be flexible during its early years—not rigid like its parents. Its thin trunk must bend, not snap, when it is kicked or when its leaves are blown or pummeled by rain. Last December, I had to put this little tree's invalid mother to rest. She was quite old, and unable to fend off attacks by fungi, carpenter ants, and woodpeckers, but she gamely followed the sage's advice to plant a tree. Her acorn, my tiny oak, grows close to her grave.

Over the years I've known many a tree. There's that hard maple by the Ring's cottage in Michigan. It was there before the Declaration of Independence was signed. When the Rings had a big bough removed, I took a chunk to a lathe, and turned a bowl. Nice color, nice grain patterns. At the entrance to Corlett's is a hard maple with a trunk wartier than a crocodile's back. A block or so away beside the Knoll road is a beech that looks to have grown as much sideways as up. Legend has it that Indians bent it to grow like that. One of our treasure hunts ended there with presents resting on the horizontal trunk.

When was it that kids stopped having fun with trees? And why did they stop? We used to climb tall trees, go higher than any house, peek into bird nests, see what was going on blocks away. The lower limbs of the better trees were usually beyond our reach, so we got started either with a ladder or with strips of wood nailed to the tree trunk or with a heavy rope tied earlier to a sturdy branch. To the bottoms of those ropes we often tied gunny sacks filled with sawdust. With my legs around one of those I could swing up and down while twirling.

If, in grade school, a girl so much as smiled at a boy, the meaning was clear. They were in love. As embarrassing as that was—for the boy at least—the scandalous news had to be reported. His initials and hers had to be carved into a tree trunk—and not just any old way. The format was this: his initials, then a plus-sign, then her initials, all inside the boundaries of a heart. Those "romances" lasted just few weeks; the carvings lasted longer than most marriages.

Early May was the right time to find a willow from which to cut a four-inch length of a branch as thick as my thumb. I cut a notch in it about a half-inch from one end, and slid the bark off like a sleeve, all in one piece. Next, I carved a little groove in front of the notch, and a cavity behind it. Then I slid the bark back on. I had just made a whistle. But why do I tell you this? You don't carry pocket knives as we did.

Trees, like people, should be judged by their character—not just by their looks. Granted, some trees are beauties: great shapes, colorful blossoms, and leaves. Others are impressive because they are kind. Red oaks give squirrels acorns and larder space. Pin oaks grow barbs sharp enough to keep cats from raiding bird nests. Some trees gracefully endure hardship: mesquites, chewed by cattle, grow on parched land; shoreline trees put up with hurricane winds; Quetico trees sprout from cracks in rocks; cypress spend a lifetime with sopping wet feet.

I like that sage's phrases: *to plant a tree, to write a book, to have a son.* Especially the tree phrase. It's so easy to plant a tree, and that tree goes on about its business with minimal help from me. Some books may be better than trees, and sons are certainly better than both books and trees, but trees are easiest.

Printed in the United States
107675LV00003B/217-219/A